African Arguments

Written by experts with an unrivalled knowledge of the continent, *African Arguments* is a series of concise, engaging books that address the key issues currently facing Africa. Topical and thought-provoking, accessible but in-depth, they provide essential reading for anyone interested in getting to the heart of both why contemporary Africa is the way it is and how it is changing.

African Arguments Online

African Arguments Online is a website managed by the Royal African Society, which hosts debates on the African Arguments series and other topical issues that affect Africa: http://africanarguments.org

Series editors

Adam Branch, University of Cambridge
Alex de Waal, World Peace Foundation
Richard Dowden, journalist and author
Alcinda Honwana, Open University
Ebenezer Obadare, University of Kansas
Carlos Oya, SOAS, University of London

Managing editor

Stephanie Kitchen, International African Institute

T0347886

Published by Zed Books and the IAI with the support of the following organisations:

The principal aim of the **International African Institute** is to promote scholarly understanding of Africa, notably its changing societies, cultures and languages. Founded in 1926 and based in London, it supports a range of seminars and publications including the journal *Africa*.
www.internationalafricaninstitute.org

The **Royal African Society** is a membership organisation that provides opportunities for people to connect, celebrate and engage critically with a wide range of topics and ideas about Africa today. Through events, publications and digital channels it shares insight, instigates debate and facilitates mutual understanding between the UK and Africa. The society amplifies African voices and interest in academia, business, politics, the arts and education, reaching a network of more than one million people globally.
www.royalafricansociety.org

The **World Peace Foundation**, founded in 1910, is located at the Fletcher School, Tufts University. The Foundation's mission is to promote innovative research and teaching, believing that these are critical to the challenges of making peace around the world, and should go hand in hand with advocacy and practical engagement with the toughest issues. Its central theme is 'reinventing peace' for the twenty-first century.
www.worldpeacefoundation.org

About the author

Rachel Ibreck is a Lecturer in Politics and International Relations at Goldsmiths, University of London. She holds a PhD in Politics and International Relations from the University of Bristol. Her research explores struggles for human rights, memory and justice in settings affected by conflict and atrocity in Africa, especially Rwanda and South Sudan. She has published in scholarly journals including *African Affairs*, the *Journal of Intervention and Statebuilding*, the *Journal of Contemporary African Studies* and *Stability*. She formerly worked in human rights advocacy, including for *Justice Africa*. She is also a research associate at the Conflict Research Programme at the London School of Economics and Political Science.

SOUTH SUDAN'S INJUSTICE SYSTEM

LAW AND ACTIVISM ON THE FRONTLINE

RACHEL IBRECK

In association with
International African Institute
Royal African Society
World Peace Foundation

ZED

South Sudan's Injustice System: Law and activism on the frontline was first published in 2019 by Zed Books Ltd, The Foundry, 17 Oval Way, London SE11 5RR, UK.

www.zedbooks.net

Typeset in Haarlemmer by seagulls.net
Index by John Barker
Cover design by Jonathan Pelham
Cover photo © Fernando Moleres, Panos Pictures

A catalogue record for this book is available from the British Library

ISBN 978-1-78699-340-3 hb
ISBN 978-1-78699-339-7 pb
ISBN 978-1-78699-341-0 pdf
ISBN 978-1-78699-342-7 epub
ISBN 978-1-78699-343-4 mobi

*For the children of the South Sudanese
court observation team.*

May they read it in peaceful times.

CONTENTS

ACKNOWLEDGEMENTS

This book emerged from a unique court observation research project involving a team of South Sudanese lawyers, paralegals and civil society activists. The idea to undertake the court observations came from a South Sudanese human rights lawyer who was handling sensitive cases in courts and prisons in Juba for most of the civil war, until he was forced to flee in January 2018. The suggestion that we should present the research findings in a book came from a South Sudanese paralegal, who recently graduated from law school, after having completed his degree during the war while living in a camp for displaced people under the protection of the United Nations. Neither these two individuals, nor any of the other 18 researchers involved in the project can be fully named here due to concerns about their security, so I will instead include them all with the initials which appear on their court reports. The book draws extensively on the work of: AJS, AKB, AMA, AW, BAB, BKY, BT, EJJ, GW, GP, JTA, LBN, SRM, TL, NG, OGL, OSM, PWG, WN and GVB. I deeply thank them. I hope that the book can be of some value for them, and that they will have other future opportunities to share their insights and pursue their ambitions. They should be fully credited for their role in this collaborative research and acknowledged for the everyday work they do for justice in their communities and the nation of South Sudan.

The book is also informed by the endeavours and experiences of many other South Sudanese research participants. Again, it would not be wise to list the names of all those who made the research possible and educated me on the subjects examined in the book, but I thank especially CW and CJ. I can name some people and organisations due to their locations or their existing public profiles. I owe much gratitude and appreciation to Justice Africa and all its staff and Flora McCrone; Angelina Daniel Seeka of End Impunity; Edmund Yakani of the Community Empowerment for Progress Organisation; Taban Romano of the South Sudan Law Society who participated in the court observation research; and Benjamin Avelino from the UK South Sudanese diaspora community. I also thank the members of the Conflict Research Programme (CRP) South Sudan 'Bridge' research team; and the members of the CRP South Sudan Panel for their extremely valuable comments on my presentations and ideas, especially David Deng.

The research for the book was supported by the Justice and Security Research Programme (2015–16), and the CRP under the exemplary leadership of Mary Kaldor; both projects were funded with UK aid from the UK government. I am hugely grateful for both the funding and intellectual opportunities the projects provided, and to all those involved in their management, administration and research teams, especially all the members of the South Sudan research team including Naomi Pendle, Hannah Logan and Alicia Luedke. I also thank Anna Macdonald for her reflections on an early draft. This research was inspired by the previous scholarship of Cherry Leonardi, Tiernan Mennen – who generously shared examples from a previous court observation project – and Mark Massoud, and by his presentation on 'law from below'. Additionally, I was fortunate to receive insightful and constructive reviews from two anonymous reviewers and Adam Branch – thank you to all of them. I am also very grateful to Stephanie Kitchen and Ken Barlow as editors for their faith, patience and advice; and to the team at Zed Books who helped to bring the book to its completion.

On a personal note, I would like to thank Rebecca Sutton and Regina Enjuto-Martinez at LSE for their inputs at an early stage in the writing process; Kiran Grewal at Goldsmiths for her powerful illustrations of the value of studying human rights in practice and for her encouragement; Liz Evans for being a feminist sister at Goldsmiths; my sisters, Siara and Susie, and my amazing children, Vannah and Kal, for listening and helping practically.

Finally, it is entirely appropriate that the book begins with a preface by Alex de Waal because, as a colleague, mentor and friend, he helped me to develop the concept for the book; discussed it with me over two years; generously commented on several drafts; and shaped my thinking about politics in the region in countless, immeasurable ways. My first lessons in the horrors of war and human rights violations in Sudan came over 20 years ago when I first went to work at African Rights and met Alex de Waal and our South Sudanese colleague Yoanes Ajawin. The JSRP court observation project is in many ways an echo of Yoanes and Alex's work in the Nuba Mountains in the 1990s. While many things have changed for many people in the region since, sadly this kind of work remains very necessary and support for it is still far too limited.

To any readers who find flaws, gaps and misunderstandings in my account, please attribute the errors solely to me. The book may not seem as familiar to its South Sudanese contributors and participants as I would wish. It was written at a distance, both in spatial and cultural terms, and can never fully represent their views and experiences; it offers snapshots of various complicated lives and experiences and positions them in academic discussions, inevitably imposing an element of abstraction. To my colleagues in the collaborative research, please accept both my thanks and apologies – in the end this book only included fractions of your research and life histories; but I still hope that it can contribute in some way to struggles for justice in South Sudan.

LIST OF ACRONYMS

ARCISS	Agreement on the Resolution of the Conflict in South Sudan
AUCISS	African Union Commission of Inquiry on South Sudan
CEPO	Community Empowerment for Progress Organisation
CoHA	Cessation of Hostilities Agreement
CPA	Comprehensive Peace Agreement
CRP	Conflict Research Programme, LSE
DFID	Department for International Development
FD	Former Detainee
IDLO	International Development Law Organisation
IDP	Internally Displaced Person
IGAD	Inter-Governmental Authority on Development
IRC	International Rescue Committee
JMEC	Joint Monitoring and Evaluation Commission
JSRP	Justice and Security Research Programme, LSE
LRA	Lord's Resistance Army
MP	Member of Parliament
NGO	Non-governmental organisation
NSS	National Security Service
OHCHR	Office of the High Commissioner for Human Rights
OLS	Operation Lifeline Sudan
PoC	Protection of Civilians site

R-ARCISS   Revitalised Agreement on the Resolution of the
            Conflict in South Sudan
SPLM-IO   Sudan People's Liberation Movement-in Opposition
SPLM/A   Sudan People's Liberation Movement/Army
SSLS   South Sudan Law Society
SSP   South Sudan Pound
SSWLA   South Sudan Women Lawyers Association
SSYLF   South Sudan Young Leaders' Forum
UN   United Nations
UNDP   United Nations Development Programme
UNHCR   United Nations High Commissioner for Refugees
UNMISS   United Nations Mission in South Sudan

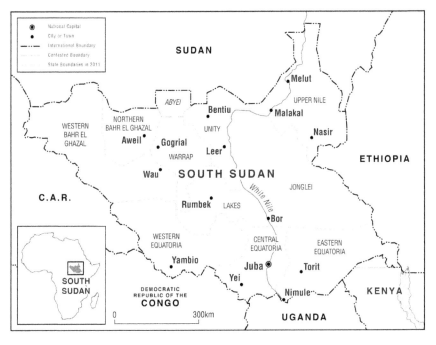

South Sudan showing state boundaries at independence in 2011.

PREFACE:
LAW FROM BELOW

Alex de Waal

For most people in South Sudan, each day brings a struggle to survive with a modicum of dignity and respectful social relationships. Despite wars, fears of new wars, and everyday violence and violation, many manage to maintain morale and insight, and persist, again and again, in reconstructing the essential elements of social functioning. Any person who writes about their situation must first acknowledge that it is not possible to fully express what it means to live surrounded by such penetrating fears and deprivations. This is the starting point for facing the extreme challenges that South Sudan poses to research ethics and methods, and to social theory.

High-status disciplines, notably economics and political science, have so far done remarkably poorly in grappling with South Sudan and in making policy recommendations. Academicians, whose analytic starting points are general models, are recurrently confounded by events. Emblematic of this is the assessment that, according to the standardised metrics of state-building, South Sudan had 'graduated' from 'crisis' to 'rebuild and reform' in October 2012,[1] just a few weeks before the eruption of civil war. The standard terminology for such analyses includes 'anarchy' and 'state breakdown', indicating analytical voids or serving as flags of intellectual surrender. But such is the metropolitan scholar's exorbitant privilege of determining the currency of analysis that such analyses can still be cashed for policy influence, even when repeatedly discredited.[2] In consequence, South Sudanese intellectuals, attuned to Western hierarchies of knowledge, often find themselves Janus-faced, trying to broker between such hegemonic but vacuous frameworks and their own lived realities.

South Sudan requires scholarship that takes seriously the perspective from the ground, alongside a dedication to the particularities of complicated and puzzling facts. Historians and anthropologists have been pre-eminent in South Sudanese studies, which is testament both to the dedication of several generations of researchers and to the enduring relevance of their methods and epistemologies. They depend upon learning from lived realities and seeking validation in detailed empirics, following the maxim that the focus of study should be the core concerns of people in the society that is being studied, and that we can only know what these are by giving considerable weight to the concepts and logics of the vernacular. Political sociology is catching up and taking it a step further by investigating power relations, contestation and resistance. Since the late colonial era, scholars of Sudan and South Sudan have turned their analytical gaze on the structures of domination as well as the lives of the dominated, interrogating the colonial apparatus, the aid and humanitarian encounters, and the wars. For academics in national universities, scholarship has also been action research – engaging with the life-and-death questions of the day in order to help people make meaningful change.

Studying South Sudan poses two particular challenges, which interleave ethics, method and epistemology. The first of these is how best to take account of, and properly acknowledge, the expertise of local people. For whom is research conducted? For whom are scholarly books and articles written? With regard to the first postcolonial generation, the metropolitan dominance over scholarship could credibly be explained away as a transitional phenomenon: in due course the national academy would answer back. And indeed, by the early 1980s, Sudan's universities – including the nascent University of Juba – were intellectual centres of world renown, especially in the emerging field of humanitarian studies and refugee policy. But the global inequity in knowledge production and valuation worsened in the subsequent generation. Foreign historians and anthropologists are acutely aware of this, but as yet no satisfactory means of rebalancing this pernicious unfairness has been found. African and Africanist scholars repeatedly provide deep insight into global predicaments, such as the post-democratic crises currently afflicting Western nations,[3] but are rarely if ever credited when mainstream Euro-American scholars belatedly arrive at similar analyses.

The second challenge is the special problem of studying violence. As Donald Donham notes in his perceptive essay 'Staring at Suffering': 'Violence is "red"'.[4] It intrudes into the process of studying it in ways quite unlike other topics of social inquiry (such as markets or religion). Violence slows down time and speeds up history: violent events expand in the subjective sense of lived experience, and they fix narratives, apparently defying the arrow of time which determines that cause should precede effect, by fixing the past in light of the present. This is particularly problematic for the scholar, who arrives on the scene well after the policeman and the journalist. As Donham notes:

> This means that almost no analyst of violence has actually observed the *process* of the creation of violence. This means that 'what happened' in any particular case of violence is typically established by after-the-fact narratives … This 'after-the-factness' of violence is not sufficiently problematized. That is, the 'data' of violence are produced by a local cultural and political process quite different from the protocols of social science.[5]

Combining these two challenges – the localisation of knowledge and the special problematics of violence – another problem arises, which is that '[t]he analyst of violence, consciously or not, steps into this fast-moving stream, with all of its undertows and cross-currents'.[6]

This is not a question of 'neutrality' but of moving from being an observer to being a participant. Every writer on South Sudan has the uncomfortable experience that analysis itself becomes part of the conflict, that the wrinkles of misgivings are ironed out into a flat narrative, and the errors become set in concrete.[7]

However, Donham's analysis does not grapple with situations in which disorder and violence are the norm, not the exception; in which people are drawing on not one shocking experience of violence but multiple, recurrent episodes; and in which they expect that such episodes will happen again. There is no 'before' and 'after'.

Where to start in studying such a situation? In this book, Rachel Ibreck takes local struggles for law as her starting point. 'Law from below' is, it transpires, a remarkable lens through which to make sense of South Sudan. The norms, principles, rules and mechanisms of law and justice are valued, performed and verily willed into being by local South Sudanese actors, including chiefs, lawyers, judges, local activists, teachers and ordinary people, who are in almost every other respect utterly without power.

In the best tradition of political sociology, this inverts the academic hierarchy. The concept of law from below is wholly missing from the hegemonic framings of states and power. For example, the World Bank's framework for understanding violence and state-building derives from Douglass North's new institutional economics.[8] This reduces law fundamentally to a managerial device for constructing and enforcing property rights and contracts. As Julio Faundez observes, in this sense 'law is closely related to political power and was historically, a device to enforce the privileges of elites. In developed capitalist democracies, the extension of the rights to all citizens came about when the elites found it in their interest to transform their privileges into impersonal rights'.[9] Remarkably, the most influential critics of such approaches to states and power surrender this terrain without a fight. For example, Giorgio Agamben writes:

Foucault contests the traditional approach to the problem of power, which is exclusively based on juridical models ('What legitimates power?') or on institutional models ('What is the State?'), and calls for a 'liberation from the theoretical privilege of sovereignty' in order to construct an analytic of power that would not take law as its model and its code.[10]

Note that both Foucault and Agamben, in refusing to endorse a juridical-institutional model of power, steer away from the possibility that law might be an arena in which elite power and privilege might be contested. They do not admit the possibility of other processes of law-formation.

Development practitioners have been more practical in engaging with the challenges of law facing poor and marginalised people. A number of international organisations, from legal advocacy groups to the World Bank, have established programmes aimed at making the mechanisms of justice more accessible, and thereby making law equitable in practice as well as in principle. As these programmes have progressed and those involved in them have learned, the importance of local knowledge and contextually sensitive approaches has increasingly been recognised.[11]

The limitation of much programming is that it treats law as a technical rather than a political challenge. Thus, for example, the metric used by the UK Independent Commission for Aid Impact to assess the Department of International Development's paralegal programmes is based on measurable outputs, rather than the processes engendered.[12] Projects to provide support to paralegals (people who have received some training in law, who are connected to legal firms and associations, but do not have formal qualifications to serve as lawyers) are therefore criticised for addressing symptoms, not systemic issues, and their normative value is discounted. Attending to the politics of legal pluralism, and contestation over law and judicial institutions, is therefore crucial to improving policy formulation, implementation and assessment in this field.

As will be clear from this book, there is a policy–theory gap. Scholars of the theory of law have much to learn from the practical experience of trying to implement rule of law programmes in the exceptionally challenging environment of South Sudan. Policy-makers also need to absorb some difficult lessons about how best to balance technocratic–professional programming with political advocacy that is informed by local activism. International promotion of the rule of law has crystallised around Sustainable Development Goal 16, which is to 'promote peaceful and inclusive societies for sustainable development, provide access to justice for all and build effective, accountable and inclusive institutions at all levels'. If this is to be pursued effectively, not only technical capacity but political strategy will be needed, and this includes activist practices of forging law from below.

From the perspective of South Sudan, the periphery of a periphery, there is no option but to understand law as a significant arena of political contestation. Indigenous traditions of the meaning and substance of law were shaped by experiences of the united Sudan, which the elites of Khartoum ruled either in partnership with colonial powers or on their own for almost two centuries until 2011. Sudan had four competing versions of legalism, drawn upon both by political authorities for legitimating their rule and manufacturing consent, and by legal activists seeking to resist and construct an alternative order. These are: military law and state of emergency; Islamic law; secular civil law (of various types); and customary law.[13]

Despite the centrality of the concept of exceptionalism in political philosophy, states of emergency and martial law are under-recognised in the sociology of law. This is an unfortunate omission. A.H. Abdelsalam argued that Sudanese constitutionalism was in reality the jurisprudence of exceptionalism; that emergency laws were the real legalism in postcolonial Sudan. He saw this as a colonial legacy, exploited to the full by both military and civilian leaders, and he argued that it was necessary to legislate emergency measures in detail partly so that those who enforced them – the army – could be kept properly in order.[14]

The Sudan People's Liberation Movement/Army (SPLM/A) was from its outset a militarised rebel force, not only using arbitrary and coercive measures but celebrating them too. As Chapter 2 shows, its penal and disciplinary codes were no less harsh than those of the government it opposed, and commanders possessed authority over courts in their areas of operation, as well as impunity for their actions, on and off the battlefield.

Across the world, British colonialism governed subject peoples using legal pluralism: secular law for the citizenry of government and commercial centres, and customary law for those governed by the indirect rule of administrative tribalism.[15] For Muslim societies, this entailed recognising Islamic family and civil law and courts. In Sudan, however, the British and Egyptian co-domini went further: they recognised Islam in the public–political sphere as well, co-opting the most senior Muslim sectarian leaders as their allies. This created a uniquely complex terrain when the Muslim Brothers began political activism in Sudan in the 1960s. On the one hand, the Islamists found a public sphere already permeated by Islam and thus receptive to the agenda of Islamisation. On the other, the Muslim Brothers as a political party had to compete with well-established Muslim sectarian parties: the Islamic seats were already taken. The consequence of this was that Sudanese Islamists were obliged to be creative.

For half a century, the single most persistent and polarising political debate in Sudan was the question of Islamic law. The dominant question was whether, how and on what basis to promote *sharia* law and Islamic courts from being the junior branch of the judiciary, concerned solely with matters of family law and personal conduct, to being the organising principle for a unified judiciary that would regulate the state itself.[16] The most influential advocate of this was Hassan al Turabi – lawyer, professor, philosopher, politician and political shape-shifter. Sometimes Turabi was the doyen of a democratic liberal Islamism and on other occasions the exponent of the 'jurisprudence of necessity',[17] which led him to embrace military rule. There were also other, contending, visions of Islamic law and Islamisation as well, and the judiciary was the site of political conflicts.[18]

Sudanese Islamists debated whether they should pursue a comprehensive civilising mission or a narrower Islamisation project in southern Sudan.[19] This encounter undoubtedly shaped southern Sudanese law-making practice, by re-legitimising customary and religious law. The very fact that elite Islamists had opened up law and the judiciary as a sphere of political contest meant that southern Sudanese were also challenged to develop their own alternatives. This was given immediate impetus by the 1990s Islamist programme named 'return to the roots', according to which, under conditions of extreme austerity, the government encouraged communities to seek authenticity in tradition. The Islamist intent was that this would reinvigorate pre-colonial Islamic local government, but for non-Muslim peoples, beginning with displaced southerners, it was a charter for celebrating customary law.

Meanwhile, in the areas controlled by the SPLM/A, commanders found that the SPLM laws were of limited use – or simply not available. A decade after it was promulgated, the SPLM administration in the Nuba Mountains had just a single copy of the 1994 code, sections of which had been hand-copied by judicial officers for their own use – but a shortage of paper meant that each one had only a few pages.[20] As a result, Governor Yousif Kuwa reinvigorated customary courts and re-codified customary law. Commanders in southern Sudan similarly improvised, in collaboration with chiefs, church leaders and officers and administrators who had some legal training and experience.

In all cases, customary law is adapted tradition, filtered through the codifications of chiefs and court clerks, colonial administrators and ethnographers – individuals, mostly men, with power, interests and world views. But while recognising the process of invention and reinvention, we should not overlook the reality of tradition also. There was a tradition of indigenous conceptualisations of law to be filtered. Customary legal systems were diverse, adaptable, and did not fit the juridical-institutional model of being an outgrowth of elite interests. This was particularly so in the case of stateless societies such as the Dinka and Nuer: their systems of law evolved so as to minimise the role of authority hierarchies other than the lineage.[21]

Rachel Ibreck's study traces historical and current legal contests in ways that are quietly but seminally subversive. It engages with the ethics of knowledge production and ownership, involving local researchers and observers who are themselves participants. One strand of the research, the simple act of observing courts and recording the proceedings, has a cumulative impact on those courts – the judges and enforcement officers are more attentive to norms and regulations. It studies violence and its regulation in real time, not 'after the fact': we can observe how the courts are creating narratives and reshaping identities. In doing so, the study of law from below allows the writer to avoid the peril of becoming an accomplice in the ways in which narratives are co-opted into the logic of conflict. Above all, this study rescues an appreciation of agency for those with limited power, or no discernible power at all, in a situation of exceptional adversity and distress. There is something that works in South Sudan. To adapt Walter Benjamin's justly famous observation, it is an exemplar of the contemporary historian with the gift of fanning the spark of hope in the *present*.[22]

INTRODUCTION

> There's no peace without justice … But simply because they
> are not warlords and they don't have guns, lawyers, paralegals
> and justices are not seen as relevant to peace. Nobody's inter-
> ested even to call them on the peace tables.[1]

South Sudan is notorious for its wars, which have proliferated on
national and local scales since the country's independence in 2011,
and date back over almost two centuries to colonialism and slavery.
Yet its people are far from 'lawless'.[2] Instead, they are wrestling with
a surfeit of laws that were made and administered in an accelerated,
incoherent manner. Legality has alternately served as either a valued
precept for social order and dignity; or a tool for political repression
and extraction. Law is implicated in successive historical systems of
oppression in the Sudans,[3] to the extent that taming and binding it
to the equal needs and rights of ordinary citizens is a prerequisite
for ending violent conflict and achieving political change.

This book explores the pervasive power of law in government
and society in wartime, featuring the remarkable histories of South
Sudanese people who continued to seek or strive for justice, despite
a violent conflict and humanitarian crisis. It concentrates on the
five years that followed the outbreak of civil war in December
2013 – a period in which some 400,000 people died;[4] and around
4 million, almost a third of the population, were displaced due to
conflict, famine, hunger and economic deprivation.[5] It looks beyond
a conventional focus on military actors and battlefields in conflict

zones, to tell a 'different kind of war story'[6] about the place of law in the plural and intersecting forms of violence suffered by South Sudanese people, their resilient legal practices; and their everyday and extraordinary forms of resistance by legal means. In spite of the war, many people still acted within the law, turning to local courts in pursuit of solutions to all manner of problems; while some tried to use law to constrain or challenge arbitrary power.

In many ways, South Sudan is an extreme case, providing a test of whether law constitutes a regulatory force, or retains an emancipatory appeal, despite exceptional levels of political violence and turbulence.[7] There is much to learn from previous work on law and activism in other former colonies troubled by conflict and political repression. Political change has generally been driven by civil struggles 'from below' in Africa,[8] although the political gains have sometimes been transitory, and civil society activists often fail to represent the concerns of the most marginalised and oppressed.[9] Africans have sometimes exemplified inventiveness in their 'legal agency'; and like other 'subalterns' they have absorbed and adapted elements of human rights law, fusing it with local vernaculars, and deploying it strategically.[10] But it is instructive for scholars if people at the margins continue to appeal to legal authorities and take cases to court in the harsh circumstances of contemporary South Sudan, all the more so if there is any evidence that courts can settle legal uncertainties and call authorities to account. More importantly, it is salient to the urgent question of how to pursue peace, civilian protection and humanitarian response in settings of seemingly intractable conflict.[11] 'Rule of law' experts have been among the international peacebuilders confounded by 'protracted conflicts'; they are wisely 'turning to the local'.[12] Naturally, the 'locals' already have their own pressing agendas, 'practical norms'[13] and eclectic knowledge and expertise, and their own legal authorities, human rights concepts and advocates.

Hopes and interventions for peace in South Sudan, at the moment of writing, rely heavily on a peace accord brokered by regional powers in Khartoum in September 2018. But, as the South Sudan Civil Society Forum lamented, the agreement did not end the 'war on civilians', and killings, abductions and mass rapes followed.[14] South Sudan's military and political elites have deliberated over the spoils of war in successive talks over more than a decade; they make promises of peace, ceasefires and reforms that they usually fail to keep. Moreover, South Sudan's conflict is multidimensional, so it is not just military campaigns but, for instance, intercommunal conflicts over land and cattle, and spiralling sexual violence that also need be addressed and resolved.[15]

Legal and judicial authorities are positioned on the frontline of multiple conflicts and their actions may be pivotal in either licensing abuses or limiting them, by addressing injustices, solving disputes and counteracting the spread of violence. It turns out that courts and prisons in South Sudan are fraught arenas for both political and existential contests. On the one hand, political and military elites use the law to repress and eliminate their opponents; on the other, the law is the last resort of victims. Committed judges, chiefs, lawyers and citizens try to reckon with everyday injustices even during a civil war. They respond to arbitrary detentions; local disputes on land rights, domestic violence in real time, trying to negotiate with plural authorities and navigate the fuzzy contours of unstable laws. Their countless, mundane struggles for justice are rarely successful and may not seem significant when set against such grievous violations as war crimes and crimes against humanity. Yet they matter not only to the people affected, but also to society and politics at large because they intuitively counteract a historically embedded system of predatory government and subvert established political practices of 'legal politics' and 'lawfare' that have perpetuated inequality and suppressed dissent over generations.[16]

The modest efforts of lawyers, paralegals and citizen activists, the threats they face, and their hard-won achievements, are wrongfully overlooked while the eyes of the world are on warring parties and peace deals. Their 'creative and improvised practices' may well be culturally distinctive, pragmatic and opaque, but they reinforce the evidence that transformative agency with the potential to incrementally alter power structures[17] can emerge even in war-torn places, where 'the mesh of violence' invariably constrains moral choices.[18] In other words, people who try to harness law to individual rights and the common good are courageously and gradually laying the foundations for sustainable peace in the longue durée, by constructing a more humane legal and political order from below.[19]

War and law

War is often represented as a time-limited 'state of emergency', during which governments may suspend certain rights and freedoms in the name of security. But this dichotomy is not as stark as it would appear. States of emergency are themselves modes of legality, and in a place such as South Sudan they have been far more prolonged and pervasive than interludes of peaceful orderliness. Many wars in Africa have been, to varying degrees, authorised, pursued and resisted by means of law. Warring parties use and abuse the law, and people observe the law and either call upon or try to circumvent legal authority. Governments and rebels cite injustices or breaches of the law to justify their actions and law also informs military conduct and the way that it is perceived. This applies not only to humanitarian 'laws of war', but also functions in two other ways: legislation generally determines who is most vulnerable to violence and what constitutes a violation; and legal consciousness and legalised violence shape relations within society and between people and government during war. It is therefore odd that policy and scholarly debates rarely analyse the relations between everyday legal practices and war, and do not tend to consider legal activism and peace negotiations in an integrated fashion. They also tend to separate routine injustices from wartime atrocities, in the way proposed by the transitional justice model, with its 'artificial time frames and zones of impunity'.[20]

War zones host multiple competing bidders for public authority, from national and subnational state actors, customary and religious authorities, armed groups and community associations to international organisations.[21] Law has a special part in their legitimation; like states they rely upon legal mechanisms and discourses to generate some degree of voluntary compliance. As the development sociologist Christian Lund argues, 'public authority' is produced in conjunction with an idea of the state (whether in alliance or opposition to this imagined entity). Legality is a central marker of stateness:

> the deployment of a language of law ... provided force to the *idea* of the state – metropolitan as well as colonial. The character of the state is intimately connected to the capacity to make distinctions, and this may just be the essence of public authority.[22]

The point applies not only to those unarmed actors who manage to govern without the direct use of violence, but equally to military actors. Authoritarian rulers and rebel forces tend to 'rule by law',[23] using it to authorise violence and criminalise opposition. Military forces are in constant interaction with legality, their status is defined by and subject to international humanitarian law (even when they are routinely breaching it), and they also make use of law for internal discipline and external justifications of their actions. Furthermore, political and social actors have inherited legal constructs that either outlaw or give license to certain forms of violence. As legal scholar Christine Bell observes:

> Law is often deeply implicated in conflict ... Conflicts are often dealt with through emergency law regimes and tweaked criminal law, denial of human rights is often a cause and a symptom of conflict and legal institutions are not understood as autonomous from those they are supposed to hold to account.[24]

Law matters profoundly to the exercise of authority and the organisation of conflict, but peace negotiations seem to be obliged to treat it as subordinate to power and external to conflict. They envisage securing a deal between political parties, then introducing law to a seemingly 'lawless' context through a top-down reform. Peace agreements set out 'legal power maps'[25] which will shape national constitutions. In the best cases, they also specify mechanisms for atrocity prosecutions or other justice provisions. However, these negotiations and agreements overlook entrenched legal practices and socio-legal understandings that might serve the ambition of peace. They also miss the iterative, protracted ways in which actual accountability relations must be generated between public authorities and the people who comply with them. This is a justification for the inclusion of civil society in peace negotiations, a recently emerging norm,[26] but there are some difficulties in establishing who fits into this category, and who they might represent, in a highly militarised and divided society.

Scholars have pondered on the constituents and legitimacy of civil society even in relatively stable countries in Africa. Critiques of civil society became rife in an era when development donors prioritised support for formal non-governmental organisations that conformed to their 'conventional view'[27] because they spoke the language of democratisation and were based on horizontal relationships. In wartime, such organisations are further disempowered; they tend to be restricted to urban areas and associated with 'transnational governmentality.'[28] They are also primary targets for repression and co-option under neo-patrimonial regimes.[29] It seems that what tends to survive and flourish are associations based on 'primordial' ideas of ethnicity,[30] which are troublingly vulnerable to the demands and exactions of violent actors mobilising around ethnic, kinship and religious ties, to the point that some definitions of civil society simply exclude them.

However, the idea of public authority offers an escape from the trap of definitions and presumptions about civil society and directs us to examine actual practices and relations empirically. In this vein, Mary Kaldor, a leading theorist of global civil society, observes that a 'logic of civicness' can survive in social networks even in the most intractable conflicts.[31] The development analyst Duncan Green calls attention to the 'power with' that is harnessed by 'citizen activists' who participate in public life with the aim to 'ensure that society and its institutions respect people's rights and meet their needs'.[32] And the anthropologist Caroline Nordstrom suggests, in her compelling account of the creativity of ordinary citizens on the frontline of the Mozambican war, that such people may prevail in the worst of times. She writes about average people engaged in a 'remarkable process of revitalization', applying 'civil traditions' to counter uncertainty, violence and a culture of militarisation. They strive to survive, she argues, by 'rebuilding humane worlds'.[33] These various perspectives provide the grounds on which to examine legal practices and legal activism, and their relations to politics during South Sudan's war.

Law and war in South Sudan

The law is a morass of plural institutions, norms and practices in South Sudan. The origins of the state, the legal system and the judiciary lie in colonial interventions designed to administer cheap authoritarian government and facilitate extraction. Since then, there have been constant and comprehensive changes to the content of law – successive governments of Sudan and South Sudan have rewritten it under the influences of British common law, Egyptian civil law, Islamic law and customary norms, as well as emergency regulations and martial law. The underlying imperative of reforms has generally been the extension of the administrative power of government, rather than the rights of citizens. As a legal and political historian of the region, Mark Massoud, acutely observed: 'law has been suborned to serve the cause of despotism'.[34]

But law has contradictory tendencies as a source both of violence and of order-making – this is true of law in a general sense, and the duality is especially stark in this region. Law, judicial actors and legal instruments have been key to historical processes of state formation at central and local levels. Statutory law has been a vehicle for authoritarian government, and yet some lawyers and legal scholars have also been at the forefront of organising political opposition.[35] Customary law has been an effective mechanism of societal regulation, and dispute resolution, providing some order and predictability at local levels, and yet the chiefly authorities that administer the law historically have an ambiguous intermediary status as both agents of control and a bulwark against the impositions of arbitrary central power.[36]

At the moment of South Sudan's independence, hopes were high for a new legal and political order. Yet the newly enshrined Transitional Constitution of the Republic of South Sudan (2011) was a disappointment. It lacked any grounding in consultation or popular participation, as it 'was pushed through at an enormous speed by several national and international actors', making it a 'handmaiden' for the interests of the ruling party.[37] It initially states that people of South Sudan are the source of the constitution and of law – that the government is governed by the constitution, which in turn 'derives its authority from the will of the people'. But this is in tension with later articles which secure excessive powers for the president and create opportunities for rule by decree, for instance licensing the president to declare and terminate a state of emergency and to appoint or dismiss state governors in a crisis,[38] while also securing him immunity from any legal proceedings while in office.

Perhaps more promisingly, the constitution recognised customary law as the foundation of the country's legal heritage, and chiefly authority as a tier of local government, enshrining legal pluralism. It positioned statutory and customary courts as equally valid forums alongside each other, albeit with the intention that they should handle different kinds of cases, dealing with criminal and civil cases respectively. This was an acknowledgement of the reality that customary authorities held popular legitimacy, already handled the vast majority of legal disputes[39] and defined people's experiences and understandings of law, but it also legalised social, ethnic and gender differences and inequalities. South Sudan is home to at least 60 ethnic groups, and customary regimes rely upon various languages and plural notions of ethnic, clan and kinship identity in their interpretations of law; and they all vigorously regulate familial relations including marriage, divorce and adultery, mostly at the cost of women's rights.[40]

However, the constitution also comprised a new, hard-won 'bill of rights' reflecting some of civil society's aspirations and long-running struggles for a people's constitution 'that guarantees respect for human rights, democracy, gender equity, good governance, accountability and the Rule of Law'.[41] The establishment of the new state brought a chance to bridge differences and transform politics, law and society. Several laws and legal institutions were substantially revised and reformed; numerous international 'rule of law' initiatives were launched, aimed at building the capacities of judicial and security actors and providing human rights training, legal aid and legal empowerment. The government promised further constitutional reforms and, in June 2012, 18 civil society organisations formed a partnership and 'resource team' to promote a participatory constitution-making process. They embarked on consultations with more than 1,000 participants across the ten states of South Sudan, fostering hopes of a civic state and political renewal.[42]

Since December 2013, the war has halted constitutional progress, implying the outright failure of rule of law projects. Military and political elites at the centre of government were manifestly looting and squandering oil wealth. They commanded power by buying and selling loyalties, and using violence to control, or to bid to enter, the 'political marketplace' in a mode of political competition and governance identified by Alex de Waal as 'real politics in the Horn of Africa'.[43] South Sudan's leaders presided over egregious violations and many judges, lawyers and activists were among the 2 million people forced to flee the country. The scale and scope of projects for human rights and legal reform narrowed considerably. The war demonstrated that military, commercial and private interests predominated in the administration of the law; it echoed and reinforced the historical tendencies of violent authoritarian government. Nevertheless, there is good reason to believe that these rule of law initiatives were not all meaningless; that they have had some unseen impacts, and that they may yet bear some fruit.

Legal activism in South Sudan's towns

This book is a study of law in action in war-torn towns and displacement sites. It finds that everyday legal processes and a commitment to legality endured despite multi-layered conflict and fragmented, 'hybrid' governance.[44] We see this in governmental invocations of the law, in the use of courts, and in the ways that people try to make them work better. It is based on my own ethnographic and documentary research from 2014 to 2019 and collaborative research with a team of court observers in statutory and customary courts in government-held towns, Juba, Nimule, Torit, Yambio, Yei, Rumbek, Wau, from July 2015 to July 2016, as well as recent interviews and court reports from other urbanised settings, including displacement sites in Melijo, Bentiu and Malakal.

In some ways the book reflects historical continuities. It is surely in South Sudan's towns, if anywhere, that we could hope to find people accessing legal forums, demanding rights and making civic claims on the state during the conflict. Towns have been 'points of articulation with the state'[45] and of social and political contestation since colonial times. Informal civic activism was often enlivened on the 'urban frontiers', with chiefs creatively negotiating with government, and students organising protests and developing new intellectual ideas and political horizons.[46] Certainly, most towns have tarnished histories as former slave-trading stations and military garrisons, and are associated with predatory government *hakuma* (government) and counter-posed to the moral values and relations of rural 'home' communities in popular perceptions.[47] But they have also been seen as places of opportunity, promising access to some services, schooling, money, markets and humanitarian aid. The duality of urban spaces, as sites of repression and innovation, remained the case after independence.

South Sudan's independence, however, was a time of change and new opportunities and it stimulated a massive influx of people into the towns. While some benefited from the new political order, the hopes of many for human development were frustrated. Dr John Garang, the SPLM's former leader, had famously promised that he would 'bring towns to people and not people to towns', but neither urban centres nor villages gained many of the promised public services and jobs.[48] Development was starkly 'uneven':[49] South Sudan's elites benefited from access to the wealth generated by oil exports and jobs in government or the international aid sector, but the majority struggled to survive petty trade and access to rural livelihoods based on land and cattle. Even Juba, the capital city, remained a ramshackle blend of concrete housing and offices with shacks or village-style *tukul* (thatched hut) housing, as well as a few mansions and hotels servicing political, military and business elites and *Khawaja* (foreigners) in the aid community. Former fighters, rural youth and returned refugees had flocked there after the Comprehensive Peace Agreement (CPA) that ended the war between the north and south of the country in 2005, hoping to escape their political and economic subjugation. Instead, most encountered massive disparities of wealth and increased competition for land and livelihoods.[50] These grievances must surely be some part of an explanation for the civil war and its dynamics, along with the interests and actions of political elites, but they were also intensified by war, as urban inequalities, deprivation and insecurity increased.

War reached South Sudan's towns in catastrophic bursts, peaking in the dry season and subsiding during the rains.[51] The fighting was persistent, but shifted from place to place according to the seasons and political geography. All of our research sites were affected at one time or another. The capital Juba was the first atrocity site in December 2013, beginning with intense fighting between different factions in the army, and culminating in house-to-house massacres of Nuer civilians by security forces[52]. Fighting flared up in Yambio in February 2016 and then Wau in June that year. The following month, war again erupted in Juba, then swept across the entire Equatoria region. The fighting reverberated around Torit,[53] then utterly devastated the formerly peaceful town of Yei, where government forces supported by the notorious *Mathiang Anyoor* militia battled with rebels, before all armed groups unleashed carnage upon civilians.[54] The displacement sites of Juba and Bentiu Protection of Civilians sites (PoCs) and Melijo internally displaced persons (IDP) camp sheltered survivors of other urban mass atrocities and warfare, including in Bor, Bentiu and Malakal, as well as people from surrounding rural areas.[55]

The towns often managed to regenerate after the worst of the fighting, returning swiftly to business as usual. But as well as sporadic warfare, towns experienced the effects of economic collapse, deprivation and hunger,[56] and of persistent forms of political and ethnic violence, intimidation and criminality. The violations and suffering of people in towns have been recorded in numerous human rights and humanitarian reports, but they are also exemplified in personal experience: all of my interviewees and most of our court observer research team had experienced threats from war and political violence by July 2016, and many had been forced to flee. At the same time, processes of law and order-making continued, both in towns and displacement sites, and a myriad of excruciating everyday problems were taken to the courts.

Legal activism

We might expect that many people in South Sudan would regard legal institutions and authorities as corrupt and repressive, and there is much evidence to support this view. But despite some six decades of cyclical warfare, instability and violent predatory government, many still act upon a hope that the law might solve disputes fairly. And remarkably, some actively struggle against the odds to promote fairer legal processes, using legal resources in efforts to promote the delivery of justice or limit injustices; they share a 'legalism from below' with people elsewhere in the world who have contested the transgressions of law by states and powerful actors 'in legal terms'.[57] This legal activism touches directly upon the relations between people and political authority and the prospects for legitimacy.

The book derives many of its insights from informal 'citizen activists' working pragmatically to limit abuses and promote justice in and around several of South Sudan's dilapidated towns, and in its capital city, Juba. The focus on government-held areas is both strategic, since opposition areas were less accessible during the war, and productive as a means to explore the relations between the law, the state and society. Their work exposes the sharp contrast between daily struggles on the ground, and the spatial and temporal abstraction of peace and policymaking processes that tend to dominate conflict resolution strategies. Legal activists work at local levels on daily disputes, violations and crimes committed within families and communities. They have specific ambitions and limited material resources. Their minor successes are often undermined by military actions and structural violence – and they require tactical compromises – yet they are tangible and 'bend towards' peace and justice.

Legal activists stand out for their intimate knowledge of how plural laws are being applied in local contexts in South Sudan, and their willingness to put this expertise at the disposal of others in their community and nation. They are ready to offer advice and support on a range of issues, including coping with demands from the security services and government officials, dealing with criminality, and disputes among neighbours and within families. Yet they are as vulnerable to violence and insecurity as the people whom they seek to assist. Numerous chiefs, judges, lawyers and paralegals were arrested or threatened and forced to flee during the research period. Every one of the activists featured in this book has

survived some form of human rights violation or war-related traumatic experience, such as the loss of a relative in fighting, abduction
or forced displacement; as historian Edward Thomas observes,
South Sudanese biographies are characterised by 'disorientating
violence and dispassionate hopefulness'.[58] Their predicament is the
consequence of recent warfare and insecurity, but it is also part of
a historical pattern of militarised colonial and Sudanese governments using and abusing the law.[59]

The struggle to make the law work in South Sudan requires political skills, knowledge of diverse cultural archives, social connections
and tenacity in the context of political and legal fragmentation and
hybridity. Successful legal activists cultivate relationships locally
and transnationally; they are able to mediate and translate between
different judicial and political actors, as well as plural ideas about
the law, finding ways to weave them into tactics for the survival of
citizens and communities. They have distinctive approaches which
are 'accustomed to turbulence and policy confusion' and understand through cultural practice what looks at a distance to be mere
disorder. In common with traders observed at the global economic
periphery, the legal activists featured in this book share 'landmarks
and navigational pathways'[60] that enable them to 'manage uncertainty'[61] and pursue 'marginal gains'.[62] They develop uniquely
'convivial' approaches through networking and negotiation.[63]
Incremental improvements in legal practices cannot halt or match
the rapid destructive force of violence, but they constitute novel and
significant responses to the dominant modes of violent, authoritarian government.

Outline

The book contributes to the evidence that everyday political
encounters and forms of resistance can reveal the concrete operation and meaning of power when seen 'from below'.[64] It is informed
by previous work that demonstrates the salience of informal and
marginal actors in the making and unmaking of political order in

conflict settings, where: 'understanding the micropolitics remains essential to understanding the subtleties and complexities of power relations'.[65] This challenge is tackled by engaging with diverse voices and influences and providing a series of vignettes, tracing specific processes of legal activism over time.

The book preserves the conventions of critical distance in its analysis, but from the outset the research was 'engaged', in the sense that it was openly undertaken in solidarity with people working against cruelty, violence and oppression, and was informed by collaborative action methodologies and the concerns of feminist legal studies. In the circumstances of a civil war it is hardly feasible for researchers to position themselves as morally above and empirically outside of the conflict; our presence and positionality is inevitably a sort of intervention in the research environment and, worryingly, our research may affect not only how we see, but what exists to 'be seen'. Nevertheless, it is surely still possible to produce valid and robust evidence from such messy and complex encounters, provided the conditions under which it was gathered are explained and taken into account, the findings are cross-checked, and some modesty about the conclusions is retained.[66]

Scholars are constantly reckoning with the significant challenges of working in war zones and trying to find ways to manage them, and this is essential to ensuring that the views and experiences of both conflict actors and marginalised people are recognised and understood. The research for this book was explicitly interested in foregrounding the concerns and perspectives of its participants as one of several ways to respond to the acute dilemmas involved in working in such difficult places. The research design was deeply influenced by what seemed possible and interesting to people on the ground. The court observation project had its origins in the concerns of a Juba-based lawyer who saw the need to monitor and document court proceedings that often went unrecorded.[67] This led to a form of collaborative action research involving 20 South Sudanese lawyers, paralegals and activists who together compiled over 600 court reports. During the research, many of these activists also continued to work in their home communities to try to provide advice and support to people facing injustices and their stories were the inspiration for further research on activism. The activist researchers also participated in seven collaborative action research workshops, designed not only to elicit views but to promote critical reflection, involving between 12 and 65 people. This research was then supplemented by focus groups, participant observation and more than 80 life histories and interviews, gathered in a series of short trips to different localities over a period of five years since April 2014. In turn, some of these encounters yielded unusual and crucial documentary sources, including letters and court judgments.

Drawing on these plural sources, the book explores wartime experiences of law and struggles for justice through a series of analyses and vignettes. It begins with an introductory vignette on violence, law and peacemaking. Chapter 1 then enters into conversation with political sociologies and ethnographies of law and government in conflict settings.[68] It also draws upon political historians and anthropologists of the region, especially seminal works that illuminate the history of law and legal politics in Sudan[69] and help to unravel the contemporary political realities of South Sudan.[70] These scholarly insights enable us to understand the power of law, the logics of government and the value of examining politics at the margins.

The remainder of the book foregrounds empirical research into different facets of the justice system and examples of legal activism. Chapter 2 examines the internal workings of the institutions of justice and the conduct of legal professionals, highlighting the political capture and domination of the institutions of justice and the persistent forms of resistance from within. Chapter 3 explores the everyday practices, processes and judgments of the town courts, mainly based on the court observations. Chapter 4 traces the processes of legal activism in three vignettes. It begins with a prolonged dispute and the mostly successful defence of a community against a land grab in Juba: 'Land belongs to the community'; it then turns to exploring 'Reforming custom in exile', examining initiatives by activists working to promote women's rights in customary courts within a Protection of Civilians site for internally displaced people, under United Nations governance. The final vignette, 'The rule of man', focuses on the voluntary initiatives by lawyers and a citizen activist who tried, and failed, to prevent the execution of two teenage boys by a statutory court. In Chapter 5, the focus is on exploring the legal consciousness, agency and resources of the activists based on detailed individual life histories. Chapter 6 also draws extensively on the life histories to present an account of the tactics of legal activists in efforts to limit violent injustices. The conclusion argues that 'no condition is permanent';[71] it considers the significance of the findings, the demands for accountability for atrocities and the possibility for a new political order based on foundational justice.

The book aims to further discussions about law and activism in academia, policy and civil society but it also calls for the extension of new forms of solidarity and support for people working for justice in South Sudan and other conflict settings. It is an attempt to communicate the scale and complexity of the injustices that judicial authorities, lawyers and citizen activists confront, and some of the artful ways in which they have responded to their predicaments. It also preserves for history experiences that might otherwise go unnoticed, because they did not manage to radically alter the immediate prospects for peace or political change. Legal activists at the margins have mostly fallen outside of humanitarian support and have been given limited attention by rule of law promoters and peacebuilders, although they are working at the intersection of all these fields. They cannot deliver the measurable, timely results that international development and humanitarian donors require. However, by working steadily for justice they promote social norms, practices and networks that might cumulatively, progressively undermine a political system founded on extraction and violence.

Law, violence and peace

There is a chasm between peace, as it is discussed and defined in high-level political negotiations, and justice for people on the ground in South Sudan. Law is implicated in this divide; but is also a means to bridge it. This applies throughout the war, but let us take the month of December 2017, and focus on two parallel events that help to reveal the manifold, concrete relations between law, violence and peace. The first event was in Ethiopia, the site of long-running peace negotiations involving political and military elites, lawyers and international officials, taking place outside the country and largely beyond the influence of its ordinary citizens. The second was a court case in Wau, which put civilians on trial for the death of a soldier. By comparing them, and considering the contexts in which they occurred, we can establish why routine legal practices in South Sudan's towns and communities are crucial to the prospects for peace in the nation.

In December 2017 in Bishoftu, Ethiopia, an attempt was underway to relaunch a failed peace deal, the Agreement on the Resolution of the Conflict in South Sudan (ARCISS) which the South Sudan People's Liberation Movement (SPLM), in government, and the rebel SPLM-in Opposition (SPLM-IO) had negotiated and signed in August 2015. The signatories had swiftly broken the ARCISS; government forces swept across the Equatoria region in pursuit of their opponents, and all parties unleashed appalling violence on civilians. Two years on, an array of smaller rebel groups had emerged and the regional mediators of the Inter-Governmental Authority on Development (IGAD) were now working hard to mediate between 14 groups.

The parties gathered together at a lakeside spa resort, funded and supported by international donors. Among them were well-paid legal experts whose task was to help draft and critique the latest texts in an ever-thickening pile of peace documentation that would produce soft law and draft legislation on the terms of future governance arrangements. Some civil society activists were valiantly trying to influence the process, including holding onto transitional justice mechanisms that they had managed to insert into the 2015 deal. The 'revitalisation' of ARCISS promised an end to the military contests plus additional measures, including a cessation of hostilities and commitments for civilian protection and prisoner releases. However, all the talking mostly proved redundant; fighting was ongoing during the process, and it resumed soon after, with many political prisoners remaining incarcerated.[72] There would, of course, be further talks and peace pacts between these 'big men', with fresh drafts of would-be legislation. Still, in December 2017 the prospects for peace did not look hopeful.

The meaning of this 'revitalisation' peace process, and other similar peace talks, can be defined by their main function, which was to reallocate power within an elite group of military and political leaders – the so-called 'gun class'.[73] The talks discursively bolstered the power and legitimacy of military actors, extending political recognition (including sovereign privileges) to a status they had gained largely through fighting, rather than by means of popular support. The voices of political and civic actors were muted, to the point that frustrated groups and individuals, with limited military experience, constituted themselves as armed groups to get a seat at the table.[74] Lawyers were corralled in to write contracts and constitutional documents, with the thinnest of pretence that this was a technical and not a political exercise.

Certainly, the transitional justice mechanisms included in the original ARCISS peace deal represented an unprecedented challenge to impunity for war crimes and crimes against humanity in this region. The parties at the peace table also dutifully promised an independent judiciary, to be strengthened by reforms and capacity-building, as well as a further attempt at constitutional review by experts.[75] But they had little to say of the ongoing exploitation of legal instruments and authorities for political violence, or the actual and plural ways in which law and governance was being administered at local levels, and the central role of customary chiefs. Moreover, in essence, the peace deal preserved a linear and historical relationship between political violence; gaining and wielding state power; and making law.

Law is associated with power and violence, on the one hand, and contrary aspirations for justice, on the other, not only in the Bishoftu peace talks, but in its daily enactments. Just before the warring parties assembled in Ethiopia, a medical doctor was put on trial in Wau, South Sudan. Doctor Anthony was accused of fraud after an operational commander of the government forces in Wau had suddenly died. He was unlucky to have been on duty when the soldier was brought to the hospital, but his apparent mistake was to have written a medical report that contradicted the lay opinions of powerful people who had stakes in the commander's life and death. The doctor attributed the cause of death to an intestinal infection, while relatives of the general and military officers were convinced that the soldier died due to food poisoning, contracted from the lunch served at a human rights workshop for military officers. The doctor was the third accused in the case of the commander's death. Previously, charges had been levelled against another unlikely suspect, a diocesan official at the Catholic Church, who had helped to organise the workshop – she was detained for two weeks, until lawyers obtained her release. The Kenyan caterer who had provided the food for the workshop was also accused and tried. The court convicted both the doctor and caterer and fined them 31 cows each, as 'blood compensation' for murder.[76]

The judgment against the doctor was predictable: the court was under pressure to defer to military authority, given the insecurity in the town. Over the previous two years, hundreds of people had been killed, raped or injured by soldiers and rebels, or attacked in intercommunal fighting, and tens of thousands had fled the town:[77] any potential form of dissent was likely to be crushed. Wau was especially salient in the politics of the independent South Sudan, because of an unusual peaceful protest against an administrative decision in December 2012, which was violently suppressed.[78] The 'government killed peaceful demonstrators who had green leaves in their hands' and in this moment the independence vision of a 'civic state' evaporated and 'a real indication of a black future for South Sudan emerged', in the words of a local MP.[79] Lawyers and human rights groups struggled hard to turn back the political tide, but their efforts to secure a fair trial for the protestors were met with intimidation. The killings of 2012 and the massacres of 2016 were peaks on a continuum of political violence. Wau had been the locus of some of the earliest and worst massacres of Sudan's second civil war in the 1980s,[80] and of atrocious violence dating back to the nineteenth century.

The Wau court was operating under severe financial constraints in December 2017, as the war had devastated lives and livelihoods, and even the judges' pay had become worthless. The prisons were overflowing with a backlog of cases. The judge's decisions to convict the doctor and value the military commander's life at 62 cows (in total), a rather high settlement by the standards of the time,[81] reflected this wider context. In a precarious economic and political situation, the court paid little heed to the evidence and rushed to settle a sensitive case with an expedient customary (and legal) norm of compensation.

We might conclude from the doctor's case that South Sudan's law was merely dysfunctional, a façade for arbitrary exercises in executive power and for settling grievances. If so, the prospects for peace and development would depend entirely upon establishing a new political and legal order at the centre, perhaps through an externally imposed solution and a second attempt to build the state from scratch.[82] Yet even if the judgment was flawed, it matters that the courts continued to function under the shadow of war and deprivation, delivering routine judgments and resolving issues in civic-minded processes. It is also significant that the relatives and colleagues of the military commander left the issue to be resolved by the judiciary, although they were capable of taking matters into their own hands. Most importantly, people did not simply accept the injustice.

The doctor's arrest was the subject of local commentary and protest from people who still believed that the law is more than a mere tool of power. His colleagues at Wau hospital went on strike for a day in support, arguing that his arrest was unlawful and that all doctors must be allowed to carry out their duties ethically. A few officials in the state government tried to intervene on the doctor's behalf. The local press produced several reports on the case, and people debated the judgment on social media. Some were critical of the doctor, suspecting he might somehow be complicit in an offence, but many deplored the decision, recognising its relevance to generalised insecurity: 'We are in a strange country anything can happen to the medical doctors because there is no law or rules that can protect them.'[83] Human rights lawyers analysed the case, critiqued the judgment, and began to strategise how to appeal against the doctor's conviction. As one lawyer explained: the judgment did not accord with either the law or the facts; no attempt was made to investigate the actual cause of death, 'a medical expert was not called to disprove the findings of the doctor ... It is just a miscarriage of justice to the ordinary citizen who has no money and no gun'.[84]

The doctor's trial and the various responses to it illustrate that the justice system is itself a source of many injustices and is largely subservient to military power and complementary to authoritarian arbitrary government. But the courts still represent a form of civil authority, while law also continues to regulate society, shaping ideas and social relations. The responses to the Wau trial demonstrate that legal consciousness does not disappear during wartime. Rather, it remains tightly connected to political agency and contention. The very fact that laws codify rights, obligations and procedures for all persons means that they provide the tools with which people with little power can challenge and criticise those in power. There are competing 'rules of law' and divergent legal imaginaries at work in South Sudan. Since legalised violations fuel grievances, stabilising the law and making it serve the interests of justice is central to resolving multi-layered violent conflicts. This means that laws and courts must be grounds for resistance.

Chapter 1

LAW AND ACTIVISM IN CONFLICT

In June 2016, the *New York Times* published a letter under the names of President Salva Kiir and Vice President Riek Machar which made the case that 'South Sudan needs truth not trials'.[1] The purpose of the letter was to head off international attempts to set up a court to bring alleged war criminals to justice. At the time, both Kiir and Machar, protagonists in the post-2013 civil war, were temporarily united in the Transitional Government of National Unity by a peace deal, the ARCISS.[2] The letter spoke of the need for dialogue and reconciliation and warned that: 'disciplinary justice – even if delivered under international law – would destabilize efforts to unite our nation by keeping alive anger and hatred'. The missive was in some ways predictable, given that both the leaders were commanders of opposing armies that had been accused of atrocity crimes and neither would want to face trial.[3] However, it soon emerged that the letter had been devised by presidential advisers and a US-based foreign public relations firm, and Machar insisted that he did not sign off on it. Just days later, Machar's spokesperson James Gatdet issued a correction: the SPLM-IO party was committed to 'justice and accountability' according to the provisions in the August 2015 peace agreement, which included a 'hybrid court'.[4]

The letter was a work of subterfuge and public relations – a blatant attempt to ensure the impunity of political elites accused of wartime atrocities. Less obviously, both the letter and the debacle surrounding it indicated that warring parties could not simply ignore demands for justice. Indeed, each of them claimed, in one way or another, to be committed to the administration of justice, and invoked the law within their political stratagems. A vivid case in point was when President Kiir broke off his alliance with the former army chief of staff Lieutenant-General Paul Malong in 2017, blaming the general for the 'breakdown of rule of law'.[5] Malong promptly responded by setting up a new political movement promising to reverse the 'total impunity' of the Kiir regime. He shamelessly pledged to establish 'democracy, development, equal citizenry and justice' – regardless of the fact that the international community had placed him under UN sanctions for violating international human rights and humanitarian law.[6]

Politicians repeatedly shrugged off such ironies and made competing claims of legality before and during the war. They referenced, and selected from, a plethora of historically familiar procedures, authorities and rules. It helped that they were operating in a complex legal environment, where both the official laws 'on the books' and unwritten 'customary' rules could apply. Legal pluralism and political hybridity have flourished to a bewildering degree in South Sudan, and the politicians have puzzled over, profited from and contributed to this maelstrom.

In typically statist, authoritarian manoeuvres, the Kiir government exploited legal instruments to silence political opponents, even reaching into neighbouring countries to extract Machar's spokesperson, James Gatdet, from Kenya. Gatdet was accused of treason, tried, convicted and sentenced to death by hanging in a Juba court, and was only released following a new peace deal signed in Khartoum (Revitalised Agreement on the Resolution of the Conflict in South Sudan – R-ARCISS) in 2018.[7] Meanwhile some opponents, including Peter Biar Ajak, an academic, and founder of the South Sudan Young Leaders' Forum (SSYLF), remained in prison at the time of writing.[8] Simultaneously, in seeming contrast, political leaders recognised the judicial authority and social legitimacy of chiefs and sought to cultivate and benefit from 'custom'.[9] They deferred to, or sought to meddle with, customary laws in accordance with political interests. Indeed, Lieutenant General Malong was a fervent practitioner and advocate of polygamous marriage and a generous contributor to bridewealth payments during the second Sudanese civil war. He gained political status partly through his attentiveness to these customary prescriptions, as explained by scholar Clémence Pinaud: 'he dominated the local war economy and used its proceeds to cement strategic allegiances ... through the practice of large-scale polygamy and by godfathering his supporters' marriages'.[10]

South Sudan's leaders are adept at converting their access to the symbolic power of both the 'juridical state'[11] and custom into political capital, and are capable of switching between distinctive legal cultures and repertoires at will. Their machinations in pursuit of power were surely implicated in destabilising law and detaching it from justice. However, the clique of political elites at the helm of South Sudan are players within a complex system, and not the architects of disorder. They are, at most, agile negotiators in a political marketplace at the global periphery; governed as well as governing. They wield forms of power that are relational and heavily reliant on fast-paced bargaining; monetised patronage; a command of identity politics; and fostering fear and threats to bring the price of loyalty down. The responses of state elites to the systemic condition of 'turbulence' usually perpetuates the problem; we know this because regimes have come and gone with reforms and revolutions, but there are many puzzling continuities and recurrent patterns over time.[12] As such, South Sudan's politics is best explained as reflective of a logic of practice rooted in 'accumulated history', adopting the insights of the eminent sociologist Pierre Bourdieu, and adapting them to this very different context.[13] In other words, the politicians competing to control the state are themselves held in the sway of culturally embedded habits and 'dispositions', and enmeshed in the recursive constitution of plural legalities.

This chapter provides the necessary conceptual tools and historical grounding to explain the power of the law, its relationship to conflict and its potential to contribute to political transformation in South Sudan. It establishes the place of law in government as a hegemonic force, one that opens up channels for resistance even as it permeates society, shaping ideas and identities and sustaining political order. It then considers why law fails to stabilise and regulate power in the case at hand. It shows that South Sudan inherited an intricate muddle of laws and legal authorities and that its previous rulers specialised in using legal mechanisms to pursue political objectives. Since the colonial era, law has been deployed in combination with violence to enable a small elite to govern a host of marginalised but recalcitrant communities. Customary and religious law, including family law, have provided firm mechanisms for regulating society, but have generally lacked jurisdiction over the political conduct of state elites. Meanwhile, statutory law has been regularly rewritten by political and military victors to serve political interests. Yet there have also been occasional but important contrary instances, in which law has been put to the service of humane and civic interests through legal activism from below.

The power of law

It is standard practice for political actors, from warlords to democrats to dictators, to turn to law to justify their government.[14] Each may have different perceptions of what it means and why it is useful, but they usually recognise the relationship between law and legitimacy and want to signal that their authority has a custodian other than the barrel of a gun. Very evidently, the modern nation-state was founded upon legalities[15] which are on display in concepts of legal sovereignty, territorial jurisdiction and legitimate violence.[16] But even imperial and colonial projects,[17] and the diverse public authorities that govern communities and territories in so-called 'fragile states', have also deployed the language of law.[18] In many different regimes law has been used to justify coercive measures and violence in order to repress political opposition and social dissent. But this authoritarian 'rule by law' generally also relies heavily on military violence and policing.[19] In contrast, the power of law, and its political utility, is defined by its capacity to persuade populations to comply with political authority. Law is a hegemonic force because it creates arenas and mechanisms for people to try to regulate each other and to provide a check on political authorities. It has 'two edges': it is a tool for power and a constraint on power.[20]

In modern Europe, the rule of law emerged from intricate, historical processes of negotiation of the meaning of state and citizenship, which produced the conviction that government must be subject to the people: 'a good law-maker, adheres to the law'.[21] In contrast, colonised societies experienced the conqueror's tyrannous 'rule by law'. The same law-making that generated the Westphalian state in Europe also legitimised the imperial seizure and settlement of colonial territories.[22] The act of colonial conquest forcibly separated sovereign power from local legitimacy and thereby created a legal dualism, in which indigenous legal mechanisms were decapitated – left to deal with social order and unable to engage with political power. Despite these alien origins, colonial lawfare has proved tenacious. In Africa, colonisers forged a legal distinction between racially privileged settlers, with access to civil law and citizens' rights, and African 'native' subjects, administered by forms of indirect rule under customary authority. As Mahmood Mamdani explains, they 'justified the subordination of subjects to a fused [local] power as the continuation of customary law'.[23] These arrangements, and the violence that often accompanied them, contributed to a sense of the public political realm as being distant from the moral codes that regulated people's social and cultural life.[24] And yet even in colonial settings people tried to use the law to secure rights. As legal anthropologist John Comaroff argues:

'To the degree that law appears to be imbricated in the empowered construction of reality, it also presents itself as the ground on which to unravel the workings of power, to disable and reconstruct received realities.'[25]

Both the hegemonic power of the law and its potential to invigorate resistance can be explained by the extent to which law operates in society, reaching beyond legal statutes and courts and permeating the 'fabric of social life'.[26] It relies on a 'legal consciousness' embedded in social norms and expressed in 'commonplace transactions and relationships'.[27] Law only becomes meaningful through action and interaction – people observe, practise, interpret or contest it – bringing cases to court and arguing, defending or judging them. One way in which this is obvious is in categorical thinking about differences between people: 'the imprint of law' carries over into 'social roles and statuses',[28] such as 'citizens' and 'migrants'. But the law and legal categories are open to interpretation:[29] political and social actors contest them, either within society, in legal forums including courts, or through social mobilisations or covert forms of resistance. People draw upon experiences of other fields, including education, religion or commerce, and upon 'social networks, organisational resources, and local cultures', as well as legal principles and reasoning[30] in their interpretations of law.

Well-elaborated insights into law in society have produced the potentially empowering recognition that law is always 'in-the-making' and we are all legal agents actively engaged in 'making law'.[31] They also reveal the symbolic power of the law, and its potential to be harnessed as a resource, a form of 'capital' in political struggles.[32] However, in postcolonial countries in Africa this making of law and the ways that people engage with it have been profoundly influenced by the impacts of colonial interventions and more recently by global governance projects. In war-torn countries law-making is an intense, decentralised, opaque and heavily contested activity, taking place amid conditions of fragmented sovereignty and in 'distinct political spaces'.[33] The results include 'assorted and diverse rule systems and institutions – some public, some private, some hybrid' – that are not necessarily subordinate to the state[34] and that are perpetually 'waxing and waning' in their authority.[35]

Conflict-affected societies have also been locations for experimentation in international intervention aimed at promoting the 'rule of law' and transitional justice. Since the 1990s, they have included support for strengthening formal 'statutory' legal systems and related initiatives aimed at making informal or customary processes 'legible and palatable',[36] including through human rights promotion. They mostly took the Weberian view that the most stable political orders are founded on legal-rational legitimacy[37] and placed the 'rule of law' at the centre of 'state-building' policies. But the rationale and impetus for these programmes arose from neoliberal concerns about property regimes and contract law, and development donors' promotion of foreign investment and the domestic private sector.[38] The programmes did not, however, engender a social contract between states and citizens, or promote human rights and justice, in the ways that some of their proponents hoped – for several reasons.[39]

International rule of law programmes generally overlooked the significance of colonial histories of 'lawfare',[40] instead focusing on institutional reforms and technical approaches,[41] and conceptualising law as an instrument rather than a contested social process.[42] But among the plural and contradictory international interventions in law, an alternative legal empowerment approach has also emerged, bringing lawyers and human rights activists into projects to promote law from below, including training community paralegals. These projects differ in their origins and impacts. They have no guarantees of success and are interpreted differently, but they are certainly shaping the social norms of those who participate in them while also providing support for citizens' struggles for justice.[43]

Despite the particular challenges of resistance by legal means in postcolonial societies and conflict-affected states, there is increasing evidence that the poor can 'engage the law … in active and creative ways'.[44] This gives weight to an argument that legal activism has 'insurgent potential' in contestations of political exclusion and violence.[45] New actors and strategies have emerged to counter neoliberal globalisation by acting at different levels and embracing both legal approaches and civic mobilisation, producing 'fervent experimentation and institutional creativity at the grassroots level'.[46] Such struggles are characterised by plurality, reflecting and producing a novel form of legal consciousness, one that sociologists Boaventura de Souza Santos and César Rodriguez-Garavito describe as 'cosmopolitan legality'.[47] Similarly, Kiran Grewal's sociology of practice reveals how international human rights frameworks may be adopted and invigorated by activists at the margins in forms of 'subversive (mis)appropriation' that produce locally meaningful 'emancipatory demands'.[48] The impacts of such struggles may be limited, and they are never immediate, but they provide a counter to the colonial and authoritarian 'rule by law' and technical 'rule of law' approaches, demonstrating the emancipatory possibilities of law and sometimes yielding 'incremental' changes.[49]

A brief history of law and politics in South Sudan

The history of Sudan exemplifies – with its own complicated twists and idiosyncrasies – the authoritarian model of 'rule by law', the problems of international interventions, and the challenges of legal activism. The government of southern Sudan had relied mainly upon the mechanisms of war-making and law-making dating as far back as the Egyptian invasion of Sudan in 1820. Since then, political entrepreneurs at the centre of the state have extracted resources from the periphery by means of violence and sent them onwards to global metropoles. They have used law to legitimise political authorities and tie people into subordinate relations with government and unequal relations with each other, fracturing them along racial, religious, ethnic and gender differences.[50] This system has sometimes managed to produce elements of civil order at local levels, but also enabled organised warfare, the mobilisation of ethnic militias and the proliferation of violence.

Law licensing war: the colonial practice

The three successive colonial-imperial conquests of southern Sudan in the nineteenth century were given (specious) justifications by the laws of the time. During the period of Ottoman-Egyptian invasion, subjugation and rule (1821–85), southern Sudan was defined in Islamic law as *dar al harb* ('land of war'), in opposition to *dar al Islam* ('land of peace'), and the right of conquest prevailed. Southern Sudanese were either slaves or enslavable people, lacking rights over their own bodies, lands, possessions and societies. The Mahdist state in Sudan (1885–98) drove out the rule of the 'Turkiyya', but southern Sudanese remained relegated to the status of the potentially enslavable. In practice, the divide between those with rights and chattel slaves was never clear-cut, as possibilities for assimilation existed, but nonetheless the division between the domains of law and war was fundamental. The Anglo-Egyptian 'reconquest' of Sudan in 1898 destroyed the Mahdist state and formally abolished slavery. However, the Anglo-Egyptian condominium rule (1898–1955, with Britain the senior partner and the de facto sole power after 1923) made rapid accommodation with the sectarian authorities in northern Sudan, while mounting extremely violent 'pacification' in the south which continued into the 1930s.

British rule in Sudan was a complex exercise in legal hybridity. Law was placed at the centre of government under this dual colonial regime: the British introduced civil law and a Civil Division, giving it higher status than the Sharia Division, whose magistrates (*qadi*s) were perpetually 'disgruntled' as a consequence.[51] Afraid of both religious uprisings and (after 1923) rebellion by modernist-nationalists, the British made a strategic alliance with conservative sectarian leaders, rewarding them with landholdings, political influence and recognition of their spiritual authority in return for loyalty to their colonial masters. Sudanese public life and law were thus never fully secularised: not only did *sharia* courts continue to adjudicate civil and family cases, but political parties based on Muslim sects (the Khatmiya and the Ansar) were legitimised. In a rich investigation of this period, Massoud uncovers a 'colonial legal politics' intent upon the creation of a legal system that was 'strong enough to encourage trust and obedience, but weak enough to support nondemocratic rule'.[52] In short order, the British administration established a legal department, appointed judges, and built courts in the north. The legal secretary was part of the colonial administration but took responsibility for the supervision of both civil and *sharia* courts, allowing for Islamic law to be applied in a manner deemed acceptable by the British. In 1900, a British common law system was applied to the civil division, and thus to district and appellate courts; judicial panels could include both British judges and Sudanese laymen.[53]

The southern Sudanese experience was significantly different. For 20 years the Condominium was little more than a military occupation, garrisoning rehabilitated nineteenth century forts. No sooner had major resistance been overcome in the south, however, than a southern Sudanese army officer, Ali Abdel Latif, led the nationalist mutiny of the White Flag League in Khartoum, along with northern Sudanese nationalists, inspired by the right of self-determination in the charter of the League of Nations, and bolstered by open sympathy from Egypt. The British promptly expelled Egyptian civil servants and army officers, and reduced their commitment to the development of an educated cadre of Sudanese (including southerners), moving towards a policy of 'native administration' that could maintain law and order cheaply and provide a bulwark against nationalism. Southern Sudan, the Nuba Mountains and Darfur became 'closed districts', where movement and access was tightly controlled.

Colonial investment in southern Sudan was scandalously low and delivered very limited public goods (such as education), even by the standards of the time.[54] In line with its policy of indirect rule, administration largely relied upon the selection, empowerment (and sometimes dismissal) of 'tribal' chiefs and the establishment of chiefly courts. In 1931, under the Chief Courts Ordinance, chiefs were instructed to 'administer the native law and custom ... provided that such ... is not contrary to justice, morality and order'.[55] Courts flourished, and colonial officials began to describe southerners as 'a litigious'[56] and a 'law-abiding' people.[57]

Individual chiefs commanded varying levels of respect. But an understanding was laid down that customary law wielded coercive power (backed by government) that could substitute for violence. Chiefs' courts dealt with a regular influx of cases and drew large crowds of participants and spectators. People took cases to court with the aim of getting 'their right' and securing some protection.[58] They invested hopes that these processes would deliver social truths and enforce dispute settlements, while reducing violence by providing an alternative means to assert honour and rights.[59] Indeed, in this period demonstrating the capacity to litigate came to be regarded as an expression of masculinity,[60] an attribute otherwise only achievable by demonstrating prowess in war or physical combat.

However, the remit of chiefs' courts was limited to local issues. Only colonial officers could try capital crimes and impose death sentences. Chiefs' performances were reviewed by colonial officers who could intervene at their discretion. Chiefs' courts were separated from the exercise of political authority. Neither colonial officers nor Sudanese civil servants could be called to account in local courts.

Warfare and lawfare in independent Sudan: 1956–2005

On 1 January 1956, Sudan won an ambiguous independence. For southern Sudanese especially, celebrations were muted. Self-government three years earlier had left southerners disadvantaged – qualifying for a tiny minority of the administrative positions handed over by the British (just six out of 800). Northern Sudanese nationalists had only begun to consider the special claims of southerners when the trajectory of decolonisation was well advanced.

The promise made to southern Sudanese members of parliament – that the independent government would embrace a federal system in return for their votes – was already looking shaky and was never in fact honoured. Meanwhile, civil war had already broken out in August 1955.

The trouble began when workers at the Zande scheme, a cotton plantation established by the British, demonstrated against the retrenchment of 300 workers. They were met with gunfire, which killed six and wounded many more. Soon after, tensions between northern officers and southerners in the Equatoria Corps were exposed, and the government decided to transfer soldiers at the barracks in Torit to Khartoum. They refused and mutinied, attacking northern merchants and government officials. More than 200 northerners and 75 southerners died in the ensuing violence.[61] It does not seem that there were any attempts to prosecute those responsible for killing civilians at the Zande scheme, but the new government exerted itself to ensure that the perpetrators and suspects of the Torit mutiny faced the full force of law.

The government's response to the Torit mutiny exemplifies a heavy-handed use of the tools of law enforcement, coupled with co-opting chiefs. Those suspected of participation in the mutiny were vigorously pursued. Many were swiftly captured, brought to court, tried and taken to prison in Khartoum – 121 southerners were tried and executed; hundreds were given prison sentences; others were simply left to languish in detention without trial. The army terrorised civilians in searches for the mutineers and their supporters: 'villages were burned, harsh interrogation methods used, and alleged supporters of the mutineers thrown into prison'.[62] Chiefs were also harnessed to track down and prosecute suspected government opponents in 'special courts'. The independent Sudanese government was showing its brutal face. In the wake of mass arrests and 'deterrent punishment' in Eastern district in 1957, one diligent northern official recorded his belief that the 'wild and savage' locals would now appreciate the new regime. He suggested that they 'have come to realize that there is a strong Government that came to stay and rule and keep peace order and give justice'.[63]

However, legalised repression had the opposite effect, leading directly towards the formation of the *Anyanya* in 1962 – an openly separatist insurgency – and full-scale civil war in 1963. Meanwhile, the parliamentary leaders handed power to the military in 1958, and martial law was imposed on the south. There was a brief reprieve and opening of political space following the 'October Revolution' of 1964 – a civil uprising demanding democracy and judicial independence. But the civilian government elected in 1965 only re-energised the military campaign, licensing a clampdown to 'restore law and order'.

The first civil war ended with a peace agreement, signed in Addis Ababa in 1972. This delivered an autonomous southern regional government, a decade of relative peace and some development. People flocked back to Juba and other towns, seeking jobs, education and trading opportunities, and southern political elites seized their chance to govern. But the peace was short-lived: the new political settlement soon began to collapse into a mire of corruption and divisions within the south, and President Nimieri reneged on promises of reform and funding. Sudan was sliding into an economic crisis[64] and he was struggling to retain power. He sought to 'emasculate the Southern region' and to secure access to recently discovered oil. By the early 1980s, tensions and violence were escalating across the south. In May 1983 soldiers in Bor mutinied against corruption and rumours that former *Anyanya* fighters were to be transferred to the north. It was from the turmoil of this period that the Sudan People's Liberation Movement and Army (SPLM/A) emerged, with its stated agenda of a 'secular and democratic Sudan'.[65] In September 1983, Nimieri declared Islamic law, polarising the political debate, fuelling conflict and making the law into a political battleground.

A second popular uprising in Khartoum in 1985 ushered in a democratic system but did not resolve the civil war or the question of Islamic law. A permanent state of emergency prevailed in southern Sudan, even while civil liberties were enjoyed in the north. The elected government, bankrupt and unstable, was overthrown in a military coup in 1989. The military–Islamist coalition that took power declared martial law and instituted a wave of repression in the north, while intensifying military campaigns in the south. Without the resources to sustain a regular army, the government resorted to licensing tribal militia and partnerships between businessmen and military officers to conduct operations that involved looting, atrocities and mass displacement. Militia leaders were given titles drawn from Islamic military ranks, merging indirect rule, jihadism and subcontracted 'counterinsurgency on the cheap'.[66]

In turn, the SPLA sought to match the state's capacity for brutality, including by dismantling social norms of accountability. It trained its fighters in the art of destruction: 'Even your mother give her a bullet! ... Food, wife, and property, wherever you find them, are to be acquired through your might.'[67] Customary ethical restraints on warfare and rape were further eroded in post-1991 wars that followed the split within the SPLA between its leader John Garang and Riek Machar and Lam Akol.[68] SPLA soldiers became notorious for raiding communities for food and for forcible recruitment. Over time they managed to control large parts of the rural south and to capture strategic towns. In large part, their capture and administration of these areas was accomplished through force, usually requiring the defeat or co-optation of local militias armed by the government.[69] The war cost hundreds of thousands of lives and devastated social life and livelihoods. The result was recurrent catastrophic famine, and the reconfiguration of the political landscape of the south through the influx of international agencies and resources associated with a UN-mandated humanitarian relief operation, Operation Lifeline Sudan (OLS).

Law-making persisted alongside the pursuit of atrocious military campaigns. In a tradition dating back to successive colonial regimes, politicians in Khartoum disputed over the legal basis of the state, while a state of emergency alongside 'native administration' remained the default option for the peripheries. While the national constitution and penal code were the focus for the most vibrant and divisive political controversies, customary law and authorities were equally a site of political contestation.

Postcolonial governments sought to change not just law but society. Family law was an arena for political controversy: it was here that Islamists and secularists fought their political battles. In the 1960s, Prime Minister Ismail al-Azhari conceived of colonialism as a 'moral injury' and mobilised discontent over the purported immoralities of city life (drunkenness, sexual vices of various kinds, immodest female dress), supposedly abetted by a secular or 'soulless' legal system divorced from customary morality, as a political cause.[70] This was the opening exploited by the Islamists, who appropriated the issue of personal morality, impotently held by the *qadis*[71] of the *sharia* courts, and used it as the starting point for advocating for an Islamic state. Hassan al Turabi, a lawyer and politician, and Sudan's foremost Islamic ideologue, presented this agenda as a means of completing decolonisation, by bringing the alien Leviathan of the state within the moral grasp of the societal values from which it had been torn by the colonial conquest. The secularists' most powerful counter-charge was that the Islamists were hypocrites, failing in practice to live up to the morality they publicly espoused. While the main prize in this conflict was the secularisation or Islamisation of the state based in Khartoum, the south was from the outset a further arena for the politicisation of law.

In the 1950s and 1960s, successive regimes tried to Arabise and Islamise southern Sudan: 'Its primary objective was to undermine Southern traditional laws and customs ... to replace African laws with Islamic laws as part of a program of Islamization in the south.' After 1960, the government proposed stripping chiefs of their administrative powers unless they converted to Islam.[72] Such actions could not be implemented at scale, but nonetheless the army in the south targeted chiefs, with those suspected of collaborating with the Anyanya facing arrest, imprisonment and sometimes torture.[73]

The 1972 Addis Ababa agreement provided respite from Arabisation and Islamisation and made provision for the governance of 'traditional law and customs',[74] reinvigorating the authority of the chiefs. However, when war returned in 1983, the old patterns resurfaced. Although *sharia* courts and penalties were never enforced consistently across the southern Sudan in this period, some courts and people were affected, most notably the several million displaced southerners in northern Sudan, who were subjected to harassment by the 'popular police' and harsh penalties for crimes such as possessing or selling alcohol.[75]

In the SPLA's 'liberated areas', the administration of justice was limited, and people were generally governed in a 'militaristic fashion',[76] with battalion commanders empowered to administer law and order in their spheres of control. Nonetheless, there were still moves to show a commitment to establishing a legal order. In 1984, the SPLA promulgated a set of penal and disciplinary laws. This code was primarily intended for internal disciplinary proceedings within the rebel army's own ranks, and not for the civilian population in general. It had no code of procedure and contained many draconian punishments, including liberal use of the death penalty. It was only printed in English and few copies were distributed. But it secured the place of customary law in the administration of justice. As a result, most court officers used customary law and procedure, what they remembered of Sudan's previous secular laws, and common sense.[77]

A former judge, Monyluak Alor Kuol, recorded and reflected upon his experiences in SPLA liberated areas from 1985 to 1994, where, he recalled, courts adjudicated on the basis of custom and took careful account of the differences between local people and their laws. Kuol was the only judge in Lakes province for four years; other areas were equally starved of staff and materials. Nevertheless, he managed to rule on numerous difficult cases, including convening a special court to resolve 'inter-tribal conflicts'. He observed that the responsibilities of chiefs increased during this period, and that they handled the majority of cases, while his court handled criminal cases and appeals. In both the Dinka and Azande areas to which he was deployed, he observed that the laws were also in flux and changing in response to the devastation of the war, and the escalating human and material losses and displacements. Both he and the chiefs faced a constant challenge in 'balancing the interests of their people and the problems created by the liberation army'.[78]

Over time, the SPLA was increasingly pressed to establish civil administration alongside the chieftaincy in the liberated areas. Against the wishes of the SPLA high command, the 1994 'New Sudan' National Convention established an 'ad hoc committee for justice and legal affairs' which pushed for an independent judiciary and legal codes for a civilian administration. It was envisaged that there would be six levels of courts, and that chiefs' courts should be formally integrated into the system as the lowest three tiers of the judiciary.[79] However, the SPLM/A leadership resisted the implementation of these commitments. Chairman John Garang made clear his reservations and stipulated that rather than an 'independent judiciary' the movement should assert the 'supremacy of the law over everyone'.[80] It was not until 1999 that efforts were made to enact the convention resolutions and appoint a chief justice and, even then, the SPLM sought to retain control by managing US aid funds allocated for judicial development.

A record of legal activism in Sudan

The historical record of adversarial forms of legal activism in South Sudan is fairly sparse. However, all sorts of authorities shaped the customary laws, which were partly devised through informal meetings between chiefs, governments and military authorities and other influential persons such as lineage heads.[81] For instance, during the second civil war, meetings with the SPLA were, according to a chief in Yei, a means to 'talk and bring out laws' in order to deal with pressing problems such as 'regulating requisitioning and conscription'.[82] This process of law-making through practice allowed for its adaptation, and surely helps to explain the tenacity of customary practice. Processes and rulings were influenced by the imperatives of the present as much as by recollection of precedent or reference to written texts; law was discussed, interpreted and partly manufactured in public and with an element of participation. And knowing about and engaging the law was regarded as empowering; young people pursued an informal legal education in the small towns in the south by 'collecting regulations' and watching 'judges settling cases, just to learn' and gained influence by becoming self-appointed court 'members' according to historian Cherry Leonardi.[83]

Town dwellers were especially vulnerable to repression from the Khartoum regime. Chiefs often used their positions to mediate on behalf of their community members, although some also acted as recruiters for SPLA or informers to Sudanese authorities in garrison towns. It was even said that in Juba: 'knowing the name of one's chief was ... the only hope for those arrested, to avoid being taken to the feared detention facilities like the "white house"'.[84] In particular, due to 'Arabisation and Islamisation' policies after 1991, many southerners were swept up in arrests, beatings and fines for breach of *sharia* laws, especially in Khartoum itself.[85] Displaced southerners needed to develop self-protection strategies and find trusted allies within the system, who might intervene covertly on their behalf when they were arrested or abducted. They turned to chiefs (as noted above) but also to their 'brothers working in the Sudanese state system', whether as militia, clerks in the judiciary or in administrative roles. These 'political middlemen' played important roles sharing information on criminal investigations or in finding and securing the release of abducted people.[86]

Strikingly, some prominent lawyers and judges in the town were at the forefront of demanding an end to the repressive regime of President Nimieri. In part they were trying to defend their own independence against constant political assaults, including the adoption and use of Islamic law as a political instrument. Many lawyers were active in the victorious civil mobilisation in Khartoum that brought down the Nimieri regime in 1985. They played important roles in supporting trade unionists, as a prominent lawyer from the south, Yoanes Ajawin, recalled: 'lawyers were also given specific assignments to pioneer civil disobedience'. In one of the earliest demonstrations, on 2 April 1985, both lawyers and judges walked at the front of mass protests in the searing heat of Khartoum 'in their full judicial regalia'.[87] Just days later, the regime collapsed when the army declared its support for the people on 6 April. The protesters had won, and they seized the moment to 'storm Kober prison' and liberate political detainees.[88]

Less visibly, legal activism was pursued by a bar association of independent lawyers that had originally been established in the 1930s and had somehow survived successive authoritarian regimes. The association took up numerous political cases, defending workers and students active in opposition to Nimieri during the 1970s and 1980s. In the wake of the failed revolution, the association lent its support to establish the Sudan Human Rights Organisation and began bringing cases against security personnel for their 'kidnapping and torture of civilians'.[89] One of its members recalled that '[independent] lawyers were very powerful in Sudan, before this [Bashir-led] government'.[90] But President Bashir was all too aware of their capabilities, and one of his first acts of government was to shut down the bar association, imprison its leaders for more than a year and torture some of them. According to Massoud, this act devastated the legal profession and paved the way for the co-optation of lawyers and judges in a series of legal manoeuvres that served to consolidate and underpin Bashir's power. Bashir revived and strengthened Nimieri's Islamisation programme, formalising the crime of apostasy in the criminal code and intervening heavily to shape the law in his political interests. He dismantled the independence of the bar association, bringing them firmly under control, and manipulating their leadership elections. Bar association leaders became known for supporting the regime, including the view that 'human rights' are 'against Islamic concepts'.[91] Sudan had a history of legal activism, but also of its vehement repression.

The new 'rules of law' in South Sudan

The period after the 2005 peace agreement was a moment of contingency and political opening in southern Sudan. The Comprehensive Peace Agreement (CPA) settlement itself was profoundly flawed: it had legitimised the authority of armed groups, established through violence, thereby endorsing 'the power of the gun – at the expense of the political class, civic associations, and the civilian population'.[92] But rule of law reforms proceeded apace and some of the most detested elements of the old order were swept away. Bashir's 'Arabisation and Islamisation' policy was reversed, Islamic law was replaced by common law and the use of English, and customary law was formally integrated into the system. South Sudan gained its own formal legislation, constitution, a bill of rights and a promise of constitutional reform.

The peace was an opportunity for justice. International organisations optimistically engaged in large-scale projects of law reform, training of the judiciary, lawyers and chiefs. Most importantly, as anthropologist Jok Madut Jok observed, the victims of the old regime seized chances to celebrate and pursue changes to the legal and political order: 'women and other marginalized groups who had been most affected by the war received this new order with elation'. Organised civil society groups continued to try to push forward the 'security' agenda they had been pressing during the war in pursuit of 'a transparent justice system and to develop a culture of respect for human and civil rights'. However, this vision of political transformation dimmed within just a few years. Jok concluded that the system of government and legal framework 'fell disastrously short of providing protection to all citizens'.[93] Perhaps the biggest failure was that, against the promise of the CPA, the feared National Intelligence and Security Service retained its powers of arrest and detention, and its paramilitary capabilities, in a national security act proposed by President Bashir's National Congress Party and agreed by the SPLM.

By February 2013, the International Committee of Jurists reported that South Sudan still lacked an independent judiciary, adequately trained personnel, proper courts, law reforms, separation of powers, an independent legal profession and a national legal aid system. It was also massively overstretched, with a mere 124 judges in place in the entire country, whose recruitment and qualifications were not open to scrutiny, raising concerns about nepotistic appointments. There were fewer than 200 lawyers on the register of the bar association.[94] Donors spent significant sums on supporting the institutions of justice and the rule of law after the CPA and in the run-up to independence. But some of the investments, including legal education, would take time to bear fruit, while others had directed funds towards security institutions and the military. As late as 2014, the United Nations Mission in South Sudan (UNMISS) claimed that its work with military police and military justice had 'contributed significantly to building the mission's relationship with the SPLA' and 'dramatically increased awareness of legal obligations under domestic and international law'.[95] The eruption of conflict suggested otherwise.

Conclusion

South Sudan is a new nation with an especially tumultuous past and present. Its conflicts, including the 2013 civil war, have been fuelled by an inherited system of government in which law was a primary 'weapon in the arsenal' of authoritarian rule.[96] This is at odds with a presumption, common to many international observers, that South Sudan's conflict was a symptom of a 'fragile state'.[97] The view that international rule of law support was 'absolutely essential to the sustainability of government' following on the first steps towards autonomy and independence[98] was a much softer echo of colonial and authoritarian notions of law as an instrument to regulate society. But it contained a similar presumption that the law would be forged at the centre of the state, without acknowledging the dilemmas provoked by a persistent relationship between statutory law and arbitrary violence, or fully confronting the tangible realties of plural and contested legal rules.

South Sudan's civil war was not simply the result of the actions of a handful of especially corrupt and violent men; it was also rooted in the logics of a historical system of government. Political leaders were obliged to pay some tribute to law, even when they stood accused of egregious crimes, but they were also accustomed to wrestling with plural 'rules of law' and with constitutional uncertainty, in a state which seemed permanently 'in transition'.[99] They clearly understood that legality is foundational for statehood, government and political legitimacy, but also that the complex and unsettled nature of law in this region created space for negotiation. The Sudanese regime had been adept in exploiting Islamic law in pursuit of power; South Sudanese leaders had challenged this partly by turning to customary law. In pursuit of power, however, they engaged in a selective exploitation of the customary law, including drawing upon patriarchal norms and ethnic discourses with legal resonances. Once in government, they could also deploy the relevant statist legal concepts to wield authority in their interactions with the international community, and to build the instruments of state security, in a similar authoritarian fashion to their Sudanese predecessors. Politicians were limited by the available symbolic resources of law, but those who were versed in these plural and diverse languages of legality and custom were best equipped to struggle in the realm of power. The most powerful harnessed particular laws to short-term political imperatives, at the same time as unleashing carnage. In so doing, they were fuelling the legalisation of violence and disorder, and sustaining a condition of chronic instability.

And yet amid these continuities there were still prospects of change as new legal resources emerged. The cataclysm of war and a litany of atrocity crimes led to vigorous demands for prosecution, putting the impunity of political and military elites in question.[100] New political and legal terrain was carved out through the inclusion of transitional justice provisions in the final chapter of the peace deal.[101] These 'Chapter V' provisions promised to bring perpetrators of war crimes and crimes against humanity to trial in a hybrid court to be staffed by a mix of South Sudanese and other African judges. Naturally, political leaders were reluctant to sign up to this agenda and sought to tighten their grasp on power, including by claiming allegiance to custom and by pushing for reconciliation and amnesty in preference to prosecutions, as illustrated by President Kiir's notorious *New York Times* letter.[102]

Less noticeably, as the remainder of the book will explore, there were more mundane legal efforts to limit the political capture of the law and channel it towards conflict prevention and the protection of human rights. As this chapter has shown, the history of Sudan, the annals of social theory and empirical research in other post-colonial settings all suggest that it is worth paying attention to everyday forms of legal activism which have incremental transformative potential. Not surprisingly, where law is complicit in subjugation, legal strategies are required to secure rights and effect political change.[103] Many civic actors had clearly understood this and were explicitly working for legal and constitutional reforms and access to justice in the new South Sudan; and some continued despite the war. But judges, lawyers and chiefs were surely the most qualified and capable of steering legal reforms and providing a check on political actors, so it makes sense to try to understand their circumstances and responses next.

Chapter 2

INSIDE THE JUSTICE SYSTEM: DOMINATION AND RESISTANCE

South Sudan's justice system is tangled and contradictory, with laws, institutions and even concepts of lawfulness that are hybrid and contested. This creates ambiguities and analytical challenges for analysts and citizens alike. For instance, two years after independence, a large-scale survey suggested that the government had 'made strides in strengthening' access to justice, since the majority of people had declared their confidence in customary courts, and almost half in the judiciary. Yet most people were only familiar with the customary courts or the police and most also described the courts as slow and expensive, and complained about ethnic discrimination and corruption.[1] The evidence of progress was relative, patchy and circumstantial.

However, these inconsistencies and fluctuations are not coincidental; they are important unifying characteristics across the justice system and signify ongoing political struggles within it. On one hand, the multiplicity of law, and the dissonance it produced, was 'functional'[2] for military and political elites, but on the other hand the plural judicial experts and their institutions could provide authoritative interpretations of law; they were not easily corralled and by default presented a nascent political threat. When the war broke out, the government attempted to revert to the authoritarian legal politics they had been schooled in, and tormented by, under the Khartoum regime. Ruling elites sought to dominate justice with 'the power of guns and money', to use a common expression,[3] although, as this chapter explains, they also encountered pockets of resistance.

The tensions within the justice system are not just a domestic matter; they also reflect some of the dilemmas of global governance in arenas of protracted conflict. Certain international agencies, including the International Development Law Organisation (IDLO) and United Nations Development Programme (UNDP), continued to support legal and judicial institution-building during the war, and listed tangible benefits for legal education and access to justice.[4] Such conscientious efforts furnished some support to reformist and critical elements within the institutions of justice. But they also meant that, on and off during the war, government officials, civil society actors and their international sponsors would converge in Juba offices and hotels around ambitious agendas for the justice system. These activities were the remnants of the former 'state-building' project, with its technocratic discourses, convenient fictions, and search for technical solutions to political problems.[5] They generally applied a formula honed for Sudan: 'more cases in the courts, and more lawyers in the streets – more law – [was] a proxy for building the rule of law'.[6] Treating government officials as if they were part of a stable bureaucracy, and strengthening and legitimising institutions, including courts, prisons and police, was problematic when ordinary people were suffering directly at the hands of the law and government. It risked presenting a 'cover of neutrality', with negative political effects.[7]

At the very same time, other internationals, including human rights organisations, the African Union Commission of Inquiry on South Sudan (AUCISS) and UN investigators vigorously documented and denounced a litany of human rights violations, including extrajudicial killings, torture, arbitrary arrests and detention, forced displacement and sexual violence. In successive reports, they presented findings that high-ranking members of the government were implicated in war crimes and violations of human rights.

They also observed that the judicial authorities were part of the problem. As the UN Panel of Experts summed up: 'the failure of the leadership in Juba to prevent or punish the abuses ... and indeed its active involvement in many instances, is a key driver of the war'.[8]

Given this complex governance context, this chapter examines the contradictions and contestations within the justice system. It focuses on some of the key institutions and actors, including the Ministry of Justice, the judiciary, the bar and chieftaincy, questioning whether and how they provided any form of checks on government. It draws upon documentary sources and interviews in an effort to understand the pressures on lawyers, judges and chiefs as well as the prevailing structures, the extent and limits of their authority, and the variations in their responses to the crisis. It attends to internal wrangling or initiatives that tried and failed to make a difference. Such micro-contestations tend to be overlooked, especially in the grand scheme of an atrocious war, but here they are examined as incipient or protean forms of resistance.

The chapter finds some truth in both of the contrary opinions that the justice system was making improvements and that it served political interests. Legal and judicial institutions were plural, and not all were similarly deficient. The task facing the institutions was overwhelming. It was not simply a matter of confronting breaches by particular individuals, since the problem was systemic: it was inherent to a logic of governance based on networks of patronage and payoff, with ongoing informal deal-making,[9] combined with the challenges of political and legal hybridity. In this context, following institutional rules and procedures was not enough: to survive in their positions, and make the justice system meaningful, judges, chiefs and lawyers would also need to have political craft.

Above the law: 'the rule of tyranny'

The SPLM/A leadership did not hold the concept of the rule of law in contempt: their notion of government still, counterintuitively, depended on legal instruments. But military law – with its corollary of impunity – was a historical norm. As one member of the judiciary observed: 'We are dealing with a government with most of them having very little idea about the independence of the judiciary. We just emerged from war where a commander was everything.'[10] For both governments and guerrillas, the emergency powers of the military commander *were* the law. By the time of the 2013 war, many senior government officials had already escaped any accountability for earlier crimes and were also suspected of grand corruption.[11] At the time of writing, none had been prosecuted for war crimes. When members of the elite brought cases against one another, it was usually for political reasons.

At independence, the Transitional Constitution provided 'unambiguous' protections for the separation of powers, but it also centralised presidential power, since the president could hire and fire supreme court justices. He was supposed to only dismiss judges in 'exceptional circumstances' and to take the advice of the Judicial Service Commission, as well as consulting parliament on appointments.[12] But even before the war broke out it was clear that these prescriptions would not be adhered to, as military and political elites intimidated or harnessed the justice system.[13] The president's abrupt dismissal of the chief justice, John Wol Makec, in 2011 was a clear signal that the judiciary was expected to be politically compliant.[14]

One problem was that many judges and lawyers were already enmeshed in the political-administrative system they were supposed to regulate. They were among the leading architects and advocates of the new regime.[15] Three individuals illustrate the revolving door between rebellion, government and civil society. The first is Justice Ambrose Riny Thiik who was appointed chief justice for southern Sudan in 2005 and was widely revered. In 2013, however, he became leader of the Dinka ethno-nationalist pressure group, the Jieng Council of Elders, frequently blamed for exacerbating the conflict.[16] The second is John Luk Jok:[17] a veteran of the SPLM and its splinters, as well as a former leading member of South Sudan Law Society

(SSLS) who had co-authored key documents advocating consti-tutionalism and legal reform.[18] John Luk took several ministerial positions after the CPA and as minister of legal and constitutional affairs he was a key drafter of the Transitional Constitution. During the disruptions of 2013 he was first purged, then detained and accused of plotting a coup; then returned to politics as a member of the Former Detainees (FD). In 2016, he was back in government, as a minister of transport. A third individual is Justice John Clement Kuc, who was an early critic of the system. In 2010, Justice Kuc was serving as an appeal court judge in Bahr el Ghazal, wrestling with the logistical and political difficulties of establishing the new legal structures in the region.[19] In 2013, he resigned his post and entered civil society as chairman of SSLS in July, publicly complaining that the 'rule of law has been replaced with [the] rule of tyranny'.[20] However, Justice Kuc's role as a human rights advocate was short-lived. He became spokesperson for the 'Taban Deng faction' of the rebel SPLA-IO,[21] and entered parliament as a deputy in 2016.[22] Yet the problems of corruption, inefficiency, nepotism and executive disregard for the rule of law he had raised in his resignation letter had simply got worse.

The ministry and the judiciary

South Sudan's institutions of justice were either bystanders or accomplices to the corruption and violence of government. The post-CPA government of southern Sudan was infamously corrupt, its oil revenues providing massive opportunities for the elite to enrich themselves. The judiciary did little to stem this and some of its members even joined in. As early as 2007–08 the payroll expend-iture of the Ministry of Legal Affairs tripled on a monthly basis for four months without any plausible reason. By 2012, corruption had become so rife that President Kiir wrote a standard-form letter to 75 current and former officials accusing them of stealing nearly US$4 billion.[23] But there was no systematic investigation into the allega-tions, let alone prosecutions – the accused individuals bargained with the president one by one. In 2015, Minister of Justice Paulino Wanawilla admitted knowledge that his own staff were implicated in taking 'bribes'.[24] Yet he did not act to clean up his own house, let alone challenge criminality in other branches of government. The ministry even stands accused of having 'hobbled' the Anti-Corruption Commission,[25] and there was a suspicious fire in the Ministry of Justice in which files on corruption cases and other documents were destroyed. As one lawyer observed frankly, the conduct of the ministry could not simply be attributed to ineptitude, rather: 'the Ministry of Justice behaves as if it is responsible to do injustice'.[26]

The judiciary was more robust than the ministry. However, judges were poorly equipped to challenge the political order, even had they wanted to. Judges had a low standing in public perceptions: 60% of people questioned for the Global Corruption Barometer in 2013 thought they were corrupt, while 12% admitted bribing a judge.[27] This situation only got worse with time. The president sought to cement his power by rewarding allies, often ethnic Dinka from his home region of Bahr el Ghazal, across the institutions of government, including the judiciary.[28] Respected and capable judges lost influence or status as they challenged the status quo. The financial and political impacts of the war steadily eroded the shreds of judicial capacity.

Nonetheless, the government still made concessions to legality that were more than symbolic, and some judges made conspicuous efforts to exert authority in order to stem the tide of corruption and violence. One example was the Supreme Court trial of four politicians – the so-called 'former detainees' accused of treason at the inception of the war in December 2013. The judges insisted that the public were given unprecedented access to the court, and the case played out transparently. Eventually the government was forced to withdraw charges in April 2014.[29] The deputy chief justice, Madol Arol Kachuol, was said to have been an important influence – he had reviewed the evidence against the detainees and declared it insufficient.[30] However, independent judges faced increasing pressures in the years that followed, and Justice Madol's principled stand in a subsequent political case seems to have precipitated his downfall.

Another case occurred in 2015, in which judicial courage and principle ultimately came to naught. The National Alliance, a grouping of 18 opposition parties chaired by Lam Akol, brought a case against the government, questioning the legal basis of a presidential decree. This case touched on a fraught political issue – the government's policy of administrative decentralisation. President Kiir had abrogated the terms of the 2015 peace agreement by unilaterally expanding the number of states from 10 to 28 (and later 32), a move blatantly designed to consolidate his power and serve the interests of his supporters. The National Alliance was not convinced that the courts could handle the case fairly because the chief justice, Chan Reech Madut, had already publicly declared his support for the 28 states decree in his capacity as a member of the Dinka Aguok community. [31] In February 2016, they brought a petition against the chief justice calling for him to recuse himself. The deputy chief justice was said to have seconded this demand, but the chief justice refused to back down. The result was a presidential intervention in March 2016: Kiir instead sacked Madol, the deputy chief justice, leaving the court case conveniently stuck in the mire.[32]

President Kiir's dismissal of the deputy chief justice without cause was proof positive of an assault on the independence of the judiciary. The remaining judges must have been aware that continuing in their posts depended upon maintaining silence about ongoing atrocities and abuses of power. Two military judges broke this code in February 2017. They wrote damning accounts of the conduct of the regime in Juba and resigned in protest. The head of South Sudan's military court, Colonel Khalid Ono Loki, accused the army chief General Paul Malong of extrajudicial arrests that targeted people on an ethnic basis, of 'fabricated cases' against non-Dinka and of establishing kangaroo courts to 'try officers on your own'. He wrote:

In your relentless endeavours to protect your own ethnicity, and founded on no single law, you always freeze and/or abolish court issuance and rulings even of murder, rape and theft cases … You have ordered arrests of civilians in military jails exterior [outside] of proper legal channels.[33]

Colonel Loki was swiftly followed by Brigadier Henry Oyay Nyago, advocate general and director of military justice, whose resignation letter informed President Kiir: 'I cannot continue to be silent … while you are finishing and slaughtering the innocent people of South Sudan.'[34] These were blunt statements, explicable partly by their timing in a wave of defections to the military opposition.

Most judges seemed to be in a bind: they could either keep their heads down or face dismissal. The Justices and Judges Committee found a way around this impasse by organising collective action. They launched a strike on 2 May, bringing the work of statutory courts to a virtual halt for five months.[35] The strikers mainly focused their demands on an end to dire working conditions and low pay – understandably since the conditions were by then untenable. As the spokesperson of the strike committee told me: 'judges are going to office on foot [or] using motorbikes … [there is] no provision of court rooms, four and five sharing one room; no tools for working, not even papers and sometimes judges buy their own. One judge is working the task of 10 judges.' Like other government employees, judges' salaries had lost their value as the local currency plummeted against the dollar and inflation spiralled. Although they were among the highest paid civil servants, their income was now below the poverty line: '[The salary] is equivalent to 20 dollars for 30 days. Now judges did not receive the salary. Judges are dying. We lost a beloved as he couldn't go for treatment.'[36]

The judges did not protest directly against interference by the executive authority, but they demanded that Chief Justice Madut must resign or be removed by the president. They blamed the chief justice for failing to address their grievances; and implied his malfeasance. The chairperson of the Judges Committee stated: 'Yes we have of course demands related to money and things related to work, but we think that the main reason of why the judiciary is not working well is the chief justice, because there is mismanagement in resource management.'[37] Their insistence that the president should step in and dismiss Chief Justice Madut, his former schoolmate and close political ally, was confrontational. The spokesperson of the striking judges commented: 'We have mentioned that he is corrupt not only in taking money but in administering the judiciary ... the hidden things we don't know.'[38] An independent lawyer was more forthright in his explanation:

> the personality of the chief justice and the minister of justice are two areas that need reform. Both cover up. There is no history of resisting. They have been in Khartoum and are comfortable with all the violations ... People reached a stage of getting angry with them.[39]

From the outset, support for the strike was solid; one of the organisers estimated that over 80% of judges turned out, with only a few Juba-based judges continuing to work.[40] This placed further stress upon a justice system which was already in dire straits. In 2016, the national human rights commission recorded that 6,500 detainees were officially imprisoned, and many others were in other unofficial places of detention; Juba Central Prison held some 1,500 in a space designed for only 400.[41] After the strike had been running for a few months, the situation in the prisons and courts was appalling, as one paralegal explained: 'the prison are full; the warders are no longer accepting more people to be there'.[42] Criminal cases piled up. The problems were so acute that even the national security officials were moved to back the judges' call for the dismissal of the chief justice.[43] A judge on the committee explained:

The security people, they are with us. It's an administrative issue not a political issue. We met with Akol Koor [the director general for internal security in the National Security Service (NSS)], his deputy and the rest and they understood our issue. That is why we are safe, and we thanked them for that.[44]

Despite the fact that the judges were united and had security agencies on their side, President Kiir sought to break the strike rather than address their issues. On 12 July 2017 he issued a republican decree for the 'removal of some judges and justices in the judiciary',[45] providing a list of five court of appeal judges, two high court judges and seven county court judges to be dismissed. The strikers had in fact anticipated this and formed a shadow committee – a tactic learned from experience in the protests against Sudan's President Nimieri in the early 1980s. The shadow committee continued to organise until 7 September 2017 when the strikers finally folded in despair, with few of their objectives met. It was clear that the political authorities would not budge, whatever the human costs. The judges caved in unconditionally 'for the sake of citizens'[46] who were affected by the 'massive backlog of cases'.[47]

The strike was a brave public protest at a time of conflict and deep uncertainty, but the consequences were devastating for ordinary people in courts and prisons, and for the judiciary. Some of the nation's most respected judges lost their positions, while the authority and political allegiances of the discredited chief justice remained intact. Another painful blow was dealt to the strikers when the president decreed the removal of an under-secretary in the Ministry of Justice, Jeremiah Swaka Moses Wani, in the early days of the strike. There was an obvious pattern to these dismissals. Wani was another independent voice and had been an ally of advocates for transitional justice. As one lawyer commented, he was 'fired on 9 May [2017] after long harassment in the ministry. He was there for four years resisting'. People of integrity were being pushed out because: 'they stick to their ethics and some people are not happy with them; some fear that they have evidence that could be used ... Some are fearing the hybrid court and looking [for] ways of destroying evidence'.[48] Tong Kot Kuocnin, a lawyer writing from Nairobi, was blunt in his accusation that the president and the chief justice had 'corrupt and dictatorial tendencies' and that: 'Justice is under fire as the rule of law is deeply buried and the rule of man reigns high.'[49] But the most devastating indictment came in the resignation letter of Supreme Court judge Justice Kukurlopita Marino Pitia in November 2017. Justice Pitia confirmed that the dismissals of judges were 'unconstitutional' and that the judiciary had been placed 'at the mercy of the executive'. He argued that 'the war cannot be used as an excuse to interfere and silence the judiciary'. In his view, the judiciary 'was no longer capable of delivering justice'[50] while its independence had become 'a mockery'.[51]

Lawyers

Like the judges, lawyers came from various backgrounds and pursued different interests. Some corporate lawyers were highly instrumental to 'facilitating South Sudan's violent kleptocratic system', according to an independent investigation.[52] But other independent and human rights lawyers were working to counteract everyday abuses of the law and human rights, despite the risks. They were able to maintain some distance from some of the malign and arbitrary practices of government through employment in private practice or funding and relationships with international aid donors. In particular, the SSLS was remarkably firm in its mandate to 'strive for justice in society and respect for human rights and the rule of law in South Sudan', undertaking politically sensitive research and advocacy, including on transitional justice. In addition, new legal organisations were formed during the conflict to promote access to justice and provide pro bono legal aid services, including the Foundation for Human Rights Initiative (FHRI), led by Taban Romano, and the Justice & Human Rights Observatory (JAHRO), chaired by Godfrey Victor Bulla. Both organisations were established in the later months of 2015, during a political hiatus in Juba while there were still hopes for the implementation of the August 2015 peace deal.

The possibilities for human rights lawyers to operate fluctuated along with the ebb and flow of South Sudan's war. At times, there was a surge of military and political violence in particular towns, involving street battles, or attacks from 'unknown gunmen' and many lawyers and activists fled to neighbouring countries. But they also tended to travel back and forth during the conflict, returning to Juba as the violence briefly quietened, seizing any opportunities to return to work. Despite the chaos, some lawyers took on pro bono cases in prisons; developed ideas on legal and human rights education and practice; and advocated for legal and judicial reforms as well as respect for the rule of law and human rights.[53] Some were also involved in human rights documentation, briefing international investigations or compiling evidence for national-level processes, as later chapters will show. The organisations and their networks were needed for mutual support.[54] The precarious situation of their members was alluded to in the report of a discussion at an FHRI meeting: 'It is a lesson learnt that even lawyers including human rights defenders do face a lot of challenges while trying to pursue and defend the rights of others, some of them have even been issued death threats, this means they, themselves need protection too.'[55]

The South Sudan Bar Association ought to have been a source of solidarity and mutual support for lawyers, but instead became a hotbed of tensions fuelled by political and security agencies. The tensions revolved around the leadership of the association, which would have the power to issue the licences for lawyers. The matter turned out to be so politically sensitive that when the organisation held leadership elections in Juba in February 2015, national security agents stormed in and seized the ballot boxes, claiming that the association needed to get permission from them to hold the vote.[56] Yoanes Ajawin was one of two lawyers competing to be chairperson of the association. He was bound to be a controversial candidate in the eyes of the government, with his background in human rights and opposition politics. His feeling was that he had a real chance of victory and 'they didn't want that'.[57] It seemed the members of a provisional executive committee sought to retain their control over the association, even though their committee had been dissolved and replaced with a steering committee in the general assembly of the association in 2013. The steering committee first organised a one-day silent strike of lawyers to protest against the disruption of the election,[58] then took the matter to court.

The Bar Association court case exemplifies both the split in the association and the laborious processes of the law, which even some of the nation's foremost advocates were apparently not able to circumvent. Before the election, two lawyers had taken the electoral and steering committees to court, questioning their legality, but the latter was deemed a 'legible' body in a court decision in January 2015. After the electoral debacle, the steering committee then decided to bring a case against the provisional executive committee to prohibit the latter from 'continuing exercising the functions, duties and powers vested in the South Sudan Bar Association'. The case reached the Court of Appeal in Juba in April 2015. Yet after much deliberation, and references to an eclectic set of legal sources – from Southern Sudan's Code of Civil Procedure Act of 2007 to experts in the UK, Kenya and South Africa – the Appeal Court determined that it did not have jurisdiction over the case. A year later, the case finally went up to the Supreme Court only for it to be determined that: 'the Courts of Appeal have jurisdiction to review administrative decisions' and the petition should be 'sent back'.[59] The courts seemed loath to handle this legal hot potato, Ajawin felt: 'they wanted to chicken out'.[60]

At stake in the dispute was the right to allocate licences to lawyers. On the surface this seemed a bureaucratic matter, but it could easily be swayed by political and commercial interests, especially given the diverse and competitive legal fraternity. As early as 2013, there were complaints against the provisional bar association chairperson Dr William Kon Bior because it seemed that only 22 lawyers had been licensed as commissioners of oaths in the entire country, a role which, he acknowledged, was commercially important, putting them 'in the market on car contracts, plots'.[61] He maintained charge of the licences in practice, even though it was officially the responsibility of the chief justice in 2013, and thereafter his authority as chairperson of the bar was being contested in the courts. In October 2016, Dr Kon died and his replacement was appointed following another disputed election.[62] In November 2016, the chief justice clamped down on 'unlicensed advocates', prohibiting their ongoing appearance before the courts.[63] This meant that lawyers themselves had no alternative but to seek the 'licence of survival', whether or not they perceived the committee as legitimate.[64] One daring lawyer, Kiir Chol Deng, refused to accept its authority and he was promptly barred from practising law in April 2017. Deng had first come to public attention when he was threatened at gunpoint in court by a national security agent, while representing individuals accused of corruption in the president's office – a case with its own intriguing backstory.[65] He was convinced the bar association's decision to ban him was 'politically motivated', perhaps to prevent him defending his clients in a retrial.[66]

From all of this, it is apparent that political interests were at play within the bar association, while lawyers were subject to monitoring and threats from security agencies, even in the courtroom. Powerful elites would not hesitate to deploy authoritarian tactics to intimidate opponents and undermine potential resistance from the legal fraternity. Their most effective manoeuvre was to engineer the passage of a new law designed to extend and reinforce the powers of the National Security Service (NSS) in October 2014. The NSS bill was a shameless copy from similar legislation in Sudan. The contents of the bill were so troubling that some members of the National Legislative Assembly staged a walkout, while human rights organisations united in protest against its provision to the NSS of 'broad and unqualified powers'.[67] Some parliamentarians fought for, and managed to secure, minor amendments, but much of the original bill passed into law in March 2015. As Augustino Ting Mayai and Jok Madut Jok of the Sudd Institute had feared, the NSS Act served to 'sanction the already existing and ghastly behavior by security agencies' and to prevent resistance from 'those who will attempt to expose or challenge these behaviors'.[68]

From 2015, the NSS Act, and an expanded security service, were primary instruments to prevent and quell any form of resistance in the urban areas.[69] Many human rights lawyers and activists were preoccupied by avoiding, documenting and responding to abuses and threats from the NSS. They had to tread carefully. The NSS wielded sweeping powers to legally conduct arrests and detentions without judicial oversight or protections of the rights of detainees.[70] Security operatives placed ordinary citizens in general, and activists in particular, under surveillance, issuing warnings or simply arresting and placing critics of the government in custody.[71] The UN Commission on Human Rights in South Sudan found that '[the NSS] has resorted to intimidation, abductions and kidnapping to clamp down on opposition activities in the region'.[72] Civil society actors were also monitored and subjected to all manner of bureaucratic and financial pressures under the NGO Act, 2016.[73] These new laws enabled the government to crush civic activism while circumventing legal and judicial scrutiny. The NSS targeted critics of the government, including those who were organising non-violently, whether they were working in politics, the media or civil society.

Among the most egregious abuses of the NSS were the detentions of some 40 individual suspects in the NSS 'blue house' compound in Juba, where they were subject to 'torture, starvation or death'.[74] Local lawyers worked to expose the plight of the detainees but were unable to gain access to them, let alone represent them. For instance, Monyluak Alor Kuol worked with Amnesty International on the investigation of the case of George Livio, a South Sudanese journalist working for a UN radio station who was detained by the NSS in Wau in August 2014. Kuol was prevented from meeting his client although he publicly described the arrest as arbitrary and without justification: an 'abuse of power, impunity, disregard for institutions'.[75] In early 2015, Edmund Yakani of the Community Empowerment for Progress Organisation (CEPO) demanded that Livio be given access to legal aid, while Livio's employers at UNMISS remained strangely silent.[76] The following year Amnesty International reported and campaigned on behalf of Livio and 34 other detainees in NSS custody in Juba. As the organisation's South Sudan researcher Elizabeth Deng argued, the detentions even manage to contravene the draconian NSS Act, which had at least required that the detainees should be brought to court within 24 hours.[77]

A handful of the detainees eventually emerged from the 'blue house', among them Professor Leonzio Angole Onek from the University of Juba, who was arrested in December 2015 and held in prolonged arbitrary detention.[78] In March 2017, after his release, he wrote a poignant appeal to the president to release his former cell-mates, including Livio, stating:

> while in custody, I met over 40 persons who were accused of being members of SPLM-IO or some other rebel groups. They too have suffered from many diseases and some of them have since died … Some of them have been in detention for over three years without being taken to court.[79]

A few months later, Livio was released without charges, while most of his fellow detainees remained in custody.

Lawyers had a chance to assist when two of the NSS 'blue house' detainees were taken to court in high-profile trials that were much criticised by human rights organisations and opposition parties alike. James Gatdet Dak, a former SPLA-IO spokesman accused of treason, had been kidnapped by South Sudanese authorities in Kenya in late 2016, in a blatant violation of international refugee law. William John Endley, a South African former adviser to opposition leader Riek Machar, was accused of spying and conspiracy. However, the first lawyer who took on the case resigned after four months, complaining of political interference. He also argued that the trial of the political detainees was itself a violation of the Cessation of Hostilities Agreement (CoHA) signed by the government in December 2017, which had promised the release of all political prisoners and detainees within two weeks.[80] The cases ran on for some five months in Juba High Court, although the prisoners did not have access to a lawyer for over a month while a replacement was appointed.[81] Judge Ladu Armenio went ahead regardless, convicting Gatdet of treason and sentencing him to both imprisonment for 21 years and death by hanging in Juba High Court. Shortly afterwards he sentenced Endley to first serve more than nine years in prison, and thereafter to be hanged.[82] Gatdet and Endley were eventually saved not by due process or legal initiatives but by a presidential pardon issued during celebrations of the Khartoum peace deal, freeing them on 2 November 2018.[83]

These prolonged arbitrary detentions and miscarriages of justice in the 'blue house' were the tip of the iceberg. The NSS also used the notorious 'white house' in Juba, a location once favoured by the former Sudanese authorities to repress their southern critics, as well as other locations elsewhere. Soldiers rounded up people in mass arrests and detentions, placing them in military custody and beyond the purview of civil processes and lawyers. Some were held for a few days and others for months; the conditions were appalling and many were tortured or beaten.[84] The South Sudan Law Society found that a staggering one-third of respondents to their survey reported losing a member of their family to enforced disappearances either before or after December 2013. Further investigations suggested that this historical continuity was no coincidence. As one survivor pointed out, sometimes the same people were responsible: 'People are now fearing ... you are seeing somebody who behaved like this before, but he is still

in the system.'[85] Beyond this, there was the basic problem of accidental injustices supplementing political detentions. Suspects on
remand in ordinary prisons could languish there for years after
their arrest, given the lack of lawyers, judges and the sheer ineffi-
ciencies of prison administration.[86]

The combination of routine injustices coupled with political
violence animated the struggles to be recounted in later chapters of
this book. But activists also faced a perpetual threat to their own
survival which of necessity shaped their responses. The lengths
to which the NSS would go to clamp down on lawyers and human
rights activists was tragically exposed in the case of one of the 'blue
house' detainees – human rights lawyer Dong Samuel Luak. Dong
Samuel had refugee status in Kenya yet he was abducted in Nairobi
and, according to Human Rights Watch, was last seen in the custody
of the NSS in Juba in January 2017.[87] A UN Panel of Experts reports
that it is now 'highly probable' that Dong Samuel and an SPLM-IO
member with whom he was abducted, Aggrey Idri, were executed
by Internal Security Bureau agents on 30 January 2017, 'highlighting
the increasingly unchecked discretionary power of the National
Security Service'.[88]

Another case in point is that of Peter Biar Ajak, an academic
and co-founder of the South Sudan Young Leaders' Forum, a
coalition advocating for the resolution of the conflict. Ajak was
arrested without charge in Juba on 28 July 2018; and remained in
detention since with only limited access to legal representation,
according to the Office of the High Commissioner for Human
Rights (OHCHR).[89] He was only brought to court on 22 March
2019, and by then had accumulated a series of charges, including
insurgency and sabotage, that were related to a prisoner protest
while under NSS detention.[90] In September 2018 the 'blue house'
inmates had become so desperate that they staged a revolt while in
custody, disarmed their guards and demanded justice. The leader
of the protestors, businessman Captain Keribino Wol, told journalists: 'we're protesting systematic injustice and oppression. All

political prisoners and detainees need to be released or given fair trial'.[91] Ajak is said not to have participated, except in calling for the negotiations which led to the peaceful resolution of the protest. He denied all the charges.[92]

Ajak's detention fitted with a wider pattern of state repression of civil society activists by the NSS, one that even led to the detention in the 'blue house' of a member of the team that contributed to this book, in the period after our research ended. He has since been released, but testified in Ajak's defence. As the Commission on Human Rights in South Sudan observed in March 2019:

> A characteristic of the conflict since 2016 has been the increasing securitization of the State with the intelligence arms of the security sector playing a pivotal role in the increasing repression, resulting in individuals being deprived of their fundamental freedoms and civic space shrinking. The Commission has documented at least 47 first-hand accounts of individuals who have been arbitrarily arrested, detained and/or subjected to torture or cruel, inhuman or degrading treatment by the National Security Service and Sudan People's Liberation Army (SPLA) Military Intelligence between December 2013 and late 2018.[93]

Political leaders displayed a veneer of legality by changing the law to enhance national security powers and using legal instruments, especially presidential decrees, to crush actual and potential resistance from lawyers and judges. They sought to harness the law and its institutions in forms of authoritarian order-making. The regular meddling of the president and his allies in micro-conflicts within legal and judicial institutions undermined the possibility for an independent judiciary and legal fraternity. Yet some judges and lawyers publicly struggled to assert their authority and, as we shall see later, others developed more covert tactics to respond to injustices.

The chieftaincy: 'essential to our survival'

Customary chiefs were South Sudan's most prolific and accessible arbiters, far outnumbering judges and lawyers and working in both towns and rural areas.[94] Chiefs were present nationwide at various levels of the local administration, including counties, and their subdivisions (*payams* and *bomas*), and in displaced communities. Their proliferation is testament to the legitimacy and durability of the chieftaincy and to the interests of both the government and 'rebel rulers' in maintaining a degree of law and order. Chiefs were constantly preoccupied with the ravages and deprivations of the war and economic crisis. They were also personally exposed to the worst impacts, as they were positioned precariously at the fringes of unstable regimes and on the frontlines of multi-layered conflicts.

Chiefs' courts proved to be the most resilient justice mechanism after December 2013. Military and political authorities continued to rely on customary authorities and law to construct legitimacy, manage populations and extend their reach into communities as they had done in the past.[95] But chiefs were constantly balancing these demands from local political and military actors with their allegiances to their communities. They had to respond to constant fluctuations in local governance arrangements, and the influx or departure of humanitarian agencies. Their authority ultimately depended upon their standing in the local community, but they risked severe consequences if they were seen to be opposed to the governing authorities.

The chieftaincy had the advantage of distance from elites at the centre of government in Juba, but they could also be subject to direct political interference. In formal terms, chiefs were integrated at the lowest tier of local government and the judiciary under the 2009 Local Government Act. Chiefs could in principle be commanded, hired and fired from above, and some chiefs were dismissed by local officials or kept in power by them against the wishes of their community. But in practice the chieftaincy was a decentralised institution that lacked a consistent hierarchy and regulation. It was not straightforward for the government to intervene, especially if a chief was esteemed and supported by powerful members of their community. In theory, chiefs received government salaries, but these payments were very unreliable, and most chiefs relied on contributions from the local community. Unlike civil servants, chiefs lived with their communities and had no option but to do so. They presided over the customary courts and involved themselves in problems arising from the war and economic crisis, from the proliferation of arms and youth violence, to food shortages. In this sense, they followed a logic of mutuality that was in stark contrast to the extractive politics of the kleptocracy.

The customary institutions are markers of historical continuity, in contrast to the novelty of other judicial institutions and the inconstancy of political authority. Their capacity to respond to intractable problems relied upon this familiarity and upon well-established relationships and practices. The chieftaincy had proved adaptable to urban and rural domains, evolving over decades of war, predation and changes of government. Chiefs have acted as 'brokers' managing the relations between people and governments since the colonial period.[96] As a result, chiefs retain their social status and value, so that even if a particular chief does not perform his (or occasionally her) duties effectively, the underlying trust in the institution endures. As a rule, chiefs have drawn legitimacy from their provision of services and their negotiations with the government, and in different contexts they could draw on the local symbolic repertoires of custom and relationships, either direct or indirect, to forms of spiritual authority.

Notably, the chiefs managed to operate during the law despite very limited material resources. Some received paltry monthly salaries, but they were not paid regularly, as one Boma chief from Nimule complained in August 2017: 'We last got a payment from the government, 902 SSP, in February.'[97] And some chiefs were not paid at all. The chiefs also received a portion of the court fees and fines but had to pay the majority to the local government.[98] Beyond this, at most, chiefs were endowed with government uniforms or sashes, paper and court stamps, and occasionally a copy of recent or historical laws. They held courts under trees, taking local cases and resolving them promptly. They could sometimes call upon soldiers or police to enforce their judgments, depending on the time and place. But they fundamentally relied upon garnering voluntary compliance and negotiating makeshift solutions within the constraints of prevailing social norms, cosmologies and power relations, in a fashion that appealed to tradition and continuity.

Naturally, chiefs varied in their legitimacy, social connections and approach to leadership. They also attained power by different means, as either elected, selected or hereditary appointments. Most came from powerful families and had brothers, uncles and nephews in politics, the army and the civil service. There could be tensions and competition between local chiefs, including between those who were literate and those who were not, or those with different political allegiances. Some chiefs were seasoned 'political-military entrepreneurs' in their own right, while many had been members of the SPLA or other fighting forces at some point in their lives.[99] And it was also often expected that rural chiefs would contribute to the war effort, assisting military authorities to mobilise young fighters. But some chiefs defied demands from government or military forces. Others publicly criticised the government or aligned themselves with opponents of the regime.[100] Several chiefs openly deplored the interventions of warring parties in their local arenas.[101]

However, the authority of chiefs was inevitably undermined and disrupted by the war, especially in rural communities. They were universally unable to address the atrocious violence arising from the civil war and mostly could not stem or punish the incessant cattle raiding either.[102] Their declining authority over young men was a constant concern, especially when the youths were armed. The relationships between chiefs and other public authorities such as local officials, generals, militia leaders, security agents, clan elders or prophets varied, depending on their location and identity. So, while chiefs were renowned for their skills as arbiters, they were by no means secure in their authority and could easily become targets of military and political schemes, or arbitrary punishments.

Before independence, President Salva Kiir had described the chiefs as 'essential to our survival', and apologised on behalf of the army for 'all the bad things we did to you' during the liberation struggle.[103] Yet this same intimate but tense relationship persisted after December 2013. Many chiefs were forced to flee their homes and were displaced with their people as refugees, internally displaced persons (IDPs) or into towns. Some were killed, others were arrested or threatened. There are no comprehensive statistics on the death toll or the impacts of the violence, but we know that the majority of South Sudanese people were affected by violence and trauma,[104] and chiefs faced specific risks.

The scandalous arrest of Chief Wilson Peni Rikito, king of the Azande in Yambio, Western Equatoria in November 2016 exemplifies the threat. The chief was especially powerful and outspoken, and from a region which had recently erupted into conflict – with a proliferation of militias, rising opposition to the government and episodes of intense state-sponsored violence.[105] Protests from local Zande leaders and international human rights organisations brought the chief's arrest to public attention and identified his whereabouts in NSS detention in Juba.[106] Some speculated that local politicians ordered his arrest, perceiving him as an ally of Joseph Bakosoro, a former governor who had previously been detained and later formed an opposition rebel group.[107] But the chief was neither charged nor tried. After a month in custody he was released on the orders of the president. Thereafter, Chief Peni circumspectly returned home to preach peace. Soon afterwards, he was appointed as a member of the South Sudan National Dialogue Steering Committee, a government-led peace initiative.[108] His arrest had clearly been a warning against opposition, and apparently the leadership then changed tack and sought to bring him into the fold.

Chief John Amba's detention was less well publicised, but it followed a similar pattern. He was the head chief from Kerepi *payam* in Eastern Equatoria and was arrested with the chief of Moli-Andru *boma* in April 2015. He recalled that they were picked up by soldiers without any explanation and 'put in prison in the barracks', where they were held with no food for two days. His community at home and in the diaspora protested: 'a message went to the governor and those people in Juba and even in Australia and the president was informed that they have arrested chiefs'. In response, the president stepped in to order the chiefs' release. The governor agreed to free them but warned them against rebellion: 'do you know that your children are in the bush? ... I will release you, but you go home and if your children are in the bush or rebels, then get out'. In the months that followed, Chief Amba had to return to the same barracks on several occasions to plead for the liberty of other detainees from his community. But by July 2016 the war had escalated in the region, there was fighting and destruction in Kerepi. The chief held on as long as he could until his life was directly under threat: 'They wanted to arrest me because everyone ran, and I remained. And one soldier told me that they want to kill you; they say that you are the one keeping the rebels.'[109]

Chiefs had moral influence and the capacity to negotiate, but no jurisdiction over the political violence and plunder committed by state elites. They were vulnerable to local conflicts and threats from within the community and rebels, and some were killed.[110] Their intermediary position was a legacy of the two-tier structures of colonial native administration policies. As a leading scholar of African politics and history Mahmood Mamdani has shown, colonisers typically secured and mitigated political domination by governing African populations 'on the cheap' under local rulers. These policies 'bifurcated' state institutions, allocating conditional rights and resources to rural, native 'subjects' under customary law; and citizenship rights to racially defined, urban-educated elites under statutory law. This premise was inserted at the foundations of the state and its legacy permeated post-independence regimes, including in South Sudan.[111] In many ways, South Sudanese chiefs broke the colonial mould: they governed in urban as well as rural spaces; they pushed back against the intrusions of predatory colonial and postcolonial states and they were generally locally legitimate and accountable.[112] But they were integral to state structures that classified people according to their ethnic and social status, legalising and politicising differences and inequalities.

Chiefs were not predisposed to act as a collective since they represented a constellation of ethnic groups divided by the conflict. There was hope that they would unite in national forums and contribute to conflict resolution, and some took a few tentative steps in this direction. In June 2014 there was an attempt to involve the chiefs in consultations to inform the IGAD-led peace process in Addis Ababa. Later on, the Joint Monitoring and Evaluation Commission (JMEC) – established to monitor the implementation of the 2015 peace agreement – brought together 655 chiefs from across South Sudan and encouraged them to serve as 'agents of peace and reconciliation' in November 2016.[113] The leader of a national Chief's Council, Deng Macham Angui Garang, optimistically promised that the 'solution to the conflict is in our hands'.[114] And representatives of the more established regional Councils of Traditional Authority Leaders (COTALs) also voiced commitments to work together and called for organisation on a national scale.[115] These were meaningful attempts, although none of them were sustained or demonstrated tangible impacts.

Chiefs were also regular participants in the energetic local peacebuilding activities of NGOs and churches. They were in great demand as highly influential local actors, and the authorities people were most likely to appeal to for justice.[116] Their limitation was that any settlements achieved at community level were prone to collapse as a result of national-level political dynamics and interventions.

During the 1983–2005 war, in the depths of the fragmentation of the SPLA and the internecine and ethnic strife of the 1990s, there had been efforts at local peacemaking and reconciliation. The most effective of these, which has subsequently become emblematic of grassroots peacemaking, was the Wunlit conference of 1999. This was inter-ethnic and regional, and provided great impetus to the legitimacy of chiefs.[117] Wunlit was driven not solely by chiefs; it was facilitated by the New Sudan Council of Churches with international support, and approval from some SPLM leaders. Its focus was upon reconciliation, not redress; it connected communities in a 'people-to-people peace' fostering relationships and providing encouragement for the north–south elite-level negotiations and the 2005 Comprehensive Peace Agreement that ended the second Sudanese civil war. However, the process leading up to the CPA focused on achieving a pact between northern and southern political elites, driven by the SPLM. It did not address the need for a 'south–south' dialogue, although there had already been some efforts to promote this, nor did it broach the issue of justice and accountability, despite calls from civil society.[118]

At Wunlit, some forthright chiefs had questioned the behaviour of their 'sons' in the SPLA, describing the 'slaughter' and 'transgressions' of restrictions on violence during the wars of the 1990s. Twenty years later, as the post-independence civil war dragged on, a number of prominent chiefs were similarly brave in voicing criticisms of the politicians in NGO forums or interviews, blaming them for the war and its impacts on civilians.[119] But not all chiefs could be relied upon to take a stand, since chiefs did not share a common position or platform and there were several different forms of violence underway – some of it directed at them personally. It was risky to protest; even contributing to discussions at an NGO peace workshop could have negative repercussions. A chief from Nimule described how he raised the issue of looting during a workshop organised by an international NGO and was threatened with arrest. Two weeks later all the chiefs were called together by the security agencies and warned: '[We said] it is our mandate to speak out the bad things that are ongoing. They said we should not have said it out.' A few months later the chief was threatened at home by armed gunmen and advised by security agencies to leave the area.[120]

Whether because of fears, beliefs or loyalties, chiefs' responses to violence were sometimes muted or ambiguous. For instance, while sexual violence escalated both in the war zones and more widely in society, some chiefs were unwilling to respond, declaring their suspicion of 'foreign' human rights interventions and asserting the sanctity of customary authorities.[121] As later chapters show, some chiefs worked with or became legal activists in efforts to limit abuses, but since the point of custom is its familiarity and indigeneity it is hardly surprising that many would grasp onto notions of tradition. Moreover, ethnic and familial loyalties underpinned their status and were bound to play a part in the calculations of individual chiefs. Perhaps this is why when the US decided to restrict arms transfers in February 2018, a select group of chiefs came out on the streets of Juba to support the government and protest against the decision.[122] In any case, these sorts of contradictions highlighted ethnic and social differences within the chieftaincy and help explain why it could not effectively challenge the system.

At Wunlit, chiefs had been advised by the SPLM officials to 'avoid matters that look like we are in a courtroom',[123] and their interactions with chiefs during the third civil war were apparently on similar conditional terms. It was politically useful for chiefs to continue in their role as arbiters at local level, as long as they did not disrupt or challenge elite interests.

Conclusion

There were certainly courageous individuals within the justice system, including judges, lawyers and chiefs, who tried to uphold the law during the conflict. They did so either simply by continuing at their posts and trying to apply the law with integrity, or by confronting political breaches of the law, sometimes at great personal risk. But for the most part, South Sudan's legal and judicial institutions and authorities have neither been independent nor an effective check on power. Some of their leading members have close ties to the ruling clique; some stand accused of corruption, a problem that was apparent even before the war. Moreover, since 2013 President Kiir has hired and fired some honourable people who displayed resistance, and security agencies have intimidated and threatened others. These various political interventions have eaten away at the leadership and internal structures of the ministry, judiciary and the bar, but preserved their shells.

However, even 'kleptocrats' recognise the need for a legal façade to be maintained during a conflict; they need effective legal institutions in all sorts of practical ways, including in negotiations with donors, lenders and international corporations interested in investing in South Sudan's resources. They also need the chieftancy, both to govern society and to mobilise political and military support. They have therefore used a variety of strategies in order to build relations and intimidate critics. But law is a slippery tool and political elites are also vulnerable to falling foul of it if they fall out of political favour. Money and might cannot fully guarantee impunity. The symbolic legality of the state still held some political sway and was a crucial instrument in the suppression of political dissent.

The cases of political opponents who ended up in court or prison during this period help to illustrate the enduring power of state legality over other forms of political authority. We can position these relations on a sliding scale. At the top sits the former deputy chief of staff, General Paul Malong Awan, who stood accused of 'planning, directing, or committing acts that violate applicable international human rights law or international humanitarian law'.[124] He had wealth, extensive kinship networks and military means at his disposal, but was briefly confined to comfortable house arrest in Juba in 2017 after a falling out with his long-term ally President Kiir. His lower-ranking supporters fared much worse, and languished in NSS detention centres long after his release.[125] Lower down the political scale comes Joseph Bakosoro, a former governor of Western Equatoria detained for four months in 2015. Further down still, a marginal player, is James Gatdet Dak, the young SPLA-IO spokesman who was subject to the full force of the law in court, convicted of treason and sentenced to death, but eventually pardoned by the president as a symbolic gesture of peace. In comparison, the countless wrongfully arrested and abused ordinary people, whose situation is explored in the remainder of the book, are entirely vulnerable to the arbitrary use of the law.

State security practices of surveillance, arrest and detention were bolstered by the NSS Act, and served as a means of neutralising opposition to the government and reducing the costs of loyalty in South Sudan's political marketplace. By creating a climate of fear and uncertainty, government elites could bargain and reward people selectively, intervening personally to free individuals at will. There may not have been a coordinated strategy behind the machinery, or cohesion between and within security agencies, but the constant threat of detention and punishment constrained agency and served government, repeating inherited practices of the use of 'law to maintain control'.[126] The continuities in the strategic use of the law by state actors were both generalised and specific; the government directly borrowed from President Omar al Bashir in the creation and content of the NSS Act and in the disruption of the 2015 bar association elections – a resounding echo of the 2006 Sudanese bar association elections which led to the silencing of lawyers critical of the government.[127]

Legal and judicial authorities wield power by virtue of their knowledge of the law. The government deployed references to the legality of the state and the use of law as a political instrument, but its legitimacy was vulnerable to being undermined by their principled critiques. This explains the intensity with which the government tried to co-opt or to suppress any form of dissent. Ultimately, as socio-legal theorists have shown us, the law is a social field; it is a domain of political struggle that political actors cannot entirely dominate, even when they have superior access to economic or military capital.[128] Moreover, law matters and becomes meaningful in the routine practices of the courts and in those arenas where people interact directly with chiefs, judges and lawyers, where we can find different political logics, pressures and struggles for justice at play.

Chapter 3

MAKESHIFT COURTS

The residents of South Sudan's towns seemed to be constantly striving to 'get justice and get even'[1] in court, regardless of the war and the government's attempt to harness the law as a tool of repression. Ordinary people brought cases to the courts on all sorts of problems, including minor arguments within families and more serious criminal matters such as murders. They also attended court as witnesses or enthusiastic spectators. Some of the criminal cases had the support of police and public prosecutors, although their involvement was neither consistent nor reliable. This chapter sifts through the records of urban court cases, compiled by South Sudanese paralegals and researchers in several of South Sudan's most populous and strategic towns and three displacement sites over the period of a year (2015–16), and also draws on material from ethnographic research from 2014 to 2019, to develop a social and political analysis of the courts.[2]

The findings suggest that town courts were productive, but paradoxical. Court hearings enabled people to raise grievances and seek recognition and redress. Judges and chiefs listened to individual concerns at length and even offered prompt solutions to their dilemmas, intended to settle the matter 'for the time being'.[3] Their processes and improvisations drew upon established practices; people evidently needed and valued these forums, and they often seemed to accept their judgments. However, the courts left people vulnerable to the violence and predation of military and political elites, while they intensely regulated relations between people, and within communities and families. In the short term they mediated and mitigated conflicts, but at the same time they were shaped by and reproduced the social conditions for war, preserving political and socio-economic inequalities while reinforcing ethnic, social, gender and generational differences.

The divergent tendencies of the courts seem bewildering, but they are meaningful in political terms. They resonate with the argument that laws and legal practices contribute to the order of things, reproducing the common sense that binds people into compliance with political domination. Historical experiences of government in southern Sudan had encouraged people to take predatory and arbitrary power for granted. But the new independent state had promised services, rights and public goods, and chances for accumulation. And whether or not they could deliver, the courts were part of this promise, holding out enticing possibilities for predictability, security and settlements. The courts had dual functions in providing moral and civil forms of local government while legalising inequalities and differences. This sustained the status quo, fostering the hegemony of violent disorder.[4] For the time being, it seemed the courts were compliant with arbitrary power, although there were many hints that they had the potential to do otherwise.

Before exploring the politics of the courts, we should register their empirical achievements. It was amazing that the courts functioned at all, given the conflict and economic crisis. Court sessions would take place in the intervals between repeated bouts of warfare and in parallel with relentless and differentiated forms of political violence. For instance, during this period people in Rumbek endured the spill-over effects of some of the worst inter-clan and intercommunal cattle raiding and violent revenge attacks. Government soldiers and security agents waged terror in the towns by means of arrests, beatings, sexual assaults, and disappearances and killings by 'unknown gunmen', especially in potential hotbeds of resistance like Juba, Wau and Nimule.[5] The character of the towns and the composition of the courts also changed as people fled to and fro, trying to evade warfare and depredations.

The chapter begins by exploring the gap between the idealised model of the judicial institutions and the actualities of courts as they existed around 2013, and in the subsequent five years. It then examines the cases people brought to the courts and the ways in which they were addressed. Stark patterns emerge from an analysis of the records of court proceedings. Firstly, only a limited number of cases have anything to do with the conflict or political authorities. Secondly, most cases centre on disputes between ordinary citizens, whether on criminal, civil or (especially) familial matters. The courts mostly worked outside of the political sphere and intensely regulated the social sphere. The discussion covers cases that were outliers, illustrating the potential of the courts to expand their authority into the political sphere; and more routine cases that show how the courts penetrated deeply into people's personal and social relations, constructing political subjectivities.

Court structures

South Sudan's courts fused legal reforms with historical practices and social initiatives. They were governed by the 2008 Judiciary Act and the 2009 Local Government Act, which together envisaged a neat hierarchy of courts and different jurisdictions for statutory and customary courts. There was to be a supreme court, three regional appeals courts, ten state-level high courts, plus county and *payam* courts.[6] The customary courts would operate at each tier of local government, from *bomas* at the bottom, up to *payam* and county levels; with multi-ethnic town bench courts as potential equivalents in towns.[7] Statutory courts would rule on criminal cases, some civil cases, and appeals from customary courts, using newly written laws and returning to a common law tradition based on precedent. Meanwhile, customary courts would judge civil cases by referring to the 'traditions, norms and ethics' of the relevant community.[8] The genesis and operation of the courts was actually far more complicated, but these legal differentiations were important in setting some parameters of what was possible.

The legal reforms preserved vestiges of the colonial legal framework that had originally politicised ethnicity,[9] while also allowing for some flexibility and innovation. Strictly speaking, the laws cemented the power of customary authorities over ethnic and moral communities, while limiting their reach over matters of state and criminality. But legal boundaries were never precisely specified, and interaction between the courts was expected, since statutory courts were encouraged to call upon customary law and authority to inform their decisions and customary courts were instructed to attend to legal statutes.[10] Leading South Sudanese jurists had seen the potential for a creative legal synthesis. Legal scholar Francis Deng anticipated 'the integration of customary law into a unified administration of justice'.[11] The former chief justice John Wol Makec perceived a legal process that would contribute to the formation of a national identity, arguing that 'just as the customs of various tribes in England became the common law in England ... our customs are going to be a common law of Southern Sudan'.[12] In any case, there was already a wealth of historical evidence that custom itself was a hybrid, partly 'invented' and reworked 'through interaction with government law and wider cultures'.[13] However, the precise content of the blend between custom and statute would depend upon everyday practices, including in the courts.

The hybridisation of customary and statutory extended beyond the content of the law. Courts on the lower rungs of the judicial hierarchy were a 'patchwork' of authorities that blurred the lines of responsibility between customary and statutory forums.[14] The legislation that aimed to regulate the courts and their ad hoc legal authorities had not succeeded before the war and had little chance of doing so thereafter.[15] The full quota of statutory courts was never realised, not a single *payam* court and only a fraction of the envisaged county courts were established, and many courts closed due to staff shortages, warfare and insecurity. The reach and authority of such courts was muddied by their association with a contested government and by perpetual confusion and contestation surrounding the administrative boundaries upon which their classifications were based.[16] In contrast, makeshift customary forums sprung up to fit with the diverse needs, identities and allegiances of communities in urban spaces and wantonly assumed responsibilities beyond their legal remit. The towns were home to an assortment of official and unofficial customary courts and they continued to handle the overwhelming majority of cases as they had done for decades.[17]

The most famous and longstanding traditional court in Juba was 'Kator B'. It was well established as part of local government, and attracted cases from most of Juba's communities, purportedly for its speed and expertise in resolving family matters, but perhaps also for its relatively low fees.[18] Our court reports show that this industrious court routinely drew crowds of up to 150, and handled cases brought by people of every ethnic background. The parties came from 13 different ethnic groups. Most were Equatorians, a common regional label, while others were Dinka, Shilluk or Balanda. There was a telling lack of Nuer – who did not appear in Kator B for the appalling reason that they had been ethnically cleansed from Juba at the start of the war – but there were people from many other backgrounds.[19] 'Kator B' was something of an anomaly in its scope and authority. It was not the only official and multi-ethnic customary court, but violent actors had increasingly deployed ethnic frames to mobilise supporters and justify violence; and as Amnesty International observed, both government and opposition forces had a record of explicitly 'targeting victims on the basis of their gender, ethnic and perceived political identities'. This was bound to fragment multi-ethnic communities, fostering differences and divisions and forcing people into enclaves of displacement. Some communities sought to distance themselves from government and, increasingly, courts were more informal and improvised.

In a stark illustration of horrendous violence spawning new courts, grassroots initiatives sprung up in the displacement sites of the UN PoCs. Almost 200,000 massacre survivors were clustered in these sites under UN protection, mainly in Juba, Bentiu and Malakal, and they created their own local forms of law and order for the purposes of 'community protection', each with local modifications. Most of the people in the PoCs had fled the government forces and were in a unique and prolonged form of internal political exile, under armed international protection. They needed mechanisms to address the spiralling disputes between individuals, families and clans in the confined spaces of the camps, where political tensions simmered, and levels of social uncertainty and trauma were rife. They established courts which relied on customary law and procedure but were also adapted to their unusual context, interacting with UN police and officials as well as accommodating different ethnic groups.[20] Similarly, other more conventional 'IDPs' activated their own customary regimes in displacement sites. Notably, the Dinka survivors of the mass killings of civilians in Bor in early 2014[21] managed to set up camps and establish their courts in their camp in Melijo, in Eastern Equatoria. Such courts were both novel and reminiscent of earlier and historical tendencies of South Sudanese communities to readily establish their own courts and authorities in adverse circumstances.

As political historian Nicki Kindersley observes, people have experience of striving for forms of law and a basic degree of 'normalcy' under successive violent governments and have developed courts as 'ways of managing complex spaces and difficult circumstances' under conditions of extreme insecurity. So the courts might come in many varieties, often ethnic in their referents – 'Nuer', 'Dinka' or 'Bari' courts, for instance – and selected by members of the relevant communities, but they are also highly local in character and reflective of the communities that constitute them. For example, in fragmented and diverse urban spaces they were also wrestling with disputes between people of different identities and could engage in negotiations with chiefly counterparts in other communities, or constitute 'mixed panels' temporarily or more regularly. They might also reflect the dominance of other social categories: for instance, Kindersley finds militarised neighbourhoods in Juba regulated by 'multi-ethnic, military-connected "customary" courts'.[22] Overall, the proliferation of customary courts reflects not only an impetus for legal forum creation and shopping, but a quest for temporary solutions to grievous insecurity, and the fragmentation of political and legal authority.

Yet for all their idiosyncrasies and variations, the customary courts tended to produce some similar approximations of the law. Customary chiefs and their panels of local notables were not legal experts, but mostly had other previous and current roles and affiliations, including military experience, and generally lacked material resources and education. They had, however, been informed by interactions over time; customary laws were adjudicated and discussed publicly, and they had evolved in deliberations between authorities in meetings and courts both historically and since.[23] Some chiefs might have had access to copies of customary codes that had been written down, such as the Nuer *Fangak* and the Dinka *Wanh-Alel*, or to the outputs of a recent ascertainment of law projects involving other ethnic groups.[24] Others might have attended one of the occasional workshops run by development and humanitarian actors to train chiefs.[25] Some retained copies or memories of current or previous statutory penal codes and used them to inform their judgments and penalties. Chiefs were often keen to acquire knowledge and copies of the written laws, although not all of them were sufficiently literate to make sense of them. Customary law was first and foremost understood through oral traditions and everyday practices might draw upon heterogeneous sources. Chiefs and court panels interpreted matters in light of the laws and precedents they were aware of, and the situations before them. In effect, the customary courts were largely concrete expressions of social dispositions and the 'logic of practice'.[26]

What certainly united the customary courts and underpinned their authority was their distinctive process of public deliberation and moral adjudication. In wartime, the courts were, as they had always been, lively community affairs, usually held beneath a tree and attended by all and sundry. Chiefs and court panels mediated, trying to find points of agreement between the parties in court by means of careful questioning and moralising. People spoke at length in their mother tongue and were listened to attentively. These procedures, even more than the content of the law, were time-honoured and commonly understood. Francis Deng once described them as 'a genuine search for truth ... [that] makes the judge the investigator of facts during a trial'. In question was not necessarily the whole truth, however, but the most socially valuable part, as the courts were oriented towards reconciliation rather than inquisition. Court panels took a look at the facts and evidence but also considered the views and identities of parties and their families, in a process of weighing and balancing. The senior chief was expected to draw out the consensus 'whose wisdom the litigants would accept',[27] in line with the prevailing conceptions of the law and the characteristics of the common good. The presence of the community underpinned the courts' authority and their judgments and underlined the moral orientation of the courts. The procedures paid heed to individual dignity, but the settlements were designed to confirm that rights were subject to the welfare and security of the community.[28]

The customary regimes were South Sudan's most abundant legal heritage and their influence seeped into high courts and county courts. These statutory forums were less transparent, flexible and participatory, but they were also under-resourced, ensuring that they took on a parochial and makeshift character. They were presided over by a single judge, and there were rarely any lawyers involved. The judge usually advised that the accused had the 'right' to an advocate but this was rhetorical, since it was not clear how they would fulfil that right – legal aid was notionally available in the most serious cases but difficult to access in practice.[29] The prescription that judges should hold cases and record judgments in English had also collapsed by the time of our court observations, since many judges had been trained under Sudan's *sharia* system and spoke only Arabic.[30] Certainly Arabic was often the lingua franca of the town courts, especially in Juba. But the crucial point was that the courts would adapt to local circumstances. Our reports show that cases in Rumbek's county court were typically heard in Dinka, while people spoke in the three local languages of Ma'di, Dinka and Arabic in some Nimule hearings.

In a similar fashion, statutory judges might call upon different sources of law as a basis for their judgments. They could reference South Sudan's recent body of legislation but they might also turn to precedents from other countries or, more commonly, to South Sudanese customary laws and chiefs for advice. As high court judge Dr Raimondo Geri Legge explained, to be a 'pro-people judge' in this 'hybrid system' you need to wear three hats and act as judge and advocate for both parties. You also need to master 'hybrid law', incorporating civil, customary and common law precepts. This explains why there were many instances in which a statutory court judged the case in line with a typical customary settlement, even for the most serious criminal cases. Judges would have to draw the line at customs that were deemed 'repugnant', in the old colonial fashion. Courts were instructed to act according to 'judicial precedents, customs, principles of justice, equity and good conscience' but this still left scope for creativity.[31] The result was that while the processes in statutory and customary courts differed substantially, their outcomes, often a mix of punishments and compensation, ranging from physical violence, the death penalty or, more commonly, corporal punishment in customary courts; to imprisonment and fines, or compensation payments, could be remarkably similar.

Law in practice

The essential point of these various insights into the plural legal regimes, their heterogeneous sources and their flexible blurring and blending, is that law in South Sudan is a largely a matter of practice.

It needs to be examined and understood on the basis of what happens in courts and through comparisons between cases. Two murder cases from Wau can help to illustrate some of the complicated overlaps and divergences which were also apparent in other localities and on different issues.

The Wau murder cases took place just months apart in 2015. The first case concerned two relatives and ran for an hour and a half in a customary court in April. The complainant accused his brother-in-law of killing his own wife and then abandoning the body.[32] The complainant said he had reported this crime 'of passion' to the police but the case went no further for some time. The customary court promptly took the matter in hand, basing its decision on the testimonies of the two parties. It found the accused guilty and ordered him to pay 16,000 SSP or 16 head of cattle based on the penal code of 2008. But the court was extemporising. The penal code actually specifies that an individual convicted of the crime of murder is to be 'sentenced to death or imprisonment for life' with an alternative of customary blood compensation with imprisonment 'for a term not exceeding ten years'.[33] The amount of compensation is not specified and therefore depends on the relevant customary norm. Notably, neither the accused nor the complainant was satisfied with the outcome, and some of the crowd that had gathered at the court thought he should have been fined more heavily, observing that the customary amount should have been at least 21,000 SSP and that he should have gone to prison.[34]

The second case came to the high court in Wau in October. Once again, a man had killed his wife but, in this instance, the case was handled by the police and then tried by the statutory court in a matter of 45 minutes. It turned out, however, that the man had himself brought his wife's death to the attention of the police in the first place. The court observation notes state:

the man asked his wife to fetch water and she refused. He proceeded to fight with her during which he pushed her, and she fell and died from her injuries. The accused ran to the police station to get the police. When they arrived at the home they found the wife dead and arrested the accused. They put him in custody for one day and then they transferred him to high court.

The case had reached the court within four days, although the sole evidence was the man's confession. The judge ruled that the accused should be imprisoned for five years for murder and pay 31,000 SSP in compensation, also based on the penal code of 2008. But again, this was a somewhat ad hoc combination of statue and custom in the sense that the confession suggested manslaughter. The court seemed to implicitly accept this, since it awarded a rather lenient prison sentence, well under the term limits for murder. In contrast, the customary payment awarded in monetary terms was fulsome. A group of family members present at the court wanted more. They stuck to their view that this was a case of murder; and they called for the accused to hang.[35]

The Wau murder cases demonstrate that trials might be equally speedy – and interrogations of evidence or witnesses similarly sketchy – in either forum. In both cases, and in standard fashion, it was the complaining party who ensured that the case reached the court, despite the fact that it concerned a criminal offence. In neither case did the accused have access to a lawyer. What both the judge and chiefs weighed up were the arguments presented by the complainant, or the prosecution, and the accused person. Their rulings were rooted in general precepts that were understood by the arbiters and other participants. They seemed less concerned with the question of whether the accused was guilty 'beyond reasonable doubt' as in procedures for criminal cases; rather they were concerned with probability and compensation in common with civil cases. In addition, the evidence was similarly sparse and there was little attention to the issue of investigation. The judges apparently took the complainants at their word and steered the judgments towards a prosecution and a settlement.

The customary settlement of 'bloodwealth' cattle compensation for murder, or its monetary equivalent, was expedient and awarded in lieu of a heavier punishment in both courts. Blood money is the 'oldest conflict resolution mechanism known to man' and has deep roots in Sudanese legal cultures. It is closely intertwined with the norms that sustain the bridewealth system (see below). But although different ethnic groups attached their own nuanced spiritual and social interpretations to the practice, town courts applied it rather sweepingly. Their main concern seemed to be to settle the matter as urgently as possible, making short shrift of the negotiation processes which are essential to the reconciliatory aims of the practice.[36] The penal code specified that blood compensation awards must be finally settled in the high court and combined with the criminal penalties, but not everyone could access the statutory courts, nor did they necessarily want to. As such, chiefs' courts continued to settle homicide cases locally when parties were willing.[37]

The Wau cases attest that people might take a similar case to a different forum and receive a similar settlement. The process differed but in both courts the decisions were informed by shared legal sensibilities and orientations, rather than the specifics of different bodies of law. The judges and chiefs were also attentive to what was socially and politically possible in the local circumstances. The crowd did not complain about the convictions; rather they thought elements of the sentence might be revised. The rulings were apparently guided by the generalities of expected norms and practices, rather than the particularities of laws, evidence and investigation.

The politics of town courts: analysing the court cases

Town courts were frantically busy, but out of hundreds of cases there were hardly any that hinted there was a war on. The courts received the cases that police and prosecutors were willing and able to bring, and those that people thought they had some chance of pursuing for the sake of social recognition or material gain. This meant only a fraction of the violations people were suffering reached the courts, and these were almost always cases that did not touch upon the public conduct of political or military authorities. Given that the regime had employed justice and security instruments to brutally silence political opposition, this makes perfect sense.[38] But the silences of the courts convey the limits of the law in practice and in popular understanding. Everyone knew that no legal remedy could be pursued for certain grievances. We can identify these legal boundaries in the gap between people's experiences of violations and the cases they took to court.

Sanctioning political violence?

The story of Edna, a businesswoman from Malakal, is harrowing and yet typical in the sense that she suffered successive traumas, in common with so many South Sudanese people.[39] However, Edna is unusual in that she was a recent migrant from Ethiopia and her choices are attributable neither simply to South Sudanese cultural norms nor to poverty, since she previously ran a successful bar and later established a thriving tea shop within the Malakal UN protection site. Her efforts to pursue justice thus speak directly to the political boundaries around the courts.

Edna was a survivor of the calamitous clashes between government and rebel forces in Malakal town at the end of December 2013, when she witnessed a series of killings perpetrated by soldiers. Human rights reports have described some of the horrors of this violence.[40] Edna simply refers to the fighting as 'cruel', and enumerates the dead:

A lot of people died in front of me including an entire family of five members ... there was Haron and I know [and] a Doctor whom they killed ... they shot him several times ... They nearly killed a pregnant woman too who refused to surrender her smart phone. They punched and kicked her all over her body till the child came out – luckily, she survived.

Edna experienced further threats to her life and financial losses. Soldiers stole all her money in 2013, she explains: 'to save my life I surrendered'. Her tea shop in the UN PoC was looted in an attack on the protection site in 2015, which left more than 30 people dead and over 100 injured.[41] In 2018, she left the PoC to take her daughter to a clinic in town, but government soldiers demanded a 'migration document'. She knew other Ethiopian traders had been arrested so she gave them all the money she had in her pocket.[42]

Edna did not regard most of the violations she suffered as justiciable. Instead, she focused her quest for justice on the betrayal of her husband, whom she said she supported financially before finding out he was seeing other women. She recalled the moment when she caught him 'red-handed' with a woman, leading her to try and gain recompense in customary courts operating within Malakal's UN protection site.

> I was devastated … I shouted at him for few minutes and left. He came home later at seven in the night and started assaulting me until I was admitted in a hospital. When I recovered, I went to sector two court with a hope that they will persuade him to give me at least some of the money I first gave him to open the business with. Unfortunately, the court officials told me I do not have the right to claim anything from my ex-husband … However, they asked him to pay 12,000 SSP for the child … I bought some bed sheets and clothes for the child … I am really disappointed by the way they handle legal issues, they told me I have no right as a woman when I took my husband to their court … I went to sector one when the sector two court couldn't look into my problem … They called my husband and asked us to sit down. There was an elder who really encouraged us to sit and solve this problem ourselves at home as Christians

... But we couldn't sit with him and I did not go back to the court again.

Edna went to court to try to recover her financial investment from her husband and to demand that he provide support for the couple's three-year-old child. She did not charge her husband with assault or adultery before the courts, although both were breaches of South Sudanese law. Perhaps she was conscious of the discrimination that a wife who accused her husband on such grounds would be likely to face in court (see below). But Malakal was also poorly served in terms of courts. Having been dismantled by the government and rebel forces there had been no statutory court in the town for four years.[43] Edna, like more than 20,000 other people from the town, had taken refuge under UN protection, and had access to only a rudimentary, unofficial customary regime within the PoC.[44] Certainly, it was easier to gain access to other judicial forums in some other towns, such as Juba or Nimule. But the fundamental political constraints applied in every government town.

Like Edna, survivors and witnesses of atrocities would not dare to report violations by soldiers or other government security forces. They did not expect to get justice and, beyond that, feared the conse-quences of voicing their grievances. Members of the army, police, wildlife service[45] and militia groups aligned to government might be locked up if they looked set to join the opposition, but people knew that they were not likely to be punished for violence against civil-ians. The painful irony was that, as Bishop Paul Yugusuk observed, the victims might be blamed: 'any report of atrocities committed by soldiers is often regarded as a crime in South Sudan'.[46]

From time to time, a member of the government would promise to exert some control and establish accountability processes. In the early days of the war the government commissioned three separate investigations into violence against civilians, but none of these ended in the courts. The Human Rights Abuses Investigation Committee, led by former chief justice John Wol Makec, was the most credible.[47] By February 2015, the committee had completed its task and filed a confidential report with the government.[48] It had gathered and preserved 'horrendous' testimony, some of it directly implicating individuals who were being 'promoted' in government, according to the deputy chairperson, lawyer Yoanes Ajawin.[49] But the report was never released, and no action was taken.

The record of prosecutions of human rights violations since South Sudan's independence was woeful; not a single senior commander or politician had been prosecuted in a civilian court, although there had been many accusations.[50] For instance, in a notorious incident in December 2012, eight students involved in peaceful protests against the relocation of Wau county headquarters were shot dead by government security forces. Mass arrests, civil unrest and more deaths followed, and 11 opponents of the relocation were sentenced to death. The security forces, however, were never brought to book for shooting unarmed civilians.[51] The army mounted a vicious campaign following a counterinsurgency in Pibor county in 2013, but only two soldiers were prosecuted in a military court for killing two women and injuring a child, and their sentences were comparatively light.[52]

Once the civil war broke out, impunity ran rife. A turnabout seemed possible when 100 soldiers were arrested in February 2014, but nothing came of this, since they all-too-conveniently escaped from military custody.[53] In February 2017, President Kiir seemed to adopt a harsh approach: he called upon the army to shoot in the head any soldiers who raped civilians. But later he backpedalled and said the soldiers should be taken to court first. In any case, this blustering was futile: government forces continued to kill and rape.[54]

Hardly any cases ran counter to this trend of impunity for the security forces during the period in question. Just one exception stands out in the trial of a dozen South Sudanese soldiers in a military court in Juba in May 2017. The soldiers were accused of gang-raping five foreign aid workers and killing a local journalist, John Gatluak, at the Terrain Hotel, in July 2016. An army spokesperson claimed the trial was proof of its 'commitment to human rights, the rule of law and transparency of the legal system'.[55] But the government had been pressured and incentivised to bring the case by foreign aid donors, themselves under pressure from survivors. The case was completed in February 2018, and 'the verdict was adjourned until further notice'.[56] Months passed without any explanation for this inordinate delay, until 6 September 2018, when the verdict was announced: ten soldiers were convicted of crimes ranging from theft to rape and murder; and awarded sentences between seven years and life imprisonment.

The process and judgment of the Terrain rape trial was precedent-setting – there was simply nothing like it in the court records. Not only were the majority of the accused soldiers convicted, but the victims were awarded compensation to be paid by the state, including over $US2 million to the Terrain Hotel for looting and damage, $4,000 to each of the five rape victims and 51 cows to the family of the journalist who was murdered in the attack. Appeals have since been filed by survivors for whom the compensation was negligible. Nevertheless, it represented a crucial achievement in holding SPLA soldiers to account for crimes committed during the conflict; and has been seen by South Sudanese and international human rights activists as a precedent that may open the way for future domestic prosecutions.[57] Well before the Terrain trial, there were public demands for justice for victims of sexual violence in South Sudan, for instance Bishop Paul Yogusuk managed to push for an investigation into the rape of women in Kubi village in 2017, although the case did not go further.[58]

The Terrain Hotel case has shown what is possible when significant international pressure is applied, and fairly low-ranking soldiers are involved. Surprisingly, there was also one other successful prosecution of soldiers for a conflict-related crime, held in Juba high court in January 2015, which is worthy of note. The case was minor in comparison to the scale of the violence and quite how it came to court and was successful is unclear, but what we do know is that it related to an act of looting gone wrong in the early days of the fighting in 2013. The military officers were accused of ordering their subordinates to loot the property of a resident in the Tongping area. The householder was absent at the time, having fled to his village to seek safety from the conflict. Men in military uniform, 'well armed and driving an SPLA land cruiser', had come to the house, broken in and begun loading his property onto their vehicle. It seems that the officers were discovered in the act of looting by another SPLA patrol, and that they reported the matter to the police. In any case, it was the police prosecutor who bravely investigated the incident and transferred the case to the court, charging them with criminal actions under 'article 48, 294 of the penal code 2008'. After the evidence was laid out, the accused officers confessed before the court. The judge ruled that they should each pay the complainant 50,000 SSP, and serve two years in prison.[59] This Juba high court case demonstrates that the civilian courts had the jurisdiction and the capacity to sanction war crimes, on the condition that they had the backing of the army and the police.[60] The fact that they hardly ever did so is testament to the political capture of the security agencies.

The courts were a local affair, so we might think that although they failed to prosecute 'big men', they might at least impose restraint on the escalating communal violence. But homicides perpetrated in the course of cattle raids rarely came to the courts, especially not to town courts. Instead armed groups pursued violent mob justice in successive revenge attacks. Many youths who had originally mobilised on a clan basis to protect cattle and community became enmeshed in larger conflict networks. They responded to the devastating human losses and meagre opportunities that were associated with the violent competition for the state. The courts could not cope. For one thing, there were simply too many killings. The old methods of settling homicide cases within and between groups by providing cattle as a form of bloodwealth compensation buckled under the numbers.[61]

This was a circular problem: law had been subordinated to military power associated with the state in the course of successive wars. Pastoralist communities had long engaged in raids upon the cows of their neighbours in local feuds that were part of their strategies for survival and growth. But these cultures, and the spiritual and social norms that had once regulated them, had mutated in encounters with violent modernity and predatory states.[62] Anthropologist Sharon Hutchinson identifies a catastrophic shift as guns supplanted spears, which was exacerbated by a split in the SPLA in the 1990s.[63] Powerful elites militarised local feuds and astutely questioned socio-legal norms and spiritual beliefs. The more they blurred the lines between government and 'home' wars, the more local violence proliferated, and the less courts could impose restraints on violence.

By 2013, chiefly and legal authority was in decline. Spiritual leaders and an assortment of other political authorities still influenced the conduct of groups like the Nuer White Army or the Dinka *Titweng*, but they might encourage violent mobilisations or try to regulate it at their personal will.[64] Violent cattle raids were endemic. Armed cattle guards had been co-opted by military and political elites for political objectives.[65] Town courts could do little to stem this host of small wars within the larger conflict. People or police occasionally took cases related to cattle raids to them, and when they did so the message was clear: revenge attacks were illegal and the perpetrators must be prosecuted and the victims compensated.[66] On the whole, however, violent contests for material assets and power lay beyond the realm of the courts, whether they were between clans battling over cattle, or politicians and generals fighting for oil wealth and the state.

Subject to security forces?

The fact that the courts hardly ever sanctioned members of armed groups was only partly due to socio-legal and cultural changes. The sparsity of statutory courts, the political assault on the judiciary and the unreliable conduct of security agencies, including the police, were also to blame. The police at street level were poorly resourced and paid and could barely handle even the most mundane problems of criminality. They were involved in prosecutions of criminal cases, but these were few and far between and their role was sometimes dubious.[67] Even in Juba, in the midst of a crime wave, only half of those who experienced an armed robbery bothered to contact the police, partly for fear of corruption.[68]

Apparently, people did not trust the police to respond, and they also anticipated that there would be additional costs for their services when they did. People talked of being asked to pay for the fuel for the police to go and pick up a suspect, or of being asked to pay for food for a prisoner who had committed a crime against them. They complained of police bias or collusion in attempts at extortion.[69] The quality of police investigations was also poor, whether as a result of trust issues or incompetence. Even when the police reacted promptly and apparently honourably, such as when gunshots were fired during a clash between clan members at a wedding in Yei, they did not always do so effectively – in the Yei wedding case, they turned up in court with 'witnesses' who had not even attended the event.[70] For the victim of a crime, getting the police or security agencies involved could be a very costly and risky business.

The tribulations of the legal route were exposed in a rare attempt to prosecute a cattle raider, in Rumbek county court, in January 2016. A pastoralist stood accused of raiding ten cows, with a group of accomplices. The police had seemingly made good progress; the accused was identified and arrested, and three cows were found. The defendant duly confessed to participation in the raid. But the complainant wondered where the rest of the cattle had gone and how he could get them back? The defendant explained that this would not be possible since the security forces and the police had already slaughtered and sold six of his cows. Indeed, he argued, the complainant had himself collaborated with them. The complainant was then called upon to explain his side of the story. Admittedly, he said, the cows had been taken by the police, but it was not his fault: 'it is a tradition of the police and security when they catch a thief to take some of his cows or money as a penalty for the crime – and this should not be counted against me as I didn't give the orders'. The judges adjourned the hearing, asking the parties to return with witnesses on the following Monday and for the police and military to present a statement.[71] The court now faced another problem of how to address this corruption within the security forces. Previous experience suggests that they were not likely to find a ready solution.

Perhaps the most troubling question for the courts was how to deal with members of 'organised forces' who brought cases against civilians on personal matters. Any attempt to confront a soldier might prove especially dangerous. A story circulating in Torit during the conflict offered a warning along the following lines. An SPLA soldier was said to have ordered a soda in a bar, but then refused to pay and beat up the female bartender. She ran home and told her husband, who went to the barracks to complain. But not only did the soldiers beat up the husband, they also followed him home, setting his house and neighbourhood on fire.[72] The story illustrates the risk attached to taking a member of any of South Sudan's armed forces or security agencies to court.

Land cases involving soldiers stood out as especially fraught. Such cases confirmed persistent political sensitivities and contestations over the control of prime urban land. In the years after the CPA, as international development scholar Naseem Badiey has shown, SPLM elites, the Central Equatorian state government and Bari community elders in Juba were all vying for the power to define land rights and influence the terms of citizenship in the new state. Vulnerable people struggled to secure their place in the harsh environment of the city. Ex-combatants claimed land rights on the basis that they had 'fought for it'. IDPs lost their homes as properties were bulldozed. A 'mafia' worked within institutions to produce documentation in a kind of 'legalised corruption' that could generate multiple papers and competing 'legal' ownership for one plot. The courts were saturated with cases involving duplicate titles, to the point that a frustrated appeal court judge described the land grabs and legal manoeuvres as a cynical 'game'.[73] None of these problems had been resolved by the time the civil war broke out, and some had only got worse.

The skeleton of a land governance framework was in place by 2013, but it left many ambiguities and there was as yet no policy for dealing with its implementation. The 2009 Land Act upheld the SPLM's mobilising slogan during the war against Khartoum: that land 'belongs to the people'. It preserved customary tenure and gave it equal legal status to public and private tenure.[74] But it also diluted it with the proviso that government should regulate the usage of all land, arousing fear in some communities. Even in Juba only half the land was registered, mainly privately by individuals.[75] Question marks also emerged over the security of community tenure as, by 2011, some members of government had begun signing away vast tracts of communal rural land to investors – a racket only interrupted by assiduous reporting and the war.[76] Relations to land were already unsettled, as recent research has established: 'customary land rights are plural, layered and changing'.[77] New kinds of land contests erupted in the conflict. Both urban and rural land has been a focus for politicised conflicts between individuals and clans, especially where the land is valuable or rich in resources.[78] Some urban dwellers targeted in ethnic violence were forced to flee their homes for displacement sites, while others took the chance to occupy these empty houses. The political contests over land contributed to the precarity of urban residents, but the courts could not do much to address them.

Even minor quarrels within families and between neighbours over land could prove difficult to resolve, and if the legal status of land was tricky to establish the best the courts could do was negotiate a compromise. When powerful individuals grabbed land, the case might become insoluble, as one of the many long-running land disputes in Juba exemplifies. Peter had the documentation to prove he purchased land in Juba. But in 2007, as the value of Juba's land was increasing, his land was confiscated by the brother of the former (now deceased) owner. Peter immediately took the matter to court and won the case. But the defendant was connected to an officer in the national security who wrote to the court warning them that 'troubles would arise' if the judgment was implemented. The case dragged on over six court hearings in a period of seven years, until Peter eventually gave up in 2015.[79] The problem was clear. The courts could be supportive of an individual claimant, even against a soldier, but they did not necessarily have the power to enforce the judgment, since the police were subordinate to the military and national security. Individuals with ties to security forces tended to respond with a mixture of legal appeals and threats, toying and tampering with the legal process while taking physical control over the plot.[80] By 2015, South Sudan Law Society researcher David Deng observed that land disputes relating to IDPs in Juba were mainly being handled by the police or newly established security committees. Some returnees did manage to get their land and homes back. The military, however, were 'instrumental in either the success or failure of efforts to reclaim land'.[81]

The courts had limited authority over security personnel, especially those who sought to use them to pursue their private interests. Even so, military officers also deferred to the courts on many occasions, for different reasons. Some sought legal recognition for their properties that had been acquired by force or intimidation while others brought legitimate cases, including the usual sorts of wrangles with neighbours over the boundaries of their plots.[82] But while courts struggled to respond to the legal confusions, intimidation and political machinations surrounding tense property disputes, they were much better equipped to respond to personal and familial issues, even when powerful security and political actors were concerned.

Regulating the social sphere?

Urban courts were deeply and persistently engaged with cases concerning relationships within communities and families. They were social problem-solvers and mediators, wrestling with the impacts of trauma, economic despair and social and political violence on a daily basis for a relatively low fee. This was especially true of chiefs' courts, which in any case handled the bulk of all court cases. The settlements they generated aimed to promote legality, order and peaceful social relations. However, they were often short-term measures, dampening down potentially explosive situations and sometimes also creating grounds for further disputes.

Not surprisingly, the courts were often preoccupied with petty criminal cases that reflected desperate social and economic circumstances. The smallest economic loss counted heavily at the margins. Take for instance the fight between two IDPs in Melijo over a loan for half a kilo of meat that ended up in Nimule's county court. One of the men, an ex-combatant, had borrowed the money for the meat from his neighbour. Two weeks later, the lender was angry that the ex-combatant had not yet repaid the loan. The two men fought each other with an iron bar and both were seriously injured. The court sentenced both men to imprisonment for three months (or a fine of 500 SSP) as well as demanding that the ex-soldier pay back the original loan. Both accepted the judgment but promised to pay the fine later, as they 'did not have the cash at hand'.[83] The case had been handled efficiently and fairly, reaching the court after just eight days. Yet it was hard to see how the individuals in such cases could ever repay the fees and fines the courts imposed, since the very reasons people ended up in court were related to abject poverty.

Under tough conditions, courts produced impromptu judgments on minor thefts, torts and informal contracts. Thefts were judged on slender evidence[84] – which was all the more worrying since some turned out to be pathetic efforts by one impoverished person to extract a small sum of money from another.[85] Most courts tended to look harshly upon accusations of stealing, and to allocate a mixture of fines, compensation and even beatings to the alleged perpetrator.[86] They offered more lenient responses to disputes about the repayment of small loans, or property that had been lost in conflict, or goods that had escalated in price due to high inflation. The legal basis for some cases was very shaky, but chiefs handled them with an eye on moral questions and a determination to prevent the disputes from escalating. They provided a sympathetic ear and tried to cool the situation, urging the complainant to be patient, preaching forgiveness of a convicted thief,[87] and even sometimes forgoing their own court fees.[88]

The courts were running a catch-all social service in a context where there were next to no other provisions for welfare, trauma or addiction. People turned to them for help with all manner of woes. Women especially brought alcoholic, neglectful and abusive husbands or sons. In one case, the chief instructed a husband with an alcohol addiction to make a ritual promise on a swearing stick to stop. In another, the husband was so ill that the chief took a harsher measure of imprisonment for six months to 'rehabilitate him'.[89] In a third, a husband was simply publicly shamed and preached to by the court panel to stop his drinking and abusive behaviour.[90]

Mostly these matters came to customary courts, but even a statutory court might be called upon to deal with serious mental health issues. A notable case involved two desperate parents who brought their son to the county court accusing him of being drunk, threatening his mother and attempting suicide. He denied all the accusations, but the courts took the word of the parents, supported by a witness, and promptly fined him and sentenced him to six months in prison. Attempted suicide was an offence under the penal code and the judgment was appropriate in these terms.[91] We can easily assume that these sorts of punitive solutions were unlikely to benefit the mental health and welfare of the individuals concerned. After all, the prison conditions were appalling. They did, however, respond to the concerns of the families and spouses who brought the cases. The fact that local courts provided a forum to air these problems and addressed them promptly, with solicitous responses, underpinned their legitimacy and authority.

Above all, customary courts were preoccupied with regulating disputes within families. Courts were overwhelmed with cases relating to familial, marital and intimate relationships. People seemed to be regularly testing and transgressing the socio-legal norms governing marriages and sexual liaisons. Many women, and some men, pleaded for divorces, which were extremely hard to get. Fathers brought cases concerning lapsed bridewealth payments or accusing young men of having 'eloped' or 'impregnated' their daughters out of wedlock. In addition, there were an astonishing number of men accusing their wives and other men of adultery. All of these cases seemed, at first sight, to be 'family matters' – peripheral to the wider conflict and indicative of people's determination to continue their lives as usual against the odds. They fit into a wider trope of towns as spaces of mixing and cultural change; where women and young people are exposed to new experiences and opportunities, and patriarchal old guards try to preserve the status quo. Courts appeared to be at the fulcrum of ongoing social and cultural changes, trying to apply the old rules to an order that was crumbling. This was perhaps part of the explanation, but there was also more to it.

What united the decisions of the courts, across different ethnic groups and a range of family issues, was their determination to uphold the sanctity of the family as a source of law and social order. They perpetuated the norms of a traditional social structure in which family and kinship ties have primary value and carry economic and political obligations.[92] It seemed that the courts drew their power and authority from their relationship to society and in turn they upheld dominant societal norms and power relations. This made sense in light of the arbitrary and predatory reputation of the state and the lack of a reliable police force to enforce judgments. It was also effective to the extent that the courts could even discipline security personnel who violated the ideals of families and kinship groups. We see court rulings against badly behaved soldier husbands, criticising them for neglect, demanding that they pay child support, or even telling them to show more respect for their in-laws.[93]

At the same time, the courts promoted a patriarchal construct of the family and routinely reinforced the authority of men over women and girls. This was dangerous in a context where violence against women had been normalised, as previous studies have shown.[94] By the time of independence, rule of law reformers were well aware that the customary courts were contributing to gender inequalities and abuses and delivering 'chronic miscarriages of justice for violence against women'.[95] International experts conceived of them quite straightforwardly as an 'an impediment to the full realization of the rights of marginalized persons'. The UNDP led the way in establishing projects to train traditional authorities to respect the bill of rights in the new constitution, while also pushing customary laws to be written down and standardised to 'reduce arbitrariness', in order to be 'harmonized' with the statutory laws.[96] There was also some evidence of social changes underway as people acquired new norms through experiences of education, and displacement in various refugee camps or global cities.[97] But none of this seemed to have had much impact upon the everyday workings of the courts by the time of our observations.

There were many cases in which women came to court to report domestic violence, seeking for their husbands to be sanctioned, or for the courts to issue a divorce. The courts usually sided with the husband, unless the woman had the support of her family. Women might try to find other means to escape a brutal husband, including running away, but they risked being found and brought to court by the husband to be publicly disciplined, especially if there was any hint of adultery. The harsh stance of the courts is evident in the case of a young Dinka Bor woman, who was accused of disappearing from her family home for two weeks. She told the court that her husband regularly beat her, and she was suicidal: 'I decided to leave his home and it's better to kill myself. I am only still alive because

I feared to go through with it.' The court did not punish her, but it also failed to offer any support or even to denounce the alleged domestic violence. The chiefs simply handed the matter back to the two families for discussion. This underlines that the central question for the courts in any such case was whether the family would be willing to pay back the brideprice and enable the wife to divorce an abusive husband.[98] The courts were implicated in a social system that trapped women in violent marriages.[99]

One reason why the courts generally failed to protect married women turns out to be the same reason why they were so popular. The courts were vigorously engaged in upholding the institution of marriage. They were consistently acting on behalf of married men who had made substantial investments in bridewealth and anticipated a bundle of rights and entitlements in return. Certainly, bridewealth systems have social and symbolic functions, expressing the value women hold for their families and encouraging the creation of new social bonds. In origins, bridewealth may be a described as a 'legitimation of marriage',[100] encouraging the view that marriage is a route to social dignity and respect, a means to become a 'full person', as one young South Sudanese man described it.[101] But bridewealth payments are also associated with displays of male power, and can become 'a crucial means through which men perform masculinity publicly and attain social status'. Marriage can become a highly competitive and exclusionary market, as political scientist Hilary Matfess shows.[102] Courts were arenas for performances of masculinity in which the legality of male authority over women's bodies was upheld. Courts were also mechanisms for participation in marriage markets and, most importantly, efforts by male elders and husbands to protect their female assets.

The courts faced immediate social imperatives to police sexual relationships outside of marriage. Cases involving young women and girls who had relationships outside of marriage were highly volatile and could easily erupt into violence.[103] As one chief in Juba put it bluntly: 'among the Dinka, the girl is source of resources for the family and so if someone come and takes her without paying anything then you will not take it easy and that is why it brings conflict that kills people ... a girl is like a bank'.[104] Fathers had invested in their wives and sought to recuperate through their daughters; brothers depended on the cattle their sisters would bring in for them to be able to marry; and other relatives and clan members supported bridewealth payments and had interests in the system. Bridewealth is usually arranged between families, so the matter only came to court when someone had breached a rule that the 'owner of the girl' – usually her father, uncle or brother – must be consulted, and a bridewealth payment must be arranged before any intimate relationship might begin. In many cases, the problem was that a couple had either begun a sexual relationship, or were suspected of doing so, without any bridewealth having been paid. Sometimes the girl was pregnant. The court rulings varied substantially between ethnic groups and even between individuals, spanning a spectrum of related offences from 'elopement' to 'impregnation' to punishments for sexual violence.

In most cases the aim of the court was to arrange a marriage and bridewealth payment. But sometimes the courts would impose a fine rather than a marriage where the boy was unwilling or incapable, or the parents were supportive of a young or reluctant daughter. For instance, in Juba PoC, a young boy insisted that he wanted to marry the girl, but admitted he had no cows to pay. The result was a punishment for the elopement: he was fined 3,000 SSP with an additional six months' imprisonment.[105] Moreover, although some fathers agreed to wait for payment and some courts agreed to split payments into instalments, it seemed that fathers were impatient in this dire economic situation. There were some cases in which courts insisted on payment within a week or two. Francis Deng has argued that insisting on full and immediate payment of debts is a sign that 'relationships are broken'.[106] But it was rarely clear how young people could pay the brideprice and fines that were heaped upon them, trapping them in debt.

Moreover, the inconsistencies in the bridewealth payments matter both in illustrating differences between groups and in identifying inconsistencies in the legal regimes operating within them. In all but one of our cases people formed relationships and marriages within their ethnic group. However, the costs and commitments to bridewealth varied between and within them. Most courts offered the payment to be made either in cattle or a monetary equivalent, although in Dinka courts some individuals rejected the money in preference for cattle, and some courts in the Equatorian region listed money or goats. In one Nuer court settlement a man was ordered to pay 80 cows or the equivalent of 80,000 SSP bridewealth, but other settlements could be significantly lower at 25,000 SSP.[107] Several Dinka Bor rulings demanded 30 cows, in line with Dinka *Wanh-Alel* laws.[108] Madi payments were usually monetary and significantly lower at 3,000 SSP for the dowry and a 5,000 SSP fine for the offence. In a Balanda case in Wau, the dowry payment was 5,000 SSP.[109] During proceedings in a Madi court in Nimule, the parents insisted that their daughter would have to go back to school before she could marry.[110] In other words, there was a great deal of variation in marriage contracts and also some evidence of variation in attitudes to women between different ethnic groups.

Secondly, the variations between and within groups are in contrast to the relative consistency of payments of fines for adultery, for children, or for blood compensation.[111] This supports wider evidence that the costs of marriage were highly differentiated and not regulated by the courts – an issue which raises all sorts of questions about the potential erosion of meaning of other compensation payments, as anthropologist Naomi Pendle has found among the western Dinka.[112] The courts might try to push back against escalating bridewealth costs in their communities, as it seems some Dinka Bor courts were doing here, and as Nuer courts in the PoCs began to do,[113] but they were under pressure and had limited control over the brideprice. Instead girls had become valuable commodities whose prices were set by competitive marriage markets operating beyond the legal regimes of the courts and dictated by local political economies shaped by war.

South Sudanese marital customs have evolved through war, social disturbance and mass death to become useful in fierce competitions for power and wealth, especially in Dinka and Nuer communities. Jok Madut Jok identified shifts in gender relations and the social norms relating to marriage and childbirth among the Dinka during the brutal wars of the 1990s. He traced the militarisation of society and the emergence of hypermasculine identities, with devastating implications for women's rights and a rise in gender-based violence. Marriage became not just desirable, but essential to social survival and the accumulation of power. The SPLM promoted the idea that getting married and having children were contributions to the struggle against the Khartoum government, in an attempted 'nationalization of the womb'.[114] They also encouraged the norm of levirate marriage or 'ghost wives' in which war widows were given as wives to their brothers-in-law.

As the human losses mounted, many men began to believe that their only source of security lay in 'marrying as many wives as possible to acquire many more children'. They sought to rapidly expand their families and clans.[115] Some SPLA commanders took this to an extreme, marrying up to 50 women. They formed a new 'military aristocracy', expanding their kinship networks through marriage and producing numerous children, including girls who could then command their own bridewealth. Commanders also paid or promised to guarantee the payment of dowries for some of their soldiers, creating 'faithful followers' by means of the social contract of bridewealth.[116] By the time of independence, the cost of bridewealth in some communities had skyrocketed. For instance, 'in 2013, government leaders in Gogrial were paying bride price of as much as 400 cattle ... It was routine for bride price to be between fifty and 100 cattle'.[117] Young men were trapped in relations of dependency to the male elders in their kinship networks or to military commanders in the SPLA. Some were priced out of the system and forced to enlist in militias or raid cattle,[118] reinforcing the evidence that 'brideprice inflation' has 'destabilising effects' and creates 'incentives for violence'.[119] By the time of the civil war, women's bodies had become tradeable commodities in a war economy, fighters described rape and abduction of women as forms of payment, and sexual violence was rife.[120]

The courts utterly failed to counteract this tidal wave of violence against women. Enlightened chiefs in various rural and communities discussed or imposed caps on brideprice through their courts, but they could not act independently or collectively on a national level.[121] Above all, the courts did not seize the opportunity to clamp down on sexual violence. Most of the rape accusations in our files were dealt with by customary courts, whose responses were inconsistent and generally weak. In one case in Kator in Juba, not only the defendant but also the woman who accused him of sexual violence ended up with a fine.[122] In Wau, one court simply dismissed the rape charges on the basis of a lack of evidence and witnesses, although the young girl was pregnant. Another court sentenced a boy accused of raping a 16-year-old girl to a fine of 6,000 SSP and six months in prison.[123] In the unusual setting of a customary court in the UN PoC, the chiefs imposed a 5,000 SSP fine upon the perpetrator and an award of 10,000 SSP compensation to the victim, although they then referred the case on to the UN police.[124] In a case of assault in Nimule, a man was simply ordered to pay the costs of medical treatment. Additionally, prospects of a conviction in statutory courts were not much better. The cases tended to be delayed or deferred.[125] The police in Wau failed to even take forward the accusation of rape of one young boy, despite the fact that he had the report of a medical examination to prove it.[126] Indeed there were few cases that demonstrated the potential of the courts to prosecute charges of sexual violence, with the exception of one extraordinary case in a Yei court which followed the prescribed procedures and duly convicted a government official of rape, imposing a sentence of six years in prison and compensation of 5,000 SSP.[127]

Overall, statutory courts proved to be inconsistent in their performance and negligible in their impacts. They were much less functional and accessible than the hardworking customary courts. Chiefs were driven by short-term imperatives to try to stabilise the social order through forms of arbitration that consistently pushed towards practical make-do settlements. They sought to cool down and contain some of the tensions generated by war, but at the same time, and inadvertently, they were implicated in the legalisation of a fragmented, discriminatory and fundamentally unstable political order.

Conclusion

The records of town court cases are a window onto the harsh realities of everyday life in a war-torn country, exposing both the dysfunctions of the legal and judicial system and its possibilities. People brought all manner of concerns to the courts, trying to find legal solutions to dire social and economic circumstances. In turn, the courts provided a listening ear and a rare public service. Under harsh conditions, they continued trying to settle quotidian criminal matters ranging from murder to petty theft, civil wrongs including injuries and damages, and highly volatile disputes within families, sometimes at personal risk.[128]

The very existence of the courts represents an achievement. The judiciary and chiefs were affected by the environment of instability and economic hardship along with the people who brought the cases to their courts. For many periods and in many places the statutory courts were closed. But chiefs laboured on, often on a semi-voluntary basis, earning only occasional salary payments of a percentage of fees from their courts.

Based on these court cases, we can debunk the notion that 'there is no law in South Sudan' – people were regularly being tried and punished, including for minor social infractions. However, the courts could not discipline the most powerful, violent and wealthy.[129] The accumulation of wealth in South Sudan was tied up with access to military power and political offices. Those who achieved these gains could mostly exempt themselves from the law or seek to instrumentalise it in their favour. With the rare exception of the Terrain trial, courts rarely handled cases that were directly related to political violence, ethnic conflict, corruption or predation. Statutory courts had the jurisdiction over such cases, but apparently not the capacity or will to exercise it. They were also vulnerable to co-option and instrumentalisation by members of the security forces. Customary courts had social power, but limited jurisdiction over the conduct of political authorities in public life; mostly they could only regulate their personal conduct within the sphere of 'home', intervening in social and family matters. Together the courts produced a great deal of law and social regulation, and some temporary solutions. But they could not provide legal certainty, except in the sense of routinely violating women's rights.

Customary courts specialised in the regulation of society. They promoted the view that, as a Nuer chief put it, 'to stop violence, you go to the court and get your right'. They were popular social rituals which bound people together as communities. Above all they sought to uphold the institution of the family, as the remaining vestige of the social fabric that had not been destroyed by cyclical wars. They were locally constituted sources of political authority that counterbalanced the constant changes and disruptions in government. Yet they also perpetuated political and social inequality and tolerated gender-based violence. Women rarely managed to divorce their husbands unless their parents were ready to relinquish the cattle or funds they had received at the time of the marriage. Men who engaged in adultery with another man's wife were 'stealing' someone who had already been 'paid for'. Young men and women were tied into relations of dependency on, or subjugation to, male elders within ethnic communities. These difference and inequalities had been shaped by experiences of war and become functional to the organisation of violence. This revealed their hegemonic function:

the courts provided a mechanism for settling conflicts, limiting abuse and upholding the dignity of individuals and communities, even as they cemented ethnic fiefdoms and gender inequalities, maintaining fertile grounds for future conflict.

Despite these larger political implications, the courts were coping mechanisms which provided ways in which people without funds, connection or education could seek protection and rights through claims on each other, if not the state.[130] Their sources of law were flexible and customary court processes were especially participatory and adaptable. On occasion, the courts could innovate, offering decisions that were progressive. Much seemed to depend on the character of the judge or chiefs and the identities of the parties in the case (and social relations or inequalities between them), as well as the quality of the arguments presented in court. This adaptive potential might well be part of the explanation for why people continued to take cases to courts; despite the fact there were so many injustices in them, these forums still offered some hope of solutions. The courts created narrow openings for the pursuit of justice in a harsh environment, so both ordinary people and legal activists tried to make use of them.

Chapter 4

LEGAL CONTESTATIONS AT THE MARGINS

Every person who brought a case to the court during the war in South Sudan was in some way trying to improve their parlous situation, and they often had to struggle hard to do so, without certainty of success. The essential problem was that 'the law is a site of contest and competition; every citizen has to be an activist to get justice', as a South Sudanese academic neatly summed up.[1] There was neglect, dysfunction, violence and corruption at the heart of government. The statutory justice institutions were crippled by both a lack of human and material resources and the intimidation or dismissal of many people of integrity. The majority of people tried to muddle along, to get some form of 'right' and resolve disputes peacefully, but they also exposed serious limitations from the point of view of justice, as the records of court cases showed. Not all of them had the knowledge, skills or connections that could help them to follow the case through, or to challenge further injustices as they arose. It was hardly surprising if some (young men especially) became so frustrated that they sought to pursue their basic rights violently; 'feelings that tribalism and corruption dominate government practices in South Sudan might have left citizens … resigned to rule of the gun trumping rule of law', as the Sudd Institute observed.[2]

However, some civil society groups and citizen activists were trying to help their fellow citizens to get justice. They were working against the grain during the conflict to monitor and contest legal injustices in and around South Sudan's courts and prisons. There were visible and vocal demands for reform from human rights and women's groups engaged in advocacy and legal empowerment campaigns.[3] Less conspicuously, individual human rights lawyers, paralegals and community activists worked at the fringes of the justice system in urban settings, questioning wrongs and trying to counter them with grassroots actions. Their responses were impromptu, disparate and often unsuccessful, but even so they cumulatively inched towards justice by defying the violent status quo. Legal and judicial reform, and the establishment of a stable and legitimate government, will partly depend upon the achievements and lessons of these various activist struggles, however marginal they might currently appear.

The town courts stand out as the principal arenas in which activists can and do challenge violent and kleptocratic politics. The potential of such activism relates to the social power of law. Courts are vectors for norms and practices that dictate the relations among the diverse peoples of South Sudan, and between them and government. Currently, local courts and regimes of law cannot govern the political realm, while the new articulations of law and rights embedded in the constitution at independence hardly permeate into society. Yet the fertile interactions between customary and written law, and some individual cases, have indicated the adaptive capacity of all local courts.[4] Changing ideas and practices of the law within social arenas, in everyday ways, can shape the cases people bring to court and the judgments they expect to receive, and can also influence the ways in which some authorities interpret law.

The 2011 Transitional Constitution was flawed;[5] however, it promised a set of civil rights that animated the struggle for independence, and were articulated by participants in a 'civil project' involving SPLM members in the latter years of the war against Sudan.[6] The bill of rights may have limited tangible consequences at present, but it is a symbolic resource for lawyers and activists.[7] It specifies the right to life and dignity; prohibits torture and cruel, inhuman and degrading treatment and arbitrary detention; establishes the right to marry and freely form a family; and states that women have the right to be 'accorded full and equal dignity of the person with men'. It also promises protections for both private property and traditionally held lands.[8] These constitutional rights are blatantly contradicted in ongoing legal processes, some with seeming popular assent. But they speak directly to violations of women's rights, land grabbing and to arbitrary detentions and the use of the death penalty. The bill of rights offered a 'political opportunity' created by a previous generation of struggles, at the same time as multiple violations of rights demanded urgent practical responses.[9]

Legal activism in process

This chapter is composed of three vignettes describing the activities of lawyers, paralegals and activists as they worked to combat injustices through practical actions at community level in the capital city, Juba, during the conflict. The struggles take place despite peripatetic warfare and forced displacement that inevitably interrupt and constrain activism. The cases merit close examination partly because they are each concerned with a critical human rights issue, namely land rights, women's rights, and deprivations of the right to life and dignity which, as the court cases revealed, were constant preoccupations for people in South Sudan's towns during the war.

There are some caveats to note. Firstly, the cases are episodes of activism in process. They are not presented as illustrative of a broader practice; instead they are exemplary cases, and important because they indicate that legal activism was possible in this extraordinarily unconducive environment. Secondly, these cases are all situated in Juba, although there were certainly other similar examples which could have been selected in other towns, as indicated elsewhere in this book.[10] We might expect activism to have the greatest chance of success, and the best access to resources in

Juba, considering that most human rights lawyers and international human rights and humanitarian organisations are concentrated there. But these cases were also chosen partly based on practical considerations, as cases that were most feasible to research over time in the context of an ongoing conflict. Thirdly the cases are valuable because in each instance there were several sources that could be triangulated, including interviews with several different activists involved, participant observation and crucial documentary evidence that could serve to corroborate claims and developments. The names of the individuals concerned in these cases is not necessary to an analysis of them, so these have generally been changed or excluded; it is worth noting that none of the cases received significant media attention or direct human rights reporting, but some of the documents I rely upon are matters of public record. Finally, the vignettes are written in a first-person, story form to reflect that my knowledge of the processes is still inevitably mediated by the perspectives of the activists involved in these struggles, and my relationships with them.

The vignettes are neither an interrogation of failures and successes nor a fully rounded and objective historical record of the events in each case. They are simply robust accounts of specific processes and practices of legal activism taking place during a time of war. While later chapters step back to critically examine the origins, scope and strategies of South Sudanese legal activism,[11] the point here is simply to establish a profile of political agency in engaging the law to challenge forms of cruelty and oppression. Importantly, both here and in later chapters I perceive and present the activists in specific roles as paralegals, lawyers and community activists, struggling in the field of law.[12] These individuals might (and generally do) have other roles and ambitions – citizens may adopt the role of a legal activist in particular situations, but may also move into another field of political and social action in short order. Especially in fragmented hybrid political orders, they can adopt and adapt different languages and registers and switch between them. What is under scrutiny here is not personal beliefs but practical actions. As Cass Sunstein explains, the public talk and actions of individuals may not reflect their private views and is a function of both 'social roles and associated norms', but it is highly significant as such.[13]

The vignettes demonstrate what can happen when civilians adopt roles as legal activists and speak out against injustices. Tracing the trajectories of these struggles reveals them to be characteristically messy and unresolved. The three cases are in many ways unique, but they all expose the complicated issues that present themselves and the improvised ways in which activists respond. Each of the encounters confirms that civilians had the power to make things happen in the courts and prisons, even as they expose the ambiguities and risks of citizen activism. Such courageous and 'conscious efforts' to effect change from below are liable to be forgotten by anyone other than their protagonists – especially when they are small-scale and appear to fail – yet as E.P. Thompson has shown, they may later turn out to be foundational steps in the 'making of history'.[14]

Land belongs to the community

This vignette follows a protracted land dispute in Hai Game, Juba, both in and out of the statutory courts. It illustrates the extraordinary difficulties facing ordinary people as they try to obtain basic land rights. Land laws and their application were in a state of confusion in post-independence South Sudan, and land contests were rife, as the previous chapter showed. However, the Hai Game case stood out for three reasons: firstly because there was an attempt to grab and commodify a large tract of land where an established community had been living for years; secondly because military actors sought to legalise this grab by bringing a court case against community leaders; and thirdly because the courts stood up for the rights of the citizens of Hai Game, following persistent, creative activism by a human rights lawyer.

The people of Hai Game live on prime land in the centre of Juba, just down the road from all the government ministries and the presidential palace, and adjacent to the headquarters of the wildlife police – the neighbourhood gets its name from the game service. In April 2014, when I first visited, Hai Game was a cluster of brightly coloured corrugated shacks, resembling a recent, informal settlement, perhaps neater and more tranquil than most. But in contrast to its temporary demeanour, Hai Game has a long heritage, so while many of its residents are poor, most were permanent. Under the shade of the tree outside his office, the energetic chief, and chairman of Hai Game quarter council, recalled the different phases of settlement marked by the political times of war and peace. The first-comers cleared part of the bush in the 1930s, since when there have been several waves of migration into Hai Game. Following the 1972 Addis Ababa agreement, former soldiers were incorporated into the wildlife police and settled there, while an assortment of different people flocked in after the 2005 peace agreement. Over time, all the land had been occupied, with up to three families on some plots and the chief estimating there were at least 3,760 people of various ethnicities living in Hai Game.

The land was described as valuable, although there were few signs of development. When I asked how much it might be worth, the chief consulted his team and did a back-of-the-envelope calculation, coming up with a figure of US$14 million. This market price estimate was surely questionable; the collapse of the local economy and currency meant that everything in Juba either cost more or was worth less. It was unlikely that there would be any buyers for land during the war – even in the optimistic independence period, most South Sudanese government elites preferred to invest in Nairobi or Kampala. However, the chief had no doubt the land was marketable because he and his council members were battling to prevent part of it being sold off to foreign investors. A syndicate of enterprising wildlife officers was attempting a land grab, and the chief and his quarter council members were standing in their way.

The story was convoluted and improbable, stretching over more than four years. The chief and his community had initiated a plan for community development back in 2010, applying for a land demarcation to create roads, divide up the land equitably and allocate titles to the residents. But the wildlife police officers had their headquarters within Hai Game and were blocking the process. It seemed a few senior officers had used their positions, and the location of their headquarters, to do some private business. They were said to have brokered a deal with foreign investors to lease a substantial plot within Hai Game that was now due to be registered to the community. Residents reported seeing the investors coming to the site in 'a big white car' on more than one occasion. Rumour had it that the officers took US$190,000 from corporate investors as 'the first instalment' for the lease, then split the money and spent it, and were now 'in trouble'.

Certainly, the wildlife officers went to extraordinary lengths to block progress on the land survey and demarcation. With support from their political and military networks, they threatened the surveyors and the local officials. In a brazen twist, they accused the community leaders of forging documents, criminal trespass and cheating, engineering their arrest and imprisonment on three separate occasions. When I met the chief and his quarter council members in 2014, the wildlife officers had taken the dispute to the courts. Godfrey, a young human rights lawyer, whose father lived in the area, had been enlisted to defend the community leaders and the 'citizens of Hai Game' on a pro-bono basis.

From this first encounter, it was clear that the Hai Game case would be an intriguing test of the possibilities for citizen activism in a time of conflict. I continued to follow developments in the case with the help of Godfrey – we employed him as a research assistant for several months alongside his legal pro-bono work, and he provided regular updates. I returned to meet the chief and community members in Hai Game in July 2015, then followed up again in January 2016. Additionally, Godfrey and the chief shared copies of the letters and court decisions they had accumulated relating to the case. These were crucial in substantiating their stories and helping to establish the order of events.

The first letter was the chief's original 'appeal for official survey' to the executive director of Juba *payam*, stating that the citizens had all agreed to the survey 'to allow ... government to deliver services to the people' and to 'finally preserve the right of ownership [of the land]'.[15] This was written at a time of high hopes for peace and development. The residents confirmed this enthusiasm for the demarcation. They told me they lacked electricity. As a result, it was dark at night and several women had been raped. There was no sanitation and they needed roads into the area – at the time there was not even a way in for a water truck or an easy route out for sick and injured people, and two people had recently died from cholera. Naturally, people longed for services and security and hoped the demarcation would improve their lives.

The citizens of Hai Game were a diverse collective of urban migrants, among them ethnic Bari, Mundari, Lokoya, Lotuko, Zande, Moru, Nuer, Dinka and Shilluk. A few were already landowners, with private plots registered in earlier years, and some were renting their houses from landlords. The majority, though, had lived for decades without papers and would now qualify for land rights.[16] Despite their differences, they seemed fairly united in support of the plan, at least at the time of my second visit in July 2015.

Admittedly, the demarcation would cause disruption. Parts of some people's houses had been knocked down because they fell on anticipated roads that were still only lines on a survey map. More troubling still, the creation of the roads and the regular 20 x 15 square metre plots meant that not everyone currently living in Hai Game could be accommodated in the tidy new development. One resident commented that 'some people were not happy and demonstrated against [the demarcation]'. But the chief was reassuring: he had made an arrangement with 'a good friend' – a Bari chief on the outskirts of Juba – to house the remainder of the community there. I spoke to a young tenant due to lose out, but he still welcomed the demarcation. The chief explained: 'we didn't forget him' – he and others like him will 'go to Northern Bari'.

Regardless of its popularity, the cabal of senior wildlife officers, including a major and three brigadiers, did all they could to frustrate the plan, purportedly because of their land deal with the foreign investors. At the outset, the demarcation excluded the

100 x 200 square metre area 'plot 50' which was officially registered to the wildlife police headquarters. The surveyors had identified this area on the masterplan of Juba town and the chief told them that they should only 'demarcate the rest'. But this was not enough, as in the words of the chief, the wildlife officials claimed that 'the rest cannot be demarcated; all belongs to them'. In March, just three months after the application, the engineers and surveyors came to Hai Game to measure up and map the area. A group of wildlife officers accosted the survey team, demanding that the official wildlife area should be allocated to them as individuals. The activity was suspended. The chief wrote to the Minister of Physical Infrastructure the same day to report the matter and to ask for a continuation of the demarcation.

This was the beginning of the tussles between the wildlife officers and the community leaders over the demarcation. The chief produced a ream of correspondence with all levels of the state government seeking their backing to implement the demarcation. The government officials responded with alternately supportive messages or obfuscations. The fact that both the definition and documentation of land rights was in disarray in Juba did not help the community's cause.[17] The directorate of survey provided a map to the Ministry of Physical Infrastructure, showing the boundaries of the area, but suggested that the dispute could 'be settled by the citizen who are there and the game authorities', implying that one side or another should produce their own documents to evidence ownership of the contested area.[18] The point of the planned land registration exercise was that no such documents existed. The bureaucratic responses and delays were Kafkaesque.

A breakthrough came with the intervention of the speaker of Juba city legislative council in October 2011, who instructed the mayor to go ahead on the basis that the 'area was not fully designated for them [Wild Life]. And the Authorities all over [CES

(Central Equatoria state)] agreed the demarcation for the area'.[19] The Ministry of Physical Infrastructure was again instructed to implement the demarcation.[20] But before they could start the process, the wildlife officers called the police to arrest the chief and his quarter council members. Seven of them were imprisoned for two days, then released. The chief made a complaint to his local MP, escalating the matter to a new level of authority.

By July 2012, the dispute had reached the highest level of the Central Equatoria state government. The Council of Ministers deliberated on the issue and passed resolution 204, ordering the demarcation to go ahead. They instructed that the wildlife forces should be relocated outside the area to a newly allocated piece of land on the east bank of the river Nile. They also called upon the various stakeholders to attend a meeting, 'for the sake of creating harmony'.[21] The stakeholders' meeting was duly held in October 2012 and once again the master plan was produced, showing the 100 x 200 square metre plot earmarked for the wildlife police and demonstrating that the rest of the area was 'unsurveyed'.[22] There was no reconciliation and tensions between the parties persisted, but the demarcation was set to proceed regardless. It seemed that the wildlife officers were now in a worse position, having lost the guarantee of their institutional claim to the land for the headquarters, let alone the larger patch that the officers were personally demanding. Moreover, the minister of physical infrastructure wrote a stern letter to the commissioner of wildlife 'to bring to your attention the activities of your officer, Major J ... [and to] prevail over this officer to avoid institutional interference'.[23]

The chief doggedly resubmitted the proposal to launch the demarcation and had got signatures and stamps of approval from an array of relevant authorities by April 2013. But in July 2013, the directorate of survey produced a budget for the demarcation, totalling 60,000 SSP,[24] which the community was asked to pay. The chief handed out forms and the residents of Hai Game pitched in funds for the survey in the expectation that this would secure their rights to a plot, with some 530 families registered. The wildlife officers took this as an opportunity to bring a criminal case against the chief and his quarter councillors on charges of trying to cheat the community. Once again, the seven local officials were arrested and taken to court. The detainees were convinced the officers had given 'money to the [police] investigation'. By this point, the chief's wife was despairing and begged him to 'leave this job', but the chief insisted he had to 'complete the process'. Godfrey defended the group in the high court. His notes on the court ruling state that the case was dismissed for lack of evidence on 12 December 2013. Just a few days later the civil war broke out.

The war only delayed proceedings for a month or so. By the end of January 2014, the wildlife officers had opened a new civil case in Juba high court against the Hai Game quarter council committee leaders aimed at securing the larger plot that they claimed was theirs. The first summons of the court asked for a survey to secure the boundaries of 'plot 50' belonging to the wildlife, as marked on the map. The parties were ordered to attend but the surveyor's 'field report' notes that Major J and his group left before the exercise was complete.[25] After this productive start, the court case halted as the high court judges had 'gone for training'. It was not until the end of September 2014 that the parties were able to present their cases in court. In the meantime, they had clashed at the site.

The push for the demarcation had continued alongside the court case, on the basis that 'the court doesn't have power to question the council of ministers'. A new date was set for February 2014. This time the chief was taking no chances; the director of Juba town helped him out by requesting that police attend. However, on the day in question, a security officer called the chief to tell him that he would have to provide fuel for the officers. The bulldozers arrived at Hai Game on time, but the police were not there, as they had gone 'to get petrol'. Major J had seen the bulldozers arriving and ran to gather his colleagues. A large group of armed wildlife soldiers (some estimated around 40) arrived and blocked the bulldozers, then 'started beating' the driver. Godfrey, the lawyer, tried to intervene, asking the officers if they had 'any papers to stop this?' The response was a direct threat: 'while I was talking he put a gun to me'. The community rallied round, the chief began calling the authorities, and the police arrived. The situation was calmed down by interventions from national security officers, the police and the minister of the interior. But the mayor also ordered that the demarcation should be suspended due to the insecurity it was causing. He warned that if the court case went in favour of the wildlife officers, all the citizens might have to evacuate the area. He then called a meeting to broker peace between the parties, but this did nothing to end the discord.

It was baffling that the community had got the backing of so many authorities for the demarcation, but none could restrain the wildlife officers. The chief explained: 'the forces that are pulling are so big that it even undermines legal authority and breaks down institutions'. Surely it was obvious to any observer that the officers were bringing the cases against the community leaders based on personal interests. As one resident put it, the 'wildlife is a curtain'. But the notorious Major J was said to have a record of violence and relatives in high places: he was apparently an 'uncle' of the governor of Central Equatoria state. The lawyer, the chief and the members of the quarter council all believed that this is why he and his group were able to continue to pose a threat.

The local officials were growing fearful: 'we don't have guns, only God protects us'. They knew that some community members had become impatient and that it would be difficult to keep the peace: 'the citizens are resolved and ready to die for this land'. All the delays were raising suspicions among the people of Hai Game and the chief was anxious for his own reputation, worrying, '[people] thought I did something underground'. In his frustration, the chief boldly wrote a memo to the governor himself in March 2014 stating: 'Hai-Game citizens are constantly being threatened by some Wildlife officers' and naming Major J as responsible.[26] The memo was copied to the state ministers, who had resolved upon the demarcation in their council, back in 2012. With this, the chief felt he had now tried every 'civilised' method.

By the time I returned to Hai Game in July 2015, the mood had changed, as the community were optimistic and celebrating a legal victory. First, the high court had followed procedures carefully and dismissed the wildlife's case against the Hai Game quarter council committee on 4 May 2015. Then the minister of finance had weighed in on the side of the people, questioning who was standing behind the officers and promising that 'whoever sits on your rights will be overcome and you will get your land'.[27] Next, the chief and his team had managed to implement part of the demarcation, and they proudly took me on a stroll down the new roads that had been constructed. It had been tough going; there had even been another spat with the wildlife officers when the bulldozers arrived, to the extent that the community leaders had had to call in the police and resorted to incentives, promising the wildlife officers private plots in the demarcation exercise. It was still a concern that the wildlife officers had appealed against the high court ruling, leading to a temporary suspension of the demarcation, but the officers had lost their original fervour and the community seemed close to a victory.

The appeal court case took some time, but it eventually upheld the original decision. It seemed that civil and legal methods could prove effective, even in this very hostile and unpredictable environment. I visited Juba again in January 2016, so tried calling the chief of Hai Game to arrange a visit and congratulate him, but he did not answer my calls. I then asked Godfrey about the chief, but his response was totally unexpected. The situation in Hai Game had deteriorated. The chief was now at loggerheads with some of his former supporters and members of his quarter council committee, and the community was divided. Godfrey was no longer involved in the case, but he advised me to meet urgently with his brother, a youth leader in Hai Game who had been appointed by the community to investigate.

I arranged a meeting with two youth leaders who updated me on the latest developments at Hai Game. They claimed that once the demarcation was completed and the 'external threat' from the wildlife and the investors had been dealt with, they were concerned that a new land grab was underway. They feared many of the original residents would be displaced. Among many vexing issues, they found out that a number of people who received tokens for their plots were told their land was no longer available when they went to finalise the registration process. The youth leaders offered a 'live example':

Plot 147 is for 'Andrew'. He was given this token to go and finish the process in Juba block, when he reached there they told him to wait. He has money, 3,500 SSP for the process, and he took the money with him and every day they told him to wait. When he came to us and explained about his case we went there and found that his number was registered by someone else's name. So he is holding the token only.

The youth leaders said that they had complained about the problems at a public meeting with the quarter council committee, but the discussion grew heated and the meeting was closed down when one of the officials called national security. This was a setback, but they said they remained determined to 'stand for the voiceless'.

The youth leader's story was troubling but needed further verification, so they suggested I spoke to a man who had lived in Hai Game since 1965. He confirmed that he too had lost his plot in exactly this fashion and was aware of other similar cases. He had joined the youth activists in a complaint to the mayor as well as writing his own lengthy complaint. From his account, it seemed that a committee had been formed to investigate and a new registration process was proposed. His account tallied with the claims made by the youth leaders and he provided letters and documents to support it. No one seemed certain who was ultimately responsible, but accusations were circulating that a particular member of the quarter council committee might be behind the land grab, or that certain council officials might have benefited. They thought the chief might have either been misled or implicated.

The central concern was that, as one youth leader put it, plots were being 'distributed to the big people'.[28] The landgrabbers seemed to be taking advantage of a political hiatus – the transitional government, promised under the 2015 peace agreement, was still being established and 'they want to finish the demarcation while government is suspended. They have a lot of hands ... who have taken a lot of plots'. The youths said that some members of the community were armed and ready to fight if the problems were not sorted out soon. But they aimed to bring a challenge in court if the committee failed to resolve the matter. Some of the residents had already launched individual court cases.

These last two interviews raised a whole new set of questions about land struggles and activism in Hai Game. They reminded me of an earlier interview I conducted in Juba back in July 2015, when Hai Game's chief suggested I should meet the chief of nearby Hai Gabat to find out more about landgrabbing in the town.

What I learned was that the Hai Gabat quarter council had also applied for the demarcation, and the implementation had begun by the time that I met their chief. But something had gone wrong in the final stages of the process, the chief said that suddenly 'the high level landgrabbers came in' claiming they had rights to a substantial area, covering 116 plots, for a commercial project. They seemed to have documents, yet it was unclear how and when they acquired them. He was trying to investigate but suspected that people in the Ministry of Physical Infrastructure might be 'participating in the issue'; he said: 'many people with money want a plot here'. I did not manage to research and confirm either the complicated issues in Hai Gabat or further developments in Hai Game. The last I heard, there was talk of another Hai Game court case being launched to contest the ownership of the former wildlife headquarters, the troublesome 'plot 50'. In all of this there seemed to be only one certainty: that contestation over land would continue, in the 'strategic location' of Hai Game, and beyond.[29]

It is tempting to write the Hai Game case off as an illustration of the quandaries surrounding land rights in the midst of political and legal uncertainty. But considering the confusions in the courts and the multi-layered violent conflicts that plagued South Sudan during the same period, we should also register its positive lessons on the existence and potential of citizen activism. It is remarkable that a multi-ethnic community remained largely united behind the effort to legalise their land rights and supported civil leadership, firstly the chief, then the youth leaders, at least for the period in question. The chief started out as a committed advocate for the community, gaining some traction for his approach. The statutory courts also played their part effectively. The lawyer defended the chief and his committee against trumped up criminal charges, and then won the civil case brought by the wildlife officers against the committee. The statutory courts were predictably slow to reach decisions, yet seemed thorough and independent when they did so.

Moreover, the next generation of activists declared their intention to challenge the latest round of land grabs and demand justice. The odds were stacked against them, but they were still willing to try. In these contests, they are thinking locally, yet confronting a fundamental governance problem with regional, global and historical dimensions. African states and economies were built upon the capture of usable land and resources at its peripheries, a colonial pattern which was cemented under neoliberal globalisation. In South Sudan, people have long sought to survive these predations by managing their livelihoods and governance arrangements at local levels and relying upon their retention of 'customary', communal and informal rights over land. These have frequently been, as political scientist Catherine Boone finds, the basis for forms of 'local citizenship' in Africa, and South Sudan is a case in point.[30]

With changing land tenure regimes and the commodification of and competition over land, various critical struggles are emerging, organised around either ethnic or civic identities, using either violent or non-violent methods, in towns and rural domains in South Sudan.[31] Whichever idiom these struggles take, and however they are ignited, they are rooted in the failure of the central state to deliver rights and citizenship, historically and in the present. David Deng documented a series of large-scale land investments by corporations in 2011, some of which were later revoked as a result of this research and community activism. His observation that it 'remains to be seen whether communities or the government will win in this battle for land' still holds true.[32] Urban struggles to secure land rights through civil and legal methods, and their outcomes, make contributions to the wider contestation and definition of land rights, and to the future terms of citizenship in South Sudan.

Reforming custom in exile

This vignette traces how paralegals and lawyers tried to promote justice processes and limit violations of women's rights within customary courts that were located inside a United Nations Protection of Civilians site. It focuses on a unique setting, but sharply illustrates wider tensions and interactions between the humanitarian and human rights regimes that govern international peace operations and locally valued customary laws and authorities.[33]

The story centres on experiences of law and activism within PoC3, near Juba airport. Among other internally displaced people, the site hosts survivors of a massacre that targeted Nuer residents of Juba in December 2013. I reflect upon the views and experiences of a group of displaced Nuer lawyers and paralegals: Chotlith, David, Andrew, Bangoang, Gach Diew and Chief William. They were also my former colleagues, acting as court observers in our research project.[34] Their story provides evidence of the potential for critical legal thinking and transformative agency among survivors and displaced people, as well as of the ingenuity and persistence required to advance rights in contexts of legal pluralism and conflict. The group were informed by legal and human rights training, but they also recognised the authority and value of customary authorities. They navigated and mediated between these competing norms and regimes and pursued new pathways to protection under exceptionally harsh conditions of displacement, social disturbance and trauma.

The people in the PoC have a unique status, akin to refugees, fleeing their state and seeking international protection, while remaining within their nation or even home town. David described it as a form of political exile: 'If you are going to the PoC you are in a different country.' The civilians must pass through a checkpoint to get into or out of the camp, a journey that many have made in pursuit of education or trade, but which is fraught with risk. Once inside the camp they are under an unprecedented form of UN governance with a degree of protection from ethnic massacres, but no guarantee of social or physical security. These circumstances, and the ways in which humanitarians and the displaced people have responded to them, have been a focus of considerable analysis and debate.[35] For our purposes, the most salient issue is that UNMISS was effectively in control of the sites and had the authority to defend their perimeters and protect people within them from incursions, but did not have the mandate to police or prosecute them for criminal actions within the sites. The UN needed mechanisms to maintain social order; but lacked the legal capacity to set up any such structures. The sites were legal and political anomalies that brought innumerable dilemmas. This helps to explain why chiefs' courts and community policing were able to flourish as mechanisms for justice and security within the sites.[36]

It is not implausible that struggles for justice should emerge in such a precarious setting. Refugee camps are generally 'warscapes', in the evocative phrase of anthropologist Bram Jansen; social relations within them are shaped by past violence and reconfigured in reaction to the politics and violence that prevails outside.[37] They are places where identities and historical consciousness are actively produced, as Lisa Malkki finds in a seminal ethnography of Burundian refugees in Tanzania. Under conditions of trauma and liminality, refugees may well turn to the past as a source of dignity and resistance, constructing divisive narratives and exclusionary identities.[38] But sites of protracted displacement are political spaces in every sense, and therefore various political projects and contestations might emerge. Some refugees look to the future while others concentrate on the past; people may innovate politically as their political ideals enter into correspondence with, or resistance to, humanitarian regimes.

As Claire Lecadet finds, 'Experimental' and 'marginal' politics, encompassing various forms of social and political organisation, can flourish in refugee settings.[39] Indeed, South Sudan's PoCs are spaces of trauma and insecurity but also of protection, care and life-affirming cultural creativity, as anthropologist Zoe Cormack eloquently observes.[40]

The paralegals with whom I worked were all survivors of the massacres at the start of the war in Juba that led to the establishment of the PoC in December 2013. Each of them had witnessed and fled violations in December 2013 and all of them had lost family and friends in the atrocity or in the war that followed. However, none of them mentioned the atrocities in any of our meetings about justice and the courts, and while their personal experiences shaped their legal consciousness and commitments, as I explain in the next chapter, they were not the focus of their activism. Certainly, they wanted accountability for atrocities, but they advised me that such talk was meaningless in the circumstances of ongoing war and displacement; according to Chotlith, it was 'just beating the drums [while] ... the people who inflicted injustices to the citizens are the ones holding power'. David added: 'After the fighting has stopped then we can talk about accountability and justice. There is nothing to talk about justice when people are still dying.' For the time being, they were still reckoning with the urgent problems of insecurity and injustice within the PoC.

Despite the constant presence of UN peacekeepers and police, and support from a host of humanitarian organisations, people in PoC3 suffered desperate and unstable circumstances. Bangoang described their predicament:

Our situation is not good. I see many people suffering and many in trauma and there is a lot of fighting within the camp and family fights. There is an economic crisis in PoC3 and people lost and confused and traumatised and there are also the 'nigga' groups [violent gangs] and they did not understand justice or have the implementation of justice. People are not living peacefully.

The insecurity was fuelled by political and social differences within a fluctuating population of more than 30,000 people. The majority of people in the camp shared a Nuer identity, but there were people of plural identities and backgrounds there, especially after July 2016, and it is important to emphasise that 'Nuer' are also diverse, including people from a complex mixture of social backgrounds, both urban and rural, with different regional, clan and kinship identities and political affiliations. The PoC was a tense environment in which fear and suspicion flourished and petty and violent conflicts could rapidly erupt.

In this context, local authorities emerged and evolved aimed at preventing conflict and establishing law and social order, including customary chiefs, a community police force and a security force known initially as the 'N4', and later as the Community Emergency Response Team (CERT). There were also official local structures established in association with UNMISS and the humanitarians for the purposes of 'camp management'.[41]

Nonetheless, several violent battles took place within the sites during the research period in which hundreds of young men fought with sticks, spears and machetes, some people died, and hundreds were injured over the years. There was a problem of gang violence, and regular altercations within the 'Nigga' youth gangs and between them and other members of the community. There were also a few threats and incursions from government soldiers outside. The most catastrophic attack came in July 2016 when two peacekeepers and more than 20 civilians were killed in fierce fighting in and around the PoCs, and many more were killed or raped in the vicinity.[42] Alongside these threats and incidents of violence, there were also the usual quota of marital disputes, petty criminality and social rivalries.

Some of the problems were a consequence of political tensions which festered within PoC3, and were fuelled by violence outside the camp. While the majority of Nuer fighters had joined the rebel SPLA-IO at the start of the civil war, some fought on the government side, most of them members of the Bul Nuer clan from Mayom, and some of them participated in an atrocious government offensive in Mayom in Unity state in 2015.[43] People in the Juba PoC, including three members of the paralegal team, had family in Unity state and lost loved ones and cattle in this military onslaught. The civil war and the machinations of elite politics, including the internal competition between Riek Machar and Taban Deng for the leadership of the SPLA-IO, inevitably impacted on social relations within the camp. Although the site hosted civilians, some among them were also former or future fighters, usually for the SPLA-IO. Suspected government supporters were subject to monitoring, threats and exclusions. The politics of the sites were also expressed in annual 15 December commemorations of the victims of the war and massacres, and in restrictions on public mourning for government soldiers: 'only those who are killed in the frontline on the side of SPLM-IO, their relatives are allowed to mourn'.[44] It was evident and inevitable that the violent conflict and atrocities outside the sites would affect the relations between individuals and within families inside, hardening clan identities and political divides.

The chiefs' courts were the main forums for managing all these political and social problems and disputes within the sites. They cultivated a shared Nuer identity and moral and legal regime. They also functioned as adaptive modes of 'customary protection', responding to conflict and social disturbance, and interacting with UN institutions and interventions. But even in this international humanitarian setting they reproduced patriarchal and gerontocratic norms. They tightly policed relationships and applied customary laws that discriminated against women and young people, breaching international human rights laws in various ways, as other similar courts routinely did in very different settings before and after the war.[45]

Remarkably, however, the courts were also adapting to their new humanitarian context and also became the focus for initiatives to reform customary law in favour of women's rights. The paralegals were at the forefront of these efforts based on their training in international human rights law. They were generally educated young men, many of them teachers, who had involved themselves in various human rights and humanitarian activities within the camp. Some of them had been training to be lawyers before the conflict erupted. Their first forays into legal activism within the PoC were in their roles as volunteers for Pact, an international development NGO that provided human rights and legal training within the PoCs before 2015 and encouraged paralegals to identify injustices, support and advise victims, and monitor the courts.[46] Their interpretations of the problems and the solutions in the sites did not appear to be consistently guided by international human rights norms and they were certainly not all similarly committed or positioned. Yet at some point all were engaged in forms of activism that related to their paralegal training.[47] Their motivations were bound to be complex and varied, but it is notable that they were all survivors of violence and injustice: as Chotlith commented, 'according to human rights, law works together with politics, when you talk about it you enter into politics. If you don't claim rights, you will be a victim forever'.[48]

The problems the paralegals wrestled with included intricate disputes within families, related to bridewealth, and abuses by members of the community security organisations or chiefs. They had some concrete impacts: for instance, one of the paralegals described how he prevented a pregnant woman, accused of adultery, from being beaten by the community watch group on the orders of a chief. But the situation was so volatile that the activists were hesitant to intervene directly in many instances. Much of what they did was information-gathering, sharing and documenting abuses – including gathering testimonies of victims of violence and rape – and monitoring court cases (some of which was sponsored by our research project). They liaised and negotiated with chiefs, UN police and international organisations, as well as convening or participating in meetings related to justice and security. Some of the activists also worked in other ways to try to change attitudes towards rights and justice in the camp. For instance, Bangoang used theatre as a means to effect change, working with his drama group to create a production that could reflect critically on the lessons of the courts, believing that 'drama is a means to bring unity ... [people] will see what is not good and think about correcting the community'. Perhaps most importantly, all the paralegals engaged in critically reflecting upon the activities and impacts of the courts, community security actors and even the humanitarians, and sought to promote improvements and solutions where they could.[49]

The paralegals' interpretations of justice were grounded in a blend of ideas about law and rights, reflecting the plural legalities with which they engaged. Following socio-legal theorist Sally Engle Merry we might think of them as localised interpretations and transformations of human rights norms, reflecting 'legal vernacularization'.[50] They were strategic and selective in their adoption of human rights principles and discourses, while also being committed to the promotion of Nuer authority and law. For instance, not all of them were necessarily opposed to the forms of corporal punishment that were being implemented by the courts and the community security organisation. Most also perceived adultery as an infraction of customary norms and did not question the need for close regulation of extra-marital relationships between men and women, although this issue was a clear source of tensions between the customary authorities and the UN's human rights regime.

However, the paralegals and some of the chiefs they worked with sought changes to the treatment of women in the courts and the bridewealth system. In contrast to a patriarchal view of girls as family assets and a source of wealth, which was readily expressed by some chiefs and routinely shaped decisions in customary forums,[51] they asserted that: 'our sisters are not resources' and 'our daughters [should] be free from harmful traditional practices'. They explicitly referenced South Sudan's bill of rights, statutory laws and international human rights laws, as well as custom. Their activism was apparently guided by beliefs that regimes of punishment should be limited and regulated by the law; and that customary courts should be oriented towards the promotion of rights and justice, taking account of both individuals and families. These were radical ideas in the context in which they were working, and they therefore had to negotiate legal and normative changes carefully and against considerable odds, as the example of the election of a female chief and the events that followed it help to illustrate.

In May 2018, Chotlith, one of the paralegals, contacted me to share a rare item of good news from the camp. He said a new woman chief, Rebecca Nyandier, had been elected. Hopes were high that this could be an opportunity for advancing women's rights. There were obvious reasons for scepticism – individual women leaders are always hard-pressed to deliver political transformation. In Nuer society women typically gain authority by becoming 'socially men' through divine possession as prophets and sometimes through advocating violence.[52] It was surely no coincidence that the new woman chief had a military record as a former SPLA general. However, women leaders are exceptionally rare in South Sudan, and there have been very few other female chiefs, so this election in itself constituted an achievement, and it was also a political opportunity, as I argued in a newspaper article at the time.[53] The activists therefore proposed to organise a chiefs' forum in an effort to promote women's rights and we agreed to treat it as a research exercise.[54]

By this point, Chotlith had completed his law degree, after daily risking the journey in and out to Juba University. His final year dissertation examined 'the impacts of custom on the life of girls and women in regard to accessibility to justice in South Sudan', with a case study of the Nuer community. He had also established a 'community-based law firm' with two other lawyers in the camp. Chotlith was engaged in a daily task of collecting cases of sexual and gender-based violence, yet he was not able to directly address the problems. The difficulties become clearer in particular cases. One case involved an underage girl who was a victim of statutory rape, having been discovered by her parents spending the night with her boyfriend. The rape was reported but the victim was left in a condition of uncertainty awaiting a remedy. Chotlith described the girl as a 'victim of rape, Nuer culture and human rights laws'. Rape and murder cases had to be referred to the UN, and could take a long time to solve, to the despair of the families concerned. In this case the family wanted an urgent customary settlement including punishment and material compensation, in either money or cows, but the courts were unable to rule on the case because the decision would need to be made by experts based in faraway UN headquarters. In the meantime, the girl was thrown out by her family and some members of the family were threatening to attack her boyfriend.

The paralegals had developed an ongoing dialogue with chiefs who were also concerned about the challenges of trying to mediate between the UN's regimes of law and popular concerns, especially on issues of women's rights. The female chief told Chotlith that she was willing to take advice from the trained lawyers; she planned to follow Nuer customary rules 'unless if some articles from the women rights are to be incorporated and approved by the Nuer community or the IDPs'. Another male chief complained that the IDPs 'entirely depend on customary law and ignore human rights laws particularly when dealing with an issue regarding marriages ... if we the chiefs consider a woman's claim for divorce then the community will not be happy with us'. Together they agreed to hold a chiefs' forum to deliberate on the issues.

The forum took place in July 2018 and involved vigorous debates about women's rights and assertions of the value of Nuer customary law, but it led to some progressive decisions. Firstly, the 65 participants, including chiefs, paralegals and youth and women's leaders had much to say about the differences between international human rights and Nuer customary law, and the fact that UNMISS neither 'believed in' nor had 'official discussions' with the community about the law. The chiefs complained that they were restricted in their ability to administer corporal punishment for fear that 'action' might be taken against them by the UN. They also discussed problems of 'clannism' and conflicts between communities within the sites. But they upheld a previous crucial decision, taken in 2017, to impose a cap on the brideprice, despite some complaints that it was too low, on the basis that in the current situation some reduction was needed to enable young men and women to exercise their right to marry and start a family. Finally, and most importantly, a decision was taken to form a committee of 25 members, including chiefs and paralegals, to review the Nuer Fangak laws and draft guidelines for customary courts and community security organisations, incorporating some articles relating to child rights and women's rights from the bill of rights in the 2011 Transitional Constitution.[55]

The achievements of the forum were considerable, but it was unclear when and whether they would have an impact in the courts. The legal committee began its work and the idea was that a second forum would be organised to review and hopefully adopt their recommendations. A month later, however, I heard from Chotlith again. The camp was in crisis, with fierce fighting, lasting over a week, between some members of the Mayom Bul Nuer community and other clans. The reasons for violence were not entirely clear and the incident was hardly reported, so my only source was the disjointed messages I received from Chotlith, with photos and videos of the fighters, and the body of a young man killed in the battle. The battles were said to have been sparked by a minor dispute relating to a stolen mobile phone, but the tensions between Mayom community and other clans were longstanding and politicised.

The inter-clan fighting in Juba PoC in August 2018 was a disaster. People were short of food and the humanitarians were not able to come in or out of the camp. The situation looked hopeless. Yet Chotlith did not lose his composure. On 24 August he sent a message to say that the situation was calm and the 'youths had peacefully accepted disarmament'. There was a photo of him smiling alongside a UN officer in front of a truck filled with the sticks and spears they had collected in an informal disarmament process. But as well as the loss of life and injuries sustained during the fighting, it also meant divisions within the chieftaincy and a problem for the reform project. It turned out that the female chief was from Mayom and she was forced out of the PoC with the rest of her community members during the battles. Another reformist chief, meanwhile, had disappeared from the camp, apparently to join the rebels on the Equatorian frontline.

Citizen activism aimed at promoting women's rights faces tough obstacles in South Sudan. The PoC became a microcosm of the problems and possibilities. It indicated emerging changes and contestations within the customary law, in sharp contrast to the static views of culture and custom that tend to be perpetuated by its beneficiaries. For instance, in 2005, confronted with the problem of a high number of cases of women in prison for adultery, the then Chief Justice Ambrose Riny Thiik suggested that the bridewealth system was, and should be, a consistent element of South Sudan's culture: 'These are arranged marriages to create an economic network of family relations. If we change these rules, our entire society could change.'[56] But there were already plural ways of arranging marriages in South Sudan and the legal activists were proposing some practical ways of making the system more compatible with human rights. In so doing they were both referencing and changing the standard practice of customary law-making which was historically processual, but typically 'made' in negotiations between male elders,[57] not women and young men.

Customary regimes are a source of dignity, identity and predictable authority to the extent that, even under UN governance, they have proven resilient. They are also frequently criticised for their role in violations of women's rights. This vignette makes clear that some male proponents and adjudicators of custom also recognise this problem; it is not simply an international concern, or a women's struggle. Paralegals and chiefs have begun pursuing their own reform agendas, which may be significant even when they do not deliver immediate results. Humanitarian and human rights actors are regarded with suspicion by customary authorities and have faced resistance and hostility to their interventions.[58] In contrast, local activists have absorbed plural regimes of law and government; they have built relationships with diverse authorities to gently press for change. In this case, they established an ambitious project to promote 'law from below' in favour of women's rights, through consistent monitoring and dialogue. Sadly, but also rather typically in this volatile context, this reform project was hindered by an eruption of conflict. Still, both South Sudan's history and social theory suggest that progress towards justice depends not only on legal reforms but upon related and overlapping struggles to change law in society, by influencing social norms and practices.[59] In this respect, something important had already changed here, exemplified by the fact of a group of young men subverting South Sudan's 'hegemonic militarized masculinities'[60] in the pursuit of women's rights.

The rule of man

This vignette focuses on an attempt to launch an appeal against imposition of the death sentence on two youths in Juba. It is important because it concerns the execution of two juveniles, a serious violation of both international human rights and domestic legislation, and because of the inventive strategies and humane actions of the lawyers and citizen activist involved. It illustrates that some lawyers have sought to address the problem of miscarriages of justice in statutory courts through the use of a customary norm, encouraging out-of-court settlements for 'blood compensation' between families. While this strategy failed in this case, it has succeeded in some others, and again shows how activists reference and blend different sources of law in pursuit of best-fit solutions.

Two boys were executed in Juba central prison on 27 June 2017. This tragedy marked a wholesale defeat in the eyes of the local activists who had tried to prevent what was a miscarriage of justice touching upon the selective and politicised character of the system. Yet the 'death of the Acholi boys', as they labelled it, was also emblematic of the inventive ways that activists were trying to respond to the excesses of the statutory courts. In what follows, I share the story of the boys' execution as it was told to me by two male lawyers and a female activist during a group meeting in August 2017, describing the efforts they invested in trying to halt the execution, and the meanings they attached to the event. I also draw upon the documentary sources substantiating their story, including letters and death certificates. The case, and the issues and debates it raised, tell us something of the painful dilemmas lawyers and activists wrestle with in South Sudan.

The Acholi boys were two brothers who had been convicted of murder and held on death row in an adult jail in Torit for two years. We can assume that the conditions during the first part of their sentence were appalling. The prisons collect and compound all the roughest elements of the justice system in South Sudan. At worst they are places of torture and starvation, while at best they are dirty and overcrowded. Their inmates include men and women on remand for years, mentally ill people, children and very many detainees who did not have a fair trial by any standards. According to Human Rights Watch, the prison population of Juba exploded between 2005 and 2012, virtually quadrupling. Their research identified appalling conditions and prisoner files 'in disarray' just before the war broke out.[61] Since then, UNMISS has continued to work with the National Prison Service in efforts to push for a 'humane and accountable prison system',[62] including taking steps to improve prison record management. The UNDP, meanwhile, has sought to reduce the backlog in cases and prolonged and arbitrary detention.[63] So perhaps some facets of prison management might be improving, but it is from a disastrously low base.

The boys were moved from Torit prison to Juba prison shortly before their execution. Juba central prison was especially crowded, holding over 1,300 prisoners in cells designed for just 400. It also held somewhere around 100 prisoners on death row, most of whom have not had a lawyer or a chance to call witnesses in their defence.[64] Despite the flaws in trial procedures, and the complaints of South Sudanese human rights lawyers, the death penalty remains on the statutes as a sentence for capital crimes. It may be applied in very serious cases such as homicide and treason and it has been implemented in a number of documented cases during the period of the war; execution takes place by hanging, and at least four prisoners were hanged in 2017.[65]

Aisha told me about her first meeting with the Acholi brothers in Juba prison. On that occasion, they seemed optimistic of a reprieve. She recalled: 'the boys did not expect they would die because they were confident that they have an appeal'. She helped work on their appeal and find a lawyer for them. She had a file of papers relating to the case which she shared with me, including their death certificates and a photo of one of the dead boys, which she had taken just after his execution. She was familiar with this and other similar cases because she worked with inmates as a prison counsellor. I had heard her talk previously about the desperate cases she saw in prison, including a previous hanging and another prisoner who died from illness. Aisha helped such prisoners with practical and legal issues, as far as possible, using her personal contacts and resources.

It turned out that the Acholi boys were from Magwi county in Eastern Equatoria. Both were accused of killing a relative during a brawl two years beforehand in July 2015. They did not deny that their relative was killed but said it was unintentional, happening 'in the course of the fighting' over an inheritance. Aisha was convinced that the boys had a strong case for appeal and she was helping to organise the petition. She had involved one human rights lawyer, Jacob, in the case and another, Godfrey, had been contacted by other prisoners because he was working on a series of death row appeals. Both lawyers were keen to defend the boys and each of them provided clarifications on aspects of the case. Aisha's files included letters from the family that helped to confirm the details. From these it seemed that the case was first heard in Torit high court. Although the details of this trial are sketchy, we do know that in March 2017 the families intervened. Wanting to settle the matter customarily by means of blood compensation, they wrote:

> the father of the deceased and the father of the boys are brothers (family matter). So in our traditional belief if you killed your brother or sister you should not be killed. So we ... the family, we feel really so much disappointed of what happened. So we are requesting the various respective offices not to kill the two boys, so we have finished the issues from home. Not to kill them.[66]

Blood compensation is a common settlement for murder cases, as explained earlier in the book, so this letter was crucial for the appeal case, although there were also many other reasons to question the fairness of the trial. None of the lawyers disputed the validity of the appeal or of the family's proposal. Here was an obvious injustice, two boys sentenced to death for what may well have been an accidental killing. The court had not treated the boys as juveniles – the penal code specifies that the death penalty should not be applied to anyone under 18.[67] No one specified their ages, and this section of their death certificates was left conveniently blank, but everyone including the family referred to them as 'boys', and the crime itself had taken place when they were two years younger. Moreover, the lawyers were looking for an expedient solution and the blood compensation settlement might provide it.

However, the court hearing took place soon after the boys arrived in Juba, and too quickly for the appeal that Aisha and the lawyers were hoping to file. Aisha reached out to her contacts in the military to try to put pressure to allow the lawyers into the case, but she was unsuccessful: 'They refused to receive the documents ... I talked to the boys, told them they have rights ... then they were calling me ... one of them was afeared to die.' Still, as soon as they heard the trial was taking place, the lawyers rushed to the court to plead with the judge to stay the sentence, as Godfrey described:

> I drove back to the prison ... I made an attempt to see the chief justice; I was blocked ... then the judge came and I entered in with the family of the deceased. I said I'm not their lawyer but I'm helping. I'm presenting an application that the family agreed they don't want the death sentence of these boys ... The judge said that these boys must be killed. I said, your honour it is so regrettable to celebrate this illegal death ... The complainant said he doesn't want them to be killed ... The execution must be halted for 72 hours and the presiding judge must tell the chief justice that I'm giving them time to document this agreement for this court ... I was pushed out by the police.

The activists were critical of the rush to administer the death sentence and suspected ethnic bias. Many prisoners had remained on death row for years, yet the court acted promptly in this case, at a time when most of the judges were on strike and very few courts were operational. The case also coincided with a period of intensified state violence and rebellion in the Equatoria region, where the boys hailed from.[68] Aisha heard someone dismissing the boys as 'rebels'. She concluded:

There is no justice in South Sudan. They made the agreement. But the court didn't wait. They said: 'they are all rebels from that side'. They are from Magwi ... We had the discussion with the director of public prosecutions. It went up to the office of the president that the conclusion that there was someone behind this case. The paper came from the president's office direct.

The case was symbolic of how little the lives of the Acholi boys counted in political terms. The government is often labelled a 'Dinkocracy' by its opponents, based on the power and wealth of a 'clique' of ethnic Dinka elites from President Kiir's home area of Bahr el Ghazal.[69] I never heard the activists use this term – Aisha, Godfrey and Jacob were all Equatorians, but they worked with many people of all ethnicities and knew Dinkas were suffering in the courts and the prisons along with everyone else. In fact, in the same meeting about the Acholi boys, Aisha had told me of her concerns for a Dinka woman prisoner, arrested on the accusations of her partner in a 'forced marriage', but too fearful to appeal and seek release in case her violent husband killed her. She recognised that the issue was not simply ethnicity; it was that some lives did not matter in the political hierarchies of South Sudan, whether because of their identity or poverty.

Yet the timing of the execution seemed politically significant. Just two months before the boys were executed, in April 2017, government troops fiercely put down what they perceived to be a rebellion in the Pajok area, Equatoria region, which was largely populated by Acholis. They massacred Acholi civilians, including children.[70] The activists were acutely aware of this recent event. Jacob had heard first-hand accounts of this atrocity because his family was from Pajok and his uncle was forced by the soldiers to bury some of the victims. Most of the Acholi had now fled to

Uganda.[71] In this context, they perceived that the courts saw
no need to uphold the rights of the Acholi boys, whether out of
intentional bias, associating the boys with 'rebels' based on their
identities, or mere judicial zeal.

The lawyers turned to customary settlement as a solution
because the community and the family valued the lives of the
boys. This was an approach that might work. Godfrey already had
a record of successful cases of this kind; by 2018 he had been
involved in the successful mediation of ten death penalty cases
leading to the prisoners' release and the organisation he worked
with had many other similar cases pending.[72] The advantage of
blood compensation was its expediency and potential for conflict
prevention, limiting the possibilities that grieving families might
try to take revenge if a prisoner's sentence was quashed.[73] There
were reasons for caution about the use of blood compensation,
as some participants in our meeting or in later interviews pointed
out. Statutory courts risked diluting its original social function
and meaning, and since the ability to pay compensation varied,
the wealthy had most to gain: they 'will compensate [so] they
can be killing all the people they want'.[74] Godfrey had written his
undergraduate law dissertation on the related issue of girl child
compensation, in which a young girl could be given to the family
in compensation for murder, which was growing less common
but could still be awarded in customary courts in some areas, a
practice which all the activists rejected. Yet although there would
be other grounds for appeal, in particular their status as juveniles,
blood compensation was seen here as the most practical approach
for an appeal.

As we know, however, the court was intransigent and the
struggle to save the lives of the Acholi boys failed. The brothers
were scheduled to be hanged without delay. Aisha was at the
execution. She said the hanging machine would not work properly

and the boys were eventually 'finished with a hammer'. Everyone was distraught, with even the prison staff and other prisoners affected. 'They had tears. Many [prisoners] refused to eat.' Ultimately, all that the activists were able to achieve was to help the family by transporting the bodies back home for burial in Jacob's car. The Acholi boys' execution was one of many injustices Aisha witnessed and reported. Yet she still felt a sense of anguish. When the case failed she said she and Jacob were 'sick completely ... There is not any killing that is honourable it is only God who has that right ... Because we are still in war and people are dying everyday let them at least stop these things'.

There was no public outcry or record of the Acholi boys' death. South Sudan has so many other victims of war and injustice and only a few agencies that are trying keep count and remember the losses.[75] Aisha, Jacob and Godfrey's stand in defence of the Acholi boys' rights and their mourning of the boys' loss count as acts of resistance to a political order which did not value their lives. Warring parties everywhere construct differences between lives that are considered valuable and to be protected and those that do not count and can be killed – usually only subjects with rights are honoured or mourned publicly, and, in feminist philosopher Judith Butler's words, treated as 'grievable lives'.[76] In the amoral logic of South Sudan's political marketplace regime, violence has become instrumentalised to the point that the lives and deaths of ordinary people may be treated as tradeable commodities in the pursuit of power, as Alex de Waal observes.[77] It therefore mattered intrinsically that the activists used their own personal resources to try to prevent the execution and then helped to arrange for the boys to be buried in dignity. They improvised humane responses to deep injustices using the best means available, in a principled rejection of the arbitrary 'rule of man'.[78]

Conclusion

The vignettes of activism in this chapter display the initiatives of lawyers, paralegals and citizen activists to invigorate rights and justice in customary and statutory courts in a time of war. They illustrate that people working voluntarily at the margins of the justice system have sought to construct the emancipatory potential of law out of the ambiguities in South Sudan's laws and legal structures. They have confronted issues that are of central importance in the violent conflict and for future peace, including land rights, women's rights and the right to life and dignity. Law is revealed as a theatre of contestation. It is a source of violations as well as of potential remedies. Legal activism is seen to be an informal activity in which people with a commitment to and education in the law and human rights act in aid of victims of violations. Such work demands particular diligence, creativity and bravery in this harsh environment and, despite considerable efforts, successes appear to be limited, transitory or negligible.

However, there were several commonalities that emerged from these very different and specific instances that indicate a wider, more optimistic, implication. In each case, plural legalities and authorities were involved. The activists engaged a blend of references to international human rights, South Sudan's constitution or statutory law, depending on the issue at hand. They seized upon opportunities presented by legal reforms and human rights interventions inaugurated in the run-up to South Sudan's independence. But what differentiated them from more conventional human rights activists was their appeal to customary law and authority. They consistently engaged respectfully with customary norms and built relationships with chiefly authority in finding solutions. It seems that they sought to draw out the most humane elements of each of the legal regimes they engaged with and to blend them in their responses. In so doing, they suggested an emergent 'vernacular rights culture'[79] and an orientation to resistance, with potential fusions of rights and law from below.

The activists in these accounts lived in a fluid and uncertain environment in which violence and political repression was a constant threat. Nevertheless, they managed to adapt and apply themselves to the changed situation. Their work demanded knowledge and skills as well as conviction. This raises questions about how and where they gained the necessary social, ideational and cultural resources to master and articulate these heterogeneous legal and political languages.

Chapter 5

CITIZENS FOR JUSTICE

South Sudanese forms of 'bottom up resistance and legal innovation'[1] have been isolated and constrained by war and shaped by a unique political and cultural context. As the previous chapter showed, activists seemed to be intent on pragmatic responses to the actualities that prevailed in real time. They worked on the frontline of the violations in striking contrast to idealist future-oriented concerns of peacemaking and transitional justice, which tend to operate at a distance, and on a different clock. They responded as best they could to concrete problems and situations, drawing upon the resources they had to hand, pursuing a trial-and-error exploration of possibilities in the present. This all helps to explain how they went about trying to use the law to respond to violations of human rights, but it does not tell us why.

The activists in question patently expressed concerns about the injustices suffered by others. We might consider this as a universal human impulse and the basis of a theory of justice, as the economist and philosopher Amartya Sen explains: 'What moves us, reasonably enough, is … that there are clearly remediable injustices around us which we want to eliminate.'[2] Yet justice has many meanings and interpretations, and can equally be used to justify very different activities and approaches, including revenge, social repression or patriarchy. This chapter explores the question of how South Sudanese legal activists thought about justice, and what enabled them to use the law to address injustices under these extraordinarily difficult circumstances. It considers their ideas and approaches and explores how these were related to their experiences and identities.

There are some existing insights into human rights, legal consciousness and citizen agency in conflict settings that help to frame and guide this analysis. Feminist political theorist Sumi Madhok has led the way in exploring 'vernacular rights cultures', which she argues represent dynamic and diverse 'sutures' of the 'multiple histories, imaginaries, subjectivities, and contexts' in which rights are formed and activated, together with 'transnational principles, practices, and imaginaries of rights'.[3] Socio-legal theorists Ewick and Sibley have explained that law becomes a tool of resistance when people shake off the notion that it is a preserve of power or a 'reified' set of rules, and instead develop a 'counter-hegemonic legal consciousness', recognising that power and legality circulate in society and can be contested through everyday interactions.[4] And political scientist Jana Krause shows how practical experiences, knowledge, beliefs and social networks are all important explanatory factors in civilian agency in conflict settings.[5] Each of these perspectives informs and resonates with my findings.

Firstly, the chapter explores individual activists' experiences and their attitudes towards the law and community, and how these evolved. It draws on a set of life history interviews, gathered mainly in 2017, and selects from these to present and compare detailed accounts from three individuals.[6] It finds that the activists are all survivors, with direct experiences of violent conflict, displacement, traumatic bereavements and human rights violations. However, they also tend to appreciate the duality of law: they critique it, partly on the basis of personal experiences of injustice, but they also commend it and have a sense of its possibilities. They have sought out and accumulated education including plural forms of legal education, and this has shaped their approach and capacity to act.

Secondly, the chapter considers the relationships among the activists and the extent to which they share agendas and elements of connectedness. It draws on a series of action research forums involving lawyers, community activists, chiefs, as well as a cohort of paralegals associated with the paralegal programmes of the South Sudan Law Society (SSLS), the Community Empowerment for Progress Organisation (CEPO) and Pact South Sudan. The forum discussions indicate shared values and approaches that suggest an emerging justice network, linking people of different ethnicities in horizontal alliances that contrast with the vertical networks of power and patronage that dominated wartime South Sudan. It also finds that the activists are adopting and cultivating vernacular concepts of rights, law and citizenship and shared tactics and approaches based on negotiation.

Survivors

Every single activist interviewed for this book had intimate knowledge of injustice and this seemed to be a crucial factor in shaping their concerns for others: they were acutely aware of the excesses of law enforcement and the costs of violence and forced displacement. Everyone had moved across county or national borders during the current or previous war, attempting to escape conflict and hunger, and to seek access to basic services, including education. Some people had lost one of their parents in the war, two were orphans. Four had been forcibly recruited or briefly abducted as children by the SPLA in separate locations and periods. Two of them fought as child soldiers in the SPLA 'red army'. One was forced to marry at the age of 13 and was a victim of statutory rape.

Several of the activists had formative experiences of the abuses of the justice system under the Khartoum regime. David described how, while he was at school as a refugee in Uganda, his aunt was killed by her husband. The family never managed to bring the matter to court and the memory of that injustice was still devastating. Aisha spoke of the occasion when she was arrested at the age of 18 and detained in the notorious 'white house' barracks in Sudan in the 1990s, accused of sending materials to the rebels because she regularly went to the post office as part of her job. Isaac was arrested when he was 11 years old, beaten with 120 lashes and detained in an adult cell for five days with a violent 'mad person' after he had defended his brother in a fight. He reflected: 'That experience was so crucial to me. That made me start advocating children's rights. I felt I must talk about rights in police custody.' In 2018, Isaac was arrested again and illegally detained in NSS custody in the 'blue house' for several months; his experience highlights the continuum of egregious violations before and after independence.

All the activists had suffered in one way or another from the effects of the civil war since December 2013. Most were directly threatened or lost family and friends in incidents of violence. Given the ethnic discourses of the warring parties, it is worth underlining that participants from diverse backgrounds were affected similarly, although each individual experienced the violence differently, and none of them mentioned these incidents until they were pressed to do so. For instance, a male Nuer paralegal said: 'In 2014 four family members were killed in Nyal [Unity]. In December 2013 I lost my nephews from Gudele [Juba]. We lost a lot. Even 2016, when there was crossfire [in UNMISS PoC] two family members were killed.' A Bari female activist was rescued by her brother in December 2013, and he was killed shortly after: 'In December 2013 ... My brother was in the National Security ... they killed him after two weeks on the other side of Mia Saba, because he took us to his house.' A Dinka paralegal described how she fled the massacre in Bor in which her father and uncle were killed, while her niece and nephews were lost and have not been seen since. An Acholi lawyer spoke about witnessing the July 2016 massacres in Juba: 'There were so many dead bodies ... I thought, how will those be buried? I saw a child being shot.' He also lost community members in a massacre in Pajok in 2017.

In contrast to their common experience of suffering, the activists stood out from the majority of South Sudanese people in that each of them had managed to get a secondary or even tertiary education in a country where the adult literacy rate was under 30%.[7] They had spent much of their lives in and around towns and had grasped at any opportunity for gaining knowledge and skills. There seemed to be a mutual relationship between their sense of injustice and their struggle for legal education, as a paralegal from Nimule explained: 'I took initiative to join training because I know my people were suffering in the area of justice; I experienced this myself.'

To be able to understand how people form their ideas and ambitions for justice and how it relates to their experiences it make sense to trace the trajectories of their lives in detail, showing how they 'navigate in and through their society'.[8] For this reason, the stories of three paralegals – Chotlith, a Nuer from Upper Nile; Awech, a Dinka from Rumbek; and Thon, a Madi from Nimule – are selected from the larger pool of life histories and compared.[9] Each story is distinctive in its own right, and all of the interviews I gathered could equally merit close study; however these three are of comparative value because they were the most different in terms of their spatial and social distance on the national and ethnic map. They can help to show whether there are commonalities and differences in experiences, conceptions of identity and interpretations of law and justice based on locality. The fact that all three are male is indicative of the gender inequalities that prevail, including in access to legal education, which dictated that the vast majority of the 80 lawyers and paralegals I interviewed were young men, and only seven were women.

Awech's story

Awech's family took him to Rumbek town in 1992, as a baby, because fierce battles between southern factions in the second Sudanese civil war had reached their village in Lakes state. Since then, his home area has been regularly devastated by cycles of killing and cattle raiding. The Agaar clan, to which Awech belongs, has lost hundreds of young men as a result of the frequent battles between it and neighbouring groups and the internal fighting among Agaar sections.[10] The raiding has its own self-perpetuating dynamic in a context where cows are the principal means of survival and are essential to customary marriage arrangements.[11] This local system of social reproduction is under constant threat from hunger and deprivation, seasonal water shortages and the resulting contests over rights to grazing land.[12] Local feuding has also been exacerbated by contests for the central state – it intensified after 2013 due to mobilisation for war. The government stands accused of supplying guns to rural youths, and of playing divide-and-rule following presidential decrees that redefined local administrative boundaries, subdividing the 10 former states into 32 new ones.[13] Over time, there have been frequent interventions aimed at brokering peace, and a few positive signs,[14] but there has been no provision for justice, as Awech and his family learned first-hand.

In 2006, Awech's brother was ambushed and killed as an innocent bystander in a 'conflict of clans'. The family tried to seek a prosecution and obtain compensation, but, as Awech explained: 'it was so complicated that the killer could not be identified, and it was just put aside. If the war killed a lot of people, then there will be no compensation and no return of cattle'. He had accepted this painful reality: 'It cannot be settled though I would have loved justice to be done. There is nothing I can do so we just move on.' At the same time, Awech emphasised that the absence of a legal process and any compensation settlement in such conflicts was also fuelling revenge attacks. His relatives in cattle camps were caught up in regular fighting and lost their lives, along with countless other young people: 'I don't know anyone taking initiative to count all these losses.'

It was Awech's education in town that saved him – 'those of us in school are the safe ones' – and he was determined to advance it. In 2007, he sought refuge in Kenya, where he managed to complete his secondary education and since then he has taken every opportunity for learning. He returned for the independence celebrations and managed to find a job as a community organiser in Rumbek for an NGO nutrition programme. At the same time, he began the voluntary work that launched his legal activism.

NPA [Norwegian People's Aid] came with this programme of land awareness, specially on women's land rights. That was the first thing we did; we came together as a group and we formed a local organisation ... We were referring back to the Land Act of 2009 and this made me interested as paralegal; you have to refer to what the land act says ... I used most of my free time ... At first, I was aware a lot of land cases arising even where I live and [people] didn't know where to get help ... I became more interested, I started to understand the conflicts in the justice system, so I did not only focus on land.

Based on a few days' training and some workshops, Awech joined the law society as a volunteer paralegal and then passed on his own training to others. He came to recognise the gap between written law and its practice in local courts, which 'has not improved from what we were using in the old Sudan ... There are a lot of compromises. It depends how the judge is interpreting'. But he also understood the challenges for judges in a context where powerful people sat above the law and chiefs and judges lacked knowledge and resources: 'the judge is aware of what he is doing is to solve the problem, but not with what the law has said'.

While Awech was not able to confront the systematic abuses in the system, he nevertheless saw some connections between his attempts to monitor the law and the problems of both local and national conflict. He intuited that his work might contribute to a larger transformative agenda, since the inconsistencies and abuses of the law were clearly undermining its potency: 'you find that someone is involved in conflict because justice is not done in the court and war is the last option'. He noted that youths in the cattle camps have detached themselves from established forms of regulation, including the chieftaincy and statist concepts of the law: 'no one can control the youth; they don't respect the law; no one will punish them if they do anything wrong'. It seemed that the government routinely neglected the Rumbek Dinka, because it could take their loyalty for granted. He suggested that the rural heartlands of the Dinka have gained little from their support for Dinka powerbrokers at the centre: the beneficiaries of the regime are 'amounting to one per cent and they don't even share with extended family'. They 'assume Rumbek is pro-government place, even if they kill themselves [i.e. fight among themselves] they know that government will come there and [SPLA] IO cannot come there'.

The twin denials of criminal and social justice were, in Awech's account, blocking development in Rumbek, resulting in a situation where 'no one is moving forward'. He faced some hostility to his scrutiny from judicial authorities, concerned that he might 'leak out the system'. But he was convinced that any effort to improve the workings of the justice system was a valuable endeavour: 'Everyone has a story like mine; the more we have a strong system and rule of law this suffering will go; it was my interest to contribute somehow.'

Chotlith's story

Chotlith is from Nasir in Upper Nile state, an area that has been at the epicentre of fighting in successive civil wars.[15] His first memory of warfare was as a young boy in 1990 when he witnessed death and devastation in the bombing of Nasir town (then under SPLA control) by the Khartoum government:

> An Antonov gunship attacked us in Nasir town ... I was with Ruei, Phot and Zuk and their mother and Kang and a visitor were inside with her sister. I was not inside and then I went to their house. I found that the bomb was dropped on part of the house. I found them all dead. And the little boy called Zuk and was hit on his leg and face. He was dusty, but he was still breathing and moving ... everyone was crying but I was not crying. I was just watching like someone surprised. I walked to the neighbour and he called 'you come to me here' and when I found him his leg was destroyed and you could see the bones

hanging on the flesh and told me bring water. I couldn't. I left him I don't know whether he is dead or not up to now and I didn't see him again. And I went to hospital and found that one of the teachers called Gatheke was killed ... I did not cry, but what made me cry more then was a woman. She was shot in the breast and the child was crying wanting to breast feed. Blood and milk mixed, and the baby was wanting to drink it.

Chotlith's family survived the attack, but one of his sisters became ill with a terrible rash within an hour of the bombing, which made the family suspect a chemical attack. Soon after the bombing, the SPLA split into Nasir and Torit factions, precipitating a new phase of warfare between and within local groups. Chotlith experienced the spiralling violence and hunger that ensued.[16] In 1994, when he was 12 years old, his village was attacked by Lou Nuer forces from Jonglei:

They were shooting guns; no one was able to stop them and our men ran away ... We lost many people in this fighting. I remember my headmaster Martin was killed. He was a very committed man who had been teaching us under the tree. He was a man I loved. There were also many others. A woman was shot in front of me. This woman was carrying a baby and it was crying. I just continued running and I could hear the gun. I saw people being killed in front of me.

The family fled to the *toch* flood plains, where they survived on fish and UN food drops; 1994 was devastating year for their community, but it was also a turning point for Chotlith as his father had decided to send him to Malakal. An uncle had offered to support his studies, and his father said: 'I don't want you to grow up here.' Chotlith walked for eight days from Nasir to Malakal to begin his education there.

Reflecting back, Chotlith identifies his father's beliefs and approach to life as determining his own values and career path:

'He is the one who encouraged me to study law or be a priest and through his words I learned that justice is important and how I chose to study law and was admitted in college.' Even as a child, Chotlith was very aware of the prestige that ownership of a gun commanded in his community:

> everyone was trying to have a gun ... The culture of the gun was adopted and when people go for dancing you had to have gun and if you don't have one you look like a weak man. Even those who killed people are more respected than those who don't have guns and those who don't have guns people call them the women. And those who have guns people fear them and women look at them as warriors and heroes.

Yet Chotlith also knew that his father did not subscribe to these views. 'My father never thought of shooting or participating in violence. If I fought with another girl or boy I was always to blame.' His father was a farmer and did not have any formal responsibility for prevention of violence, but he was also a devout Christian and an evangelist, and was unusual in his efforts to discourage his son from fighting and his advocacy for justice in the community:

> My father was talking about justice during the civil war. In my area people were fighting, especially in 1994 between Nuer of Jonglei and us [Jikany Nuer], and our cattle were raided. When the community gathered, my father was called to contribute his view on whether we should declare war on the Nuer of Jonglei. And he said it was a crime according to the Bible. And he suggested that the Nuer of Nasir should collect the cows and give to the Nuer of Jonglei [in the interests of peace]. But my father was isolated. He always contributed to justice. He doesn't believe in fighting ... My father said to fight brings more violence and more suffering; we cannot learn through that.

Over the years, other relatives and friends were caught up in the southern wars – one of his cousins lost his life after he was captured and taken to fight for the forces of the Nuer commander, Paulino Matiep. In contrast, Chotlith managed to continue his studies, supporting himself by working as a labourer in Khartoum in the holidays. By 2008 he knew he wanted to be a lawyer. His first opportunity for training arose when a friend connected him to a prominent civil society activist, Edmund Yakani, who was then running a rule of law promotion programme through the 'justice and confidence centres'. He worked at the centre for a year as a rule of law promoter and paralegal, receiving his first clients there.

Chotlith was still pursuing his legal education and working as a deputy head in his brother's school in Juba when the civil war broke out in December 2013. He was staying with his new wife, together with his brother, sister-in-law and their new-born baby, in a house near the military barracks where the first shots were fired. Chotlith's wife hid under the bed while he phoned friends and family to try to find out the cause of the trouble and make a plan. In the morning, he got a call from his friend James, who informed him that the fighting was not only between security personnel but that civilians in Gudele were also being targeted. No one was sure where they should go, or whether it might be best to hide at home. But when Chotlith called James back later to continue the conversation, a stranger picked up the phone and told Chotlith that 'he is no longer alive, I killed him'.

The family decided to move, despite the intense gunfire. They prayed and then went outside, carrying all their money. Their first thought was to seek protection at the home of a friend who was a soldier in military intelligence. When they reached there, they found him surrounded by a group of Dinka soldiers. Yet they received a warm welcome, and assurances from the men that they were 'proper soldiers'. By the following day, there was more terrible news – Nuer civilians were being systematically targeted and many were on the run. They decided to stock up and stay in the house, but when one of their party went out to get food he was captured and threatened that he would be killed and dumped in the 'big hole near Gumbo' with other Nuer soldiers and civilians. He only escaped by the sheer good fortune that a colleague of his turned out to be among his captors: 'He told him to come out. He told him to throw away your ID card and speak with any other language [not Nuer].' With this shocking evidence, the family realised they must seek refuge at the UN headquarters in Tongping and made a successful appeal to the Dinka soldiers at their friend's house, who had 'claimed to be professional', to help to drive them there. The soldiers agreed and this was how Chotlith and his family became long-term residents of what was to become Juba PoC3.

In the five years that followed the return to civil war, Chotlith worked as a teacher in the PoC. It was there that he was trained as a paralegal and he also managed to graduate as a lawyer from the University of Juba. The decisions that Chotlith took to remain in the PoC and work for education and justice were unusual. A more straightforward route to political activism was to join the opposition. One of Chotlith's brothers defected to the opposition and was killed in fighting in Upper Nile. Chotlith lost 11 close relatives either in massacres or warfare in the period after war broke out in 2013. His narrative did not dwell on these decisions or losses, although he was involved in the organisation of an annual commemoration of the victims on 15 December. His approach was not judgemental but practical – injustices were collective problems to be solved and his own efforts were felt as obligations to his community: 'I just took the risk because of my people.'

Thon's story

Thon was born in Anzara boma, Nimule, in 1980, in a period of relative peace, under the southern regional government. But the second Sudan civil war caught up with him when he was in primary school in Mogali in 1989. Since then he has lived with the turmoil of war and forced displacement: 'up to now my life has been throughout in a war zone'. While many local people fled to the camps in Uganda immediately, Thon's father was determined to stay: 'We stayed in the bush for six months hiding from the soldiers. We could only go to fish and hunt wild animals.' After two years of this hardship, Thon was sent across the border to his uncle's home near Atiak, where he resumed primary education. But this part of northern Uganda was soon overwhelmed by the brutal insurgency of the Lord's Resistance Army (LRA). Thon felt its effects: 'I entered into a terrible situation during the LRA conflict: we could go to sleep in the bush, people were abducted by the LRA, even our teacher was killed. We saw human beings killed by the roadside.' The family fled back to Mogali, but there were troubles there too: 'Life was not easy because the SPLA were abducting young children for war. I was abducted in Nimule, detained for three days and the commander realised I was young and [he] could not take me for war.' The commander advised Thon to go to the refugee camps in northern Uganda, and he agreed to do so.

However, even the refugee camp was not a place of safety. Thon saw other young refugee boys being abducted by the LRA, and also suffered the loss of his mother in this period. But he managed to progress academically. He was awarded a UNHCR scholarship to attend secondary school and spent four years as a boarder. By 2000, he had graduated and returned to the refugee camp, but soon moved on due to food shortages. In 2001, he was caught up in LRA raids on Oluwa refugee settlement camp in Adjumani district. The camp was eventually closed due to attacks on the refugees. Thon continued to apply for educational opportunities and in 2003 he was awarded a scholarship by the Jesuit refugee service to train as a teacher in Gulu. While in college, he witnessed a brutal assault by the LRA: 'I knew many people who died in the conflict. One time when they met in fighting there were many killed.' Around the same time, his father and his sister-in-law were abducted by the LRA. His father was badly beaten and left in a coma; his sister-in-law was held captive by the LRA for five years in the bush before she was rescued.

Thon returned to his native town of Nimule in 2007, two years after the peace deal between the Khartoum government and the SPLM/A. He helped with the registration of other returning refugees and then found employment as a teacher: 'Pay was low, but as a government teacher I was receiving 700 SSP. It was great, by then it could be worth about 300 US dollars per month.' Despite the benefits, he soon noted 'a kind of injustice' in the allocation of posts and scholarships for training within his profession. Former refugees seemed to be placed at a disadvantage: 'They said to us, "during the war we were one suffering here [while] you were in the camp; you wait your time".' Like other members of the Madi community, he was worried about discrimination and landgrabbing within the town. So in 2012 Thon joined the Madi community council, an ethnic association advocating for community development and rights, and was elected as a youth leader. In that role, he found himself at the forefront of contention when a land dispute flared up in 2013, leading to the murder of a chief, the arrest and transfer of some of his colleagues, and generalised repression. By then, he had also joined the group of paralegals trained by the SSLS, and this was his path into legal activism.

By 2017, Nimule was a ghost town. Most of the Madi had returned to the Ugandan refugee camps, including Thon's wife and four children, escaping increased surveillance, arbitrary arrests, attacks by 'unknown gunmen' in the town, and the eruption of war in the surrounding region. From time to time, cases still came to court and Thon sometimes went to observe them, or to visit prisoners. But the Madi community council had dispersed and Thon mainly focused on education. He kept his job in the school and worked in the youth centre, coaching football and encouraging young people to avoid violence. He regularly crossed the border into Uganda to sleep in safety at night, but he felt a duty to continue as deputy head at the secondary school, although the salary by then was irregular, and worth a pittance.

Over the years, Thon was exposed to the influences of the church, customary authorities and community elders, educational institutions and human rights lawyers. He moved across borders in efforts both to escape conflict and to gain further education and training. He attributed his ability to survive, and interact with the law and political authorities, to his access to diverse sources of knowledge and ideas, and to his constructive approach.

> I grew up in the church. This helps the profession I am in and my exposure to the community. Also, the training I had with SSLS – I went to Juba two times and Nairobi. That helped me to build my approach. I want not to hurt anyone but to send a message ... [by] criticising positively and talking generally, not in a way that people could feel offended.

As deputy head and chairperson for discipline in his school, Thon had to apply these skills of negotiation on a routine basis. His task was made more difficult by rising tensions within the school following the spread of the war and the ethnic discourses of the warring parties: 'If you want to discipline [a student], they bring this thing of Equatorian versus Dinka.' The conflict not only affected relationships among students but also their attitudes towards their teachers: 'It went down to the extent that three teachers were beaten in school.' Added to this were complications that the school was now being patrolled by soldiers and some security personnel were enrolled as students. Thon explained how he coped – by building relationships with students, their parents and the security personnel across the ethnic divides:

> I am safe because of the other side. I have a different face in school and community centre, I teach them there and play football. In the eyes of the community they see that I'm helping their children, even if there's false accusation they may back me up. I don't want to dissociate so much ... I feel now that that could be the only way we could make change, if we keep making ourselves distant then the situation could be worse than were we are. So it is better we try to manage it.

In this daily struggle to manage and avert conflict, Thon presented his roles as teacher, youth representative and legal activist as complementary. The skills and knowledge acquired in each of these roles were transferable; serving in one capacity enabled him to forge relationships and networks, gain trust and be effective in other spheres. This social capital was integral to his survival in the town. For instance, he considered leaving with his family when the situation was at its worst: 'Accusations were happening, and many people disappeared in April, May and June [2017]. In August I went to Bweyale [in Uganda] with my family. I stayed for two months.' During this period the school had closed down for lack of teachers and local officials were pleading for them to return, promising that they 'would not be intimidated'. Thon was convinced to return by a government official. Thon still felt that he was at constant risk – he used to regularly cross the Ugandan border to sleep nearby on the other side. He said: 'I personally don't feel secure at night.' But his personal security and his practical ability to move around the town and across borders were aided by his relationships with Dinka pupils and their families at the school. I observed the strength of these social bonds myself when two local *boda boda* drivers in Nimule town offered him lifts and refused to take payment. And he explained that some of the border guards were also willing to wave him through without question or payment because, they said, 'teachers are for everyone'.

Thon described allegiances to both ethnic and civic communities, and despite the fractures of the conflict he did not see these as incompatible. He persisted with his efforts in the educational and legal domains out of a sense of belonging to the place and to the Madi people: 'If all of us have gone there will be nobody who knows information on the ground. Our children will have lost their identity, and no one will tell the story in the future.' But he also described his work for justice as a civic duty: 'I feel being a citizen it is my duty to be a voice for the voiceless and to be exemplary ... We cannot wait; better we act now.' He was socially rooted in Nimule and his Madi identity, but open to ideas and cultural norms from different sources, and to building relations across the ethnic divides in South Sudan.

Shared experiences

All the activists had been directly affected by the horrors of conflict and by the failure of the justice system. Yet they presented their experiences as ordinary matters. They were part of the realities of life in a country where the average citizen has survived repeated traumatic events.[17] No one spoke of their suffering openly, and they generally did not speak at length. Instead, they mentioned events such as bereavements, threats, abductions, rape and forced displacement without elaboration. Even the death of a loved one tended to be mentioned only 'in passing' in South Sudan.[18] Physical and economic insecurity was a constant for all of them. But they had also developed strategies to survive in the conflict arena. Awech depended on his connections to schooling and urban life to avoid being drawn into clan wars. Chotlith's life was saved thanks to his connections with a friend in military intelligence, while his everyday legal activism in the PoC required strong, positive relationships with the chieftaincy. Thon relied on forging positive relationships with his Dinka students, their families and security personnel at the school, and on respect for his status as a teacher.

The activists' knowledge of the law and ideas about justice was assembled from various sources and encounters. They were shaped by familial, religious and educational influences and by cultural and geographic mobility. They were used to cross social and geographical boundaries, from village to refugee camp to town; into neighbouring regions or countries; in and out of different educational spheres and jobs. None of them were in a stable situation, but they typically had both paid and voluntary jobs and academic qualifications. Many worked as teachers, which provided a small income, but this was not always regular. They were staunch members of their ethnic groups, in these three cases Dinka, Nuer and Madi, but also had plural affiliations as teachers, paralegals, refugees or IDPs. They spoke of a sense of duty to work for their communities based upon a very concrete understanding of a shared predicament.

Justice networks

We now look beyond the individuals or small groups engaged at community level, and towards the growing and potential linkages among activists. In the first place, there are not many of them, since the cadre of lawyers and paralegals in South Sudan is small. There were fewer than 100 lawyers registered with the South Sudan Law Society and some 200 members of the Bar Association before the war.[19] The war forced most of them into the largest towns, or into exile. As a high court judge reported:

> If you go to Raja now, there is no lawyer, the whole of Rumbek east is without a lawyer. In Minkamann there [are] no lawyers. We are lacking lawyers even within the towns. In Bentiu town there were only two before the crisis. In Torit there were a few; in Kapoeta, none.[20]

To supplement the lawyers, national and international organisations established various paralegal programmes providing hundreds of educated young people, usually men, with a basic training in the law. They encouraged participants to work in informal advisory roles in the community and to advocate for human rights. Pact South Sudan began this work as early as in 2002, then expanded its programme in the years that followed.[21] The International Rescue Committee (IRC) and UNDP stepped in around 2003 to fund 'justice and confidence centres' across Sudan, including in Juba, Malakal and Wau. After 2010, CEPO took up some of this work,[22] and the UNDP established its own programmes.[23] The SSLS trained some 280 paralegals as part of its access to justice programme in 2015.[24] But the work of the courts was suspended in some localities and periods, some paralegals fled, and funding for paralegal training programmes declined.[25] We do not know how many were left during the war, and without support or further training many may not have continued this work. However, some did clearly did continue to try.[26]

My research for JSRP involved and paralegals in a series of action research forums, with support from SSLS, CEPO and Justice Africa, between 2014 and 2017. These events included participants from the towns of Torit, Nimule, Rumbek, Yei, Wau, Yambio, Juba town and Juba UNMISS PoC. The forums were designed to enable paralegals and lawyers to share knowledge and experiences, to reflect critically on the administration of justice, and to support a collaborative research exercise documenting court cases.[27] Over time I also interacted with a wider pool of activists. These meetings supplemented the life history interviews as a window onto relationships between activists from different localities and ethnic groups. They helped to establish the extent to which they had common interests, commitments and values that might qualify them as an existing or potential network.[28]

The meetings indicated a sense of mutual understanding of the problems, their causes, and a shared mission that transcended obvious differences. The participants from different localities and ethnic groups, alongside the conflict dynamics, meant that ethnicity was treated as a political marker of support for either the government or the opposition. Regardless of beliefs, people were 'tagged'.[29] This might have made participants in the forums wary of discussing the politics of the conflict, but it did not prevent them from speaking out and finding common ground on the failings of the justice system and the injustices experienced by ordinary people. As one participant argued:

> If we want to advocate for justice we need to find out exactly what is going on. People are in need of justice … We need to compare how those chiefs of Wau do handle cases and how the chiefs of Torit do handle cases. From there you will be able to

fix the national agenda and educate about the rights of women
… I want to take South Sudan to the position that all the people
are living without discrimination. People need to talk and know
each other.

In this spirit, the activists dissected the problems of courts, police
and prisons. The customary courts, explained one paralegal
from Juba, 'contradict the constitution', especially with regard to
women's rights. The decisions of the court were too easily swayed
by 'vocal' complainants: 'normally the accuser … wins the case'.
Statutory cases, they all agreed, dragged on 'without end'. But they
also deplored the 'lack of respect of the courts', which meant that
even if a just settlement could be achieved, there was no guarantee
of implementation. They gave examples of threats and extortion. Several paralegals had been asked to find the funds to feed a
prisoner or to pay police 'facilitation' money to enable an arrest. In
one egregious case, a woman activist was threatened by the police
and commanded to pay 30,000 SSP as 'blood compensation' when
she managed to secure the release of a detainee who had been falsely
accused of murder.

They also agreed on the fundamental political obstacles. A
paralegal from Torit observed: 'Rule of law requires government to
be subject to the law not law subject to government. But government will not be called to the court; they will not be prosecuted.'
In a similar vein, an activist from Melijo IDP camp referred to the
impossibility of dealing with cases involving military and political elites: 'Superpower is the one thing we face.' Activists spoke
of cases of people being arrested at night and taken to the military
barracks: 'When you try to make follow-up you are told you will also
be arrested.' It emerged that even one of the original paralegal team
was now under detention. His colleague explained: 'When I tried
to mention it, I was told it was a security issue I should not tamper
with.' The chiefs faced a similar issue: 'People don't respect us when
we're doing our work … We have no guards … the soldiers interfere

in our work. I have been arrested by soldiers and taken to the detention facility, the situation was horrible.'

In the forums, activists presented themselves as both adher-
ents and critics of the law, finding commonalities that transcended
ethnic and political ties. They agreed upon the nature and sources
of injustices and upon the need to respond. They also saw the value
of collective enterprise in order to counteract persistent inequalities
and discrimination on a national scale, despite the political turmoil
in their fractured state. They saw themselves as part of the solution.

Volunteers for the community

The activists took it for granted that they would freely give their own
time to work for the common good. This was a badge of honour. A
handful of those interviewed had paid jobs in a civil society organisation, or earned money as a lawyer, but undertook voluntary work on
the side. A lawyer employed at SSLS explained that he had left a more
lucrative post in an international organisation to join the law society
at 'three times less than my original salary'. Most of the activists
worked purely on a voluntary basis as paralegals or pro-bono lawyers,
and some had formed voluntary community associations. A paralegal
who had formed his own local community human rights organisation, staffed by community volunteers, acknowledged that the work
had taken a toll on his personal life but he was ready to continue:

> People think I'm paid for the things I do. They don't understand
> the voluntary work. There was a time I wasn't eating ... Some
> people mocked me for working for them for free but I'm doing
> it for the community. I was doing it at the cost of my family.

Similarly, a women activist described how she worked in several
voluntary positions, and used her own money to support this:

> I have been working without pay. We have houses for rent in
> Juba and using that money to help orphans. My parents had

these houses and gave those to me and people rent those houses … we are surviving on this money.

No doubt, some individuals also perceived their voluntary work as a step towards a career in a national or international NGO or towards a future career in the public sector or government. Some of the activists did speak about their hopes of getting a job in a related field. In some cases, voluntary activism had already yielded some paid work, including for a period as researchers for the court monitoring project described earlier. Isaac spoke of a short stint of paid work assisting UNMISS with human rights training, and Aisha said she hoped to find a paid position advocating for women's rights with UNMISS. Both of them, though, freely and regularly provided information to UNMISS about human rights abuses – information they gathered and shared at personal risk. Above all, altruism and independent initiative were highly valued. For instance, Isaac spoke of his admiration for Aisha: 'If there is a Christian paradise then surely she will be there.'

This autonomous voluntary work was revered, in contrast to paid positions within government, the public sector or in NGOs, which several activists had held at one time or another. They described problems in each of these sectors. A few had seen corruption and abuse of office in the upper echelons of power at close range. One worked in a logistical role on a programme for the president's office and recalled witnessing the theft of US$40,000 of public funds: 'You cannot say [anything] against the cousins of the president. I made my report, and after they remove that out and they take the money. So, I went for leave and then I didn't return to that job.' Another was chairperson of the trade union while working for an international NGO in Juba in 2012. He said he raised a complaint about the practice of paying non-nationals higher salaries than the nationals, but it was ignored, and he left in protest. A third described how his salary as head of a school had suddenly been cut to a lower pay grade with no explanation. When he complained, he was sacked and had to find work as a casual labourer. However, his interest and training in the law helped him to bring his own successful case: 'I wrote to the Public Prosecutor with the intention to sue the Minister of Education. He advised them to either deny the allegation or solve my issues. They returned me to my job and my grade was restored in 2015.'

The activists were all committed to community service. Several of them also held elected positions in other voluntary roles such as community youth leader or women's representative, and some were either already chiefs or had been proposed to stand as a chief. Each of these roles was voluntary, or in the case of chiefs lowly and irregularly paid, but they were highly regarded as emblems of service to and respect from the community.[30] My observations suggest the activists were warmly received and esteemed by the communities they sought to support.[31] It seemed that what drove and sustained them was the fact that they were building relationships of respect, trust and solidarity within their communities, and increasingly with each other.

Advocates for change

In the forum discussions, the participants compiled a record of struggle, with only occasional achievements, usually on individual cases. They also achieved rare examples of a wider change in practice. For instance, a paralegal from Yambio felt that his presence at the courts provided scrutiny and improved their conduct: 'It may give much work for the judge if he is not presiding well over the cases. That will make them accountable.' An activist from Nimule spoke of an initiative to improve the flow of information within the justice system; he had been asked by the judge to track and report back on cases that had been referred to the customary courts. The gains were generally small-scale and tentative, but this did not appear to affect their willingness to continue and their firm commitment. It was clear that it was not only immediate legal victories or political change that motivated them. Rather, they also sought social transformation.

This normative project, or moral agenda, is expressed in the parable a paralegal shared about a man who went to the bush with his son and his dog to kill a beast. Along the way the pair ran out of water, so the man left his son to search for more, but while he was gone, the beast found the boy and attacked him. The dog fought off the beast 'seriously', saving the boy's life, allowing him to escape. When the man came back he found only the dog and the dead beast. After searching for his son for just five minutes he thought he must be dead, so he blamed the dog, and killed him. When the son came back he was angry with his father, asking him why did you kill the dog? The moral of the tale was transparent. His account emphasised not only the value of reasoned judgment for each person, but also his sense of obligation to promote this kind of careful analysis within his community.

> Our community, they can do something before they analyse things ... You may kill somebody. My contribution is to give them to know about how to analyse things, to encourage them to think more about the problem before they take action.

Other activists agreed on this need to attend to the welfare of a group of people beyond themselves and their families. This was core to their definition of justice, even if they used different language, and the boundaries of their concern were not always clear. On the whole, they were less interested in specifying which laws should apply, among the inconsistent plethora available to the South Sudanese courts, than they were with finding humane solutions to disputes and conflicts as they occurred. A paralegal from Yei described the task of securing justice as a process of restoring humanity:

> We are all human beings, but attitudes differ. It comes from how you position yourself. What we are trying to do is to try to understand what happened and how it happened and how we can go about that. When we talk about justice, what we

are looking for exactly is that we want to mend broken relationships that happened based on people's misunderstanding perceiving one another from another angle, from seeing someone in a subhuman way.

There were political dimensions to their agendas which were articulated most powerfully by a paralegal from Torit:

> If citizens could really say 'enough is enough'. People are just dying ... if we are to be killed all, we could just demonstrate. Mobilise enough; let us make history. This is now unbecoming. People don't have voices to say anything. [Some] people are now getting more richer and others suffering as victims ... When are we going to come up as citizens and voice our voices?

Activists spoke of their motivations to 'take care of people in my country in the future'; or to 'encourage the youth that we come together and talk together and make reconciliation, so we can live and open a new state'. They emphasised persistent inequalities that subjugated 'the common person' and generally made them 'victims' of law and authority.

The struggle for justice was conceptualised as a long-term project and their role in it as a civic duty. They were clearly reflecting on the need to find ways to end the conflict, but were looking beyond political elites to find them. Change needed to take place within the justice system and the community and they felt they could play a part in this. In the words of a paralegal from Melijo, change would require: 'a serious commitment from the citizens of the country ... We are ever calling for peace; but peace will not come when we don't make it ... To be a good person you start from your home and it goes out. You can extend it to other people.'

The forum discussions revealed that legal activists were working in most of the main towns of South Sudan during the conflict with similar aims and values. Their focus was on specific cases within their communities, but they presented this as part of an agenda for social and political transformation in the future. As one paralegal expressed it: 'We will make positive things ... this will not come in short time or free of charge; we will have to pay a high price for that.' Activists from different localities had overlapping concerns and a common vision of injustices. They encouraged each other to continue their efforts, recognising that these needed to be collective and cumulative. As one participant concluded: 'Activism is not easy ... We have to stand tall and talk about those things that are affecting our community and then there will be change ... It does not come [at] once.'

Conclusion

This chapter finds commonalities in the legal activists' ideas and experiences. Their ideas about law and power, and the relations between them; their 'legal consciousness' was both critical and engaged. By virtue of their personal suffering at the hands of the law they were acutely aware of the dysfunctions, tensions and contradictions within the justice system. But they also understood that law was more than a set of rules associated with power. Their legal education and knowledge of plural sources of law enabled them to see possibilities for the pursuit of justice by means of law. They had accumulated plural cultural resources and practical skills that could enable them to act on their determination to combat injustice for themselves and others. They understood law as a site of 'contest and struggle',[32] and sought to equip themselves to engage effectively in this arena.

There is certainly reason to believe that active citizenship has been 'fragmented' by the conflict in South Sudan, but my research dispels fears that it has entirely 'collapsed'.[33] By definition, the participants were outliers, including because they had access to secondary and sometimes tertiary education and training in various forms of law. They were also individuals with multiple identities and allegiances and accustomed to engaging with international humanitarian and human rights activists and adjusting their linguistic

and normative registers accordingly. But they consistently emphasised the high value they placed on their citizenship and espoused a
commitment 'to the public good'. And this commitment was being
routinely translated into practical action. Not only did they work
voluntarily but they also valued this autonomy highly, in themselves
and each other, and they asserted it as a source of dignity. The
forums revealed the willingness of activists of diverse backgrounds
to work together across the ethnic and social divides marked out
by the conflict and to collaborate in projects towards legal and
normative change. They indicated the emergence and potential of
a network of citizen activists with shared values and commitments
to work for justice.

The activists clearly spoke about and acted on issues of rights and
law from the perspective of concrete locations and practical experiences at the margins. But their struggles diverge from the 'vernacular
rights' struggles identified in other postcolonial contexts in the global
South. They expressed shared values and commitments to humanity,
to the nation, and to their particular communities, drawing on a
multicultural blend of conceptions of rights and law. They recognised that threats, vulnerabilities and injustices were the shared
conditions of life in South Sudan. However, they were not part of a
social movement; they did not articulate a coherent agenda for political change; and they had not developed 'legal strategies'.[34] Instead
they were responsive to concrete violations as they arose, and they
offered modest and pragmatic tactical responses to injustice, rooted
in a sense of social need, interdependence and mutuality, which
Francis B. Nyamnjoh has defined, and celebrated, as 'conviviality'.
In 'cosmopolitan' urban contexts, and under conditions of violence
and uncertainty, he observes, 'frontier Africans' live with contingency, interdependence and 'incompleteness'. They forge 'tactical
alliances informed by mutual needs and aspirations'; they cultivate
social networks of 'cooperation' and relationships defined by 'negotiation'.[35] For the South Sudanese activists, such flexible 'convivial'
approaches were not a matter of choice, but of survival.

Chapter 6

BROKERING SURVIVAL

People working for justice need a multiplicity of skills, resources and tactics to survive in South Sudan. This chapter examines their methods. It explores the threats that legal activists confront, and the tactics they have developed in response. Civil society activist Edmund Yakani captured something of their general orientation when he described his work as 'bargaining on behalf of the citizens',[1] but the stakes are extraordinarily high. It is hard to imagine a more inhospitable environment in which to try to secure basic rights, let alone try to effect legal and political change. Unpredictable, opaque and shifting threats can emanate from various sources in an unstable and fragmented state. In this context, assisting victims of injustice, and indeed simply surviving as an activist, requires fostering extensive and diverse social connections, including relationships with powerful allies, as well as cultivating deep cultural understandings and knowledge of the laws.

In some ways, the predicament of South Sudanese activists will be familiar to those who work in and study other African countries characterised by hybridity, where plural, unstable and competing forms of public authorities rule.[2] The responses are also similar; people find inventive ways to forge relationships across social and institutional boundaries; they adjust approaches according to the situation and develop 'contradictory modalities of getting things done'.[3] To make a difference, people cross categorical and institutional boundaries and are flexible and responsive, exploiting possibilities for exercising agency at the interstices of power. This fluidity makes it especially difficult to sustain social movements that can challenge intransigent and violent regimes, and activists are vulnerable to co-optation into power, to the pursuit of personalised agendas, and to collusion with violent forms of order-making.[4] People rely on heterogeneous norms and identities to act in multiple public spheres, as political theorist Achille Mbembe observes. They learn 'to bargain in this conceptual market place ... [and] to manage not just a single identity for themselves but several, which are flexible enough for them to negotiate'.[5] Those with access to material resources are best placed to do so, but good information and networks are also essential: 'the more affluent, the better connected and the more knowledgeable tend to have the upper hand'.[6]

South Sudan's legal activists need to be adaptable and tactical in order to reckon with the complex problems of legal, social and economic uncertainty, plural authorities and threats from a government and society that was mobilised for war.[7] The struggle for justice has turned out to be its own particular 'type of war'.[8] In a memorable speech at a forum in Juba in July 2015, a prominent high court judge bluntly laid out the issues and paid tribute to the group of assembled paralegals and human rights lawyers:

> Your life may be at risk from powerful individuals. It is a government of chaos and injustices. The government has forgotten its mission and vision ... It's not an easy job to be a paralegal, or human rights activist; you may die at any time. You are martyrs of building this nation. Be ready for that and God will bless.[9]

In the sections to follow, the risks experienced by activists based on life histories, interviews and their contributions to action research forums are explored, along with patterns in their attempts to manage them. The focus here is on experiences during the period of the war, when the problems intensified, but it is worth emphasising that many activists had experienced similar problems prior to this period and some had developed their methods long before the war broke out. A few had been active under the Khartoum regime and it was there that they had learned the art of manoeuvre. Indeed, Sudan served as a baptism of fire for activists, since the Khartoum regime was exceptionally restrictive, especially so for southerners. To act in the public interest, Yakani recalled, it became essential to innovate, avoid confrontation and 'infiltrate', finding partners within the regime in what he labelled 'political entrepreneurship ... mobilising allies within your enemies' constituencies'.[10]

Legal activism did not begin with the war, and it looked set to continue in a similar vein thereafter. It is of course not the only form of civic struggle underway, and runs parallel to or intersects with advocacy aimed at securing peace; or the practical initiatives to sustain civil society, such as those of church leaders, academics and teachers. But it is distinctive in its explicit focus on engaging and transforming law, an endeavour which is defined by long-term horizons and holds out the possibility of transforming structures. Beyond this, activists do not seem to have consistent strategies or organisational platforms, as the previous chapter showed. Instead they have tactics defined by negotiation and orientations towards a social network-based, 'convivial' approach.[11] This approach is not only relevant to trying to work against injustices in particular cases, but also a means towards personal survival. Activists need to foster diverse alliances, to call upon the law and social ties, and to gather an eclectic store of legal and cultural knowledge for their own protection and to assist others. They leverage social and cultural forms of capital, and the symbolic capital of the law, in order to sustain themselves in forms of resistance to power.

Survival tactics

War and displacement have marked activists' biographies and life chances and define the context in which they operate. All of the research participants were affected directly by the civil war in one way or another, as the examples in Chapter 5 illustrated. But they also faced specific hazards as a result of their activism during the civil war. Legal activists experienced the impacts of repression and violence in the same way as other South Sudanese civilians and were conscious of this shared precarity. As one of my interviewees explained, war 'is something that has happened not only to one person, but to everyone'. Violent conflict has also persisted for so long that many people are accustomed to regular disruptions and threats: 'life has always been in a warzone'. The life histories I collected provided overwhelming evidence of this, to the point that it is impossible to capture all the troubling and traumatic instances they raised.

Most of the activists, at one time or another, were intimidated, threatened or harmed. All had to devise strategies to protect themselves or others within their networks. At the same time, they were striving to promote the welfare and survival of others. There was an implicit reciprocity in this, although no one described it as such. The activists used similar tactics to protect themselves as they did for others, focusing on building good relationships in all the spheres in which they worked. In turn, these relationships encouraged solidarity and sometimes even helped to protect them. The severity of the threats and the ways that people responded to them varied, depending on their localities, identities and commitments. My interviewees were a diverse group: mostly paralegals, with some professionally trained lawyers, and a few were elected as community representatives, with varying degrees of legal training. Those further up the legal or social ladder managed to air their criticisms publicly to a greater degree and had also developed wider strategies and relationships that helped them manage the risk. The better positioned activists were often also part of the network that the less well-established activists could call upon in difficult circumstances.

Whatever their locality or status, activists felt that they were being routinely monitored and had examples to prove it. They relied heavily on their mobile phones as a means of communication, information and networking on social media. But the government had purchased the technology to tap phones and national security was using it liberally. Eventually an important court of appeal case in May 2017 declared the practice 'unconstitutional', but most of my research was before this and it is not clear whether the authorities acted upon it thereafter.[12] Many activists mentioned receiving strange calls, messages or direct threats on their mobile phones. One also described how his camera and computer were confiscated and released later after some of their contents had been deleted.

As the conflict continued, especially after 2015, activists increasingly complained that they had 'no freedom' to meet in groups and organise, since any civil society meeting had to be approved by the security services. They felt they were under surveillance, not only from government officials and security services, but also potentially from anyone within their communities, or in organised civil society, who may be reporting on them. They explained that 'the government has spies; people fear each other and are losing trust'. There was a sense that people might turn on each other for different reasons, political or personal. This monitoring was corrosive, limiting spaces for public deliberation and impeding collective action; trust was constantly being eroded.

A number of activists were directly threatened or abused at the hands of government soldiers, national security operatives or armed men whose identity was unclear during the research period.[13] A female activist in Juba described how she was detained and tortured for several days after she witnessed the murder of three people just outside her house. She had been seen taking photos of their corpses for documentation purposes:

At the prison they asked why I took the photos. I told them: 'I had right to take photos. Why did you kill?' And then they tortured me for three days. They bent the fingers back and hurt my wrists and knocked my head against the wall.[14]

Other activists also reported similar incidents involving detention or violence. For instance, a paralegal in Wau was held in detention for several days; three lawyers or paralegals were directly threatened with a gun put to their head either by a soldier or armed civilian at one time or another; and several community activists were taken to military barracks or prisons where they described being 'flogged', or receiving cuts to their ears, among other human rights violations.

My interviewees tended to describe the threats in matter-of-fact accounts and to carry on with their work pragmatically. Isaac commented that: 'someone harassed me on the way home putting a gun to my head. My work put me in a dangerous place'. Steve was detained, threatened and displaced, but still returned to work in his home town, explaining: 'My life is a free gift; if I give it for a bigger cause, then there is no problem.' Hardly any of the activists identified the individual perpetrators or mentioned pursuit of justice for the crimes committed against them. Rather they hoped for better times in which other steps might be taken, as a paralegal from Yei observed: 'the situation is not permanent; we may get a better administration'. In the meantime, they tried to build a store of information and powerful connections that could help them to respond. Jacob described how he handled an attempt to intimidate him:

> Someone sent a text message saying 'I will kill you' and that's when [my colleague] received calls threatening his life. We had a meeting with the management with SSLS and we met the Dutch embassy and told them the situation. We took the stand that we will not leave the country ... [We also explained to the] Non-Violent Peaceforce and Open Society Institute and UNDP. I said [to my colleague:] let me go to national security and talk to them in case they have problem with you. We had a nice meeting with them. I explained to them situation and what I actually do; and said I don't want to run out of the country. They said we don't have any problem with you and we aren't looking for you. I asked how about this message and can they investigate the source? But nothing much happened.[15]

The situation was so radically unstable partly because of such inconsistencies. The administration itself included different factions, as well as some officials who were trying to do their jobs effectively. Threats might come from diverse sources, government officials and security operatives, armed civilians or rebels. Meanwhile, straightforward efforts to prevent injustices or uphold the law could easily inadvertently challenge the interests of powerful political and military elites and produce a backlash, as the experiences of a lawyer from Yambio illustrate. The lawyer had been appointed to chair a land disputes tribunal in 2016, when the town was fairly peaceful, and for a few months they were working quite effectively. However, in May 2016 a case was brought to the tribunal relating to a prime plot of land along the town's main road. It turned out that the dispute was between a military commander and a civilian; there was no evidence of the military officer's claim, while the actual owner presented a lease issued in 1989, which was deemed by the tribunal to be legitimate. As soon as the commander lost the case, he began to mobilise against the tribunal. He started by threatening the local commissioner, a member of the tribunal, and within two days he had arranged for the commissioner to be fired by the governor. Immediately afterwards, the lawyer was attacked and injured in his home at night, while getting ready for bed.

> I saw someone with a veiled face like a ninja. I just saw the barrel of gun. I started screaming. I dived inside the house. We went into the room; my wife was there with small kid. I cried; I fell between two beds, my wife's and mine, and then I was screaming. He stood at the door and said (in Arabic) 'your work has finished today' and he released three bullets. He was aiming at my head. Then five bullets. It hit my hand and I was shot; my wife was on bed and light was on. Then I fell down and kept quiet; he thought he blasted my head and I could not talk anymore.

The gunman fled, and the lawyer was successfully treated for his physical injuries, but he and his family were left severely traumatised. He pushed for an investigation and the mayor and the police seemed supportive in this. The commander was still in town. However, no one was arrested. After that, the land tribunal collapsed when its other members were too afraid to 'expose themselves'. Later on, the doctor who had treated the lawyer for his bullet wounds was killed. The lawyer felt his life was constantly at risk and he eventually left for a refugee camp in Uganda.

It seemed that any citizen activist who challenged the political or personal interests of the military and political 'kleptocracy' might be vulnerable to violence. The fear of being targeted preceded the war, and was fuelled by the assassination of the outspoken investigative journalist Isaiah Abraham by 'unidentified men' in December 2012.[16] Reports of attacks by so-called 'unknown gunmen' escalated during the war, and among the victims was human rights activist Emmanuel Wani, who was killed a week after he briefed a United Nations Security Council delegation about human rights abuses.[17] Speculation was rife that such attacks were the work of 'government operatives'. But there were no investigations or prosecutions to prove this. However, there was strong and clear evidence that the instruments of the security services and of arbitrary detention were being used systematically to crush dissent, as discussed in Chapter 2.

While some lawyers tried to respond to the arbitrary detentions of activists formally through the courts, often without success, citizen activists, including chiefs and community leaders, were also employing local forms of humanitarian negotiation, using back-channels to try to secure prisoner releases. We can better understand this approach, and its potential to deliver results, through an example of the illegal detention and torture of a community leader, the deputy *Loprigo*[18] of the Madi community. The deputy *Loprigo* was a citizen activist on land rights issues. He was picked up by soldiers in January 2015, during a wave of government repression against 'suspected rebels' and was held for four months in horrendous conditions. He was taken first to military barracks in the town of Nimule but later was moved to the 'white house' detention centre in Juba. Much of his detention was spent in an underground pit. He described this as a prolonged form of torture and deprivation, which some of his fellow prisoners did not survive:

> There were holes four or five metres deep like a latrine, or septic tank; they will push you in … They gave you one bottle of water per day, like a cup of water. It was fetched from river Nile not treated. At 10pm you got water 1pm food – we ate *posho* [maize meal] without sauce … In prison seven brothers [fellow prisoners] died. Three Nuer were others Equatorian, one Dinka … Every time you are moving death is not far from you.

However, after four months in these conditions, the deputy *Loprigo* was eventually released due to the consistent and prolonged efforts of Madi community leaders to negotiate on his behalf. They mobilised all their contacts and eventually secured a meeting with the head of military intelligence. In that meeting they were able to convince him that there was no case to answer and to negotiate the deputy *Loprigo*'s release. Indeed, they were even offered an apology. The deputy *Loprigo* fled to Uganda soon afterwards. He was deeply traumatised and scarred; the torture had left him with physical injuries and problems with his sight.[19] Nevertheless, the case illustrates the use and efficacy of networking and negotiation.

Another case in point is that of a human rights lawyer in Juba who was forced to flee in January 2018 after he provided legal aid to a woman involved in a land dispute against a high-ranking military officer. The day after the court case he realised he was being was followed by a car and saw that the men in the car were armed with rifles. He suspected they were from the national security. He managed to reach an embassy, abandoned his car and fled on a motorbike. In the hours that followed, the lawyer searched for information and contacts that could help him. He turned to a friend in government with connections inside the national security service; through them, the lawyer learned that an order had been sent to target him in order to undermine his client in the court case. Yet it also emerged that some members of the NSS were opposed to the move. Ultimately, the lawyer was able to mobilise influential allies – including a governor, and high-ranking member of the national security – and others in his social network for support. This rapidly and informally constituted network then arranged for him to be evacuated the same night. One of the other human rights lawyers provided a car, while allies in the national security and armed soldiers accompanied the lawyer for protection across the Ugandan border in a convoy of two cars. The lawyer relied on connections he had made through his work, and his reputation for helping people of various backgrounds in court, in order to secure his escape.[20]

Mobility was also essential to survival; many activists were forced to flee South Sudan during the research period either temporarily or for a prolonged period, usually to refugee camps or to towns in the region, Kampala, Cairo or Nairobi. But threats could also emerge in these places of refuge. The case of Dong Samuel Luak, a human rights activist abducted in Kenya, discussed in Chapter 2, was one stark example. Another more fortunate activist described how he managed to escape an attempted kidnap in Kampala: 'I was in a tea shop [in Kampala]. They came with three cars. They told me I'm a threat to national security. They grabbed me and told me to enter the car.' The activist's friend called the Ugandan police, who intervened to stop the kidnap, and revealed that the would-be abductors held ID cards identifying them as officers from the South Sudan embassy.[21]

Activists were constantly vulnerable to threats and violence, but reliant upon their social connections and tactics of persuasion and negotiation, rather than advocacy and confrontation, to respond. They exploited splits and tensions within the institutions at the heart of 'the system' and found individuals inside who were willing to covertly assist individuals on a personal level.

Networking and negotiation

Fostering and leveraging social connections with heterogeneous political authorities, and people from different backgrounds, was crucial both to the self-protection of activists and to their agenda of using and influencing the law to combat injustices. They fostered connections with religious leaders, and with international organisations or 'foreign officials with clout'.[22] They also cultivated linkages to customary authorities and elders; as one activist put it, 'to solve problems you need the relationship with the chief'.[23] Government officials or security actors 'in the system' could make for especially powerful allies. Many could name people in an array of positions within the government who had helped them on occasion, warning them of threats or identifying people in need of their assistance. They emphasised that there were some good people 'in the system' who 'don't want to harm you. They just need to inform you'.

Activists had to move with discretion and caution and try to find ways to tap into trust networks. There were administrative muddles and divisions within the institutions that could be exploited and religious and familial connections could also help to influence decisions. A Madi civil society activist explained how she helped on a number of occasions when a member of their community had been illegally detained in the barracks, where there was no point in trying to secure a lawyer's visit and other methods had to be found.

> We tried to see who we should meet and talk to and carefully find people we know to go through them. My husband was able to go with the arrest warrant that was issued by the police to get to the security office. He went with a bishop who happened to be from Dinka tribe. He has weight in such a place and knows other people. He was able to go there with my husband and meet the deputy director general for security to find that he had no idea to find that such case had been brought … There was no file opened for them, no written case … They were stressing and torturing

people, wasting government resources for no reason. If follow up is not done, they could just die there. In the higher offices they don't know; and these are junior and medium ranks …

It is individual courage to really move when some of these arrests happen. What we usually do is that the information snowballs around and we talk to people individually to get to a certain level. If I know someone in the office … you have to build trust. If you are someone who doesn't command respect, people may not take you seriously. You extend your network outside of your community. We have forever done that by going through Dinka friends; they do have their own network.[24]

A paralegal and youth leader from Yei described a similar initiative to extract youths accused of 'being rebels' from military custody, using influential allies. Sway with the relevant authorities enabled them to access the barracks, and after that they used monetary resources to 'bail' the detainees out of custody, despite the fact that there had been no investigation, charges or trial:

The commissioner on the ground he will give us the authorisation to go the barracks … when they [the commissioner and other government officials] are the ones who go to the military barracks the military always tell them these youth are suspected to be rebels so they also think it might be true statement … But [when we went] the army will ask for money, come and pay and take your boy and he will report here every day, and he is given a time to report to MI [military intelligence] after they have taken your money.

In the confusion about authority and in an atmosphere of uncertainty, activists seized chances to garner assistance from influential individuals who were 'not happy with what is happening' and wanted to 'contribute to the work' the activists were doing. Some of these connections were based on ethnicity or kinship ties, others were attributable to solidarity and friendship. The motives and behaviour of the unexpected allies who provided covert support were not always honourable, but the activists took a practical view on the need for their support: 'We cannot succeed without involving people responsible for human rights violations.' They were ready to work with 'sympathisers within the system'.[25]

More generally, activists were quiet about their own political allegiances. They undoubtedly held opinions, but I did not probe and they did not declare them voluntarily. They carefully distinguished between the ongoing political competition and their work in the legal field. They seemed to walk a tightrope. Many had relatives, friends or peers working in government, or fighting in the opposition forces, or both. They had also lost relatives or friends in political violence and suffered from intimidation or displacement themselves. They tended to express sympathy for the predicament of foot-soldiers on both sides, blaming their lack of access to education, or suggesting that 'people are fighting … [because they are] lost and confused and traumatised'. One activist was unusually outspoken in his belief that rebels were fighting against oppression: 'They don't have rights, you don't have a say and when you talk of it you're taken for prison … You're accused of what you have not done – that makes them go in the bush. We look at it is correct.'[26] Most explicitly positioned themselves in opposition to 'the system' rather than particular warring parties or ethnic groups.

At the same time, the activists seized on any opportunities for relationships, support or training with international organisations that could also help them to leverage social power. One activist gave an example of how he was trained by UNMISS and had gained knowledge, opportunities and social connections as a result. On one occasion he was called upon to participate in training police and SPLA prison guards on human rights and their responsibilities. The participants appreciated his efforts in the training and later on became useful connections for him. International organisations were also a source of material assistance. Several activists turned to organisations such as the East and Horn of Africa Human Rights Defenders Project and Nonviolent Peaceforce, for example, including for temporary evacuations. They also reported to international human rights organisations such as Amnesty International and human rights investigators from UNMISS in efforts to expose violations. Members of formal civil society organisations were often recipients of donor funding, although this was not consistently the case for many of my research participants, who were often working voluntarily, alongside other jobs as teachers, or journalists.

Relationships with international organisations could also be a source of frustration. Three activists mentioned that they felt the information they provided to UNMISS voluntarily about human rights violations was not fully used or reciprocated, since they did not receive information back: 'we don't see the output'.[27] Additionally, they welcomed the invitations to train as human rights activists as chances for networking, but felt they could not apply the strategies they were taught: 'The templates and concepts are not applicable on the ground. You have to go a different way to achieve your goal.' Sometimes they realised that the internationals themselves lacked the requisite knowledge. As one activist from Yei observed: 'South Sudan is a training ground and there are a lot of expats come ... not to do the actual work but to learn so they can do better jobs outside.'[28] In this context, civil society 'training' could become surreal occasions on which human rights violations or legal problems were examined in the abstract and expert advice was provided to local legal activists who were already witnessing, experiencing and responding to them directly. Activists were also critical of elements in civil society that were drawing on international support and treating their work as a business: 'The organisations were ... just saying they are giving life skills but there is nothing. The money was divided between government and those in the organisations ... staff are engaging in trading.' They saw the need to develop independent and novel approaches.

Using law in practice

The approaches pursued by the South Sudanese activists were quite distinct from the established 'naming and shaming' approach in international human rights advocacy,[29] and from some international approaches to legal empowerment. The limitations of external models for legal education are neatly captured in Mark Massoud's account of international legal empowerment workshops run by humanitarian organisations for displaced people in Khartoum. He found that people valued these workshops as a chance for education but knew that the legal training they provided could not be applied on the ground. As one NGO worker explained, to get your rights you had only two possible avenues. Either 'give something reasonable ... and they will leave you' or appeal to your most influential social connections, tapping 'family, neighbourhood or village connections within the various levels of the bureaucracy'.[30] This thorny issue that 'law on the books' had limited sway when it encountered the configurations of power on the ground preoccupied the activists and defined their tactics.

In contrast locally defined approaches to legal empowerment involved dissecting the actualities of power and producing practical strategies to respond to them. This was apparent in the discussions at a paralegal training session run by local human rights lawyers in Nimule in April 2015. The workshop discussion began with some rather generalised and abstract accounts of human rights and the law, but the paralegals soon pushed the discussion towards matters of practice. The human rights lawyers were bombarded with questions on what to do when faced with tangible muddles, manipulations of the law and local 'superpowers', including military officers and political officials.

Both organisers and participants were increasingly frank about the political challenges, and the human rights lawyers described some of the compromises and tactics that would be required to negotiate solutions. They emphasised the importance of looking beyond the statutes and building relationships with chiefs: they 'had power' and it was crucial that any paralegal should 'understand the local traditions and customs of the place. He must be from the place, because he understands the local environment'. They advised that the policy and institutions were 'not in place' and that to help resolve land disputes they should 'ensure you are as much as possible impartial, with integrity – a good listener' and to appreciate that 'traditional customs are sources of the law ... follow the elders'. Yet this same approach might only exacerbate the difficulties surrounding cases of rape, defilement and gender-based violence. For these, the paralegals were advised to turn to a women's officer in police stations; but they complained: 'If we go to the statutory system we are told it has to go to customary system, this is our culture. The police refer back to the customary.' The lawyers could provide no remedy but suggested the answer lay in involving more women in the legal system. Most of the paralegals were male, and they were asked to 'bring your sisters. We will not deny them to sit and receive the training. Women have many meeting points, they can share the knowledge they have acquired'.

Together, the lawyers and paralegals explored how they could manage the entanglements of law to get the best outcome in particular situations. They knew that they could not rely on a standard procedure. They spoke of law in all its plurality, fusing customary, statist and human rights principles and sifting them to identify the most humane. But they also spoke of the 'real politics'[31] of the people in authority who would determine the outcomes. They knew that much depended on the social identities of the parties in the case, especially if a military officer or his relative was concerned. This might either prevent an accused from being brought to book – 'if the arrested has a brother who's a general he's released' – or the reverse might apply:

> One of our teachers was on the ground with us. Some big general, a military man, sent soldiers to the site and he was

taken by force. It was very difficult to follow up because they can arrest you in the same way. He was taken to the barracks in Juba. We followed it up. He was then taken to the police. [Later] the one who was pushing his arrest disappeared and he was released because there was no case.

Overall, the lawyers suggested that there might be two alternative approaches to reckoning with power in the interests of justice:

Option one: You play a low card ... you keep a low profile, follow up slowly, get the information and move it with quietly. Get people you can contact. Option two: you play a higher one. You make a follow up openly, meet the concerned institutions, tell them this and this is happening. You will be more exposed, they will know who is making the follow up; if those institutions know you they might fear. My humble opinion is the best option is to confront these institutions. If you tell them the right things maybe they will follow. Inform them, at the end there may be a positive outcome.

The group were meeting at a time of escalating repression, a local land dispute and a civil war. They knew some of their colleagues had been arrested and there was a history of 'ethnic tensions' between the Madi host community and Dinka Bor IDPs that was bound to affect relations of trust among the paralegals.[32] One of the Dinka Bor paralegals was in detention, one of the Madi had been recently released, while several others had been warned or intimidated. Yet the group united in condemning arbitrary power in the meeting. And since some chiefs and local officials were present they were already, in a sense, playing a 'high card', with some positive results. The chiefs appeared supportive and engaged, with similar concerns to those of the paralegals. One government official present at the meeting was also responsive. He warned them: 'We are in a critical situation where there is an issue of rebellion. Your role as a citizen is not to turn against your community.' But he also promised to follow up cases of illegal detentions in the barracks (which he later did leading to some releases), saying: 'They will be released if there is no evidence ... Don't fear me, let us not fear each other; bring me your problems ... you are the agents of change.'[33]

Several other legal activists described this process of 'playing a high card' to try to persuade individuals within relevant institutions to uphold rights. They emphasised that everything depended on a 'good approach'. It would not work to condemn and criticise, instead they often tried to gently educate the relevant person, gaining their buy-in through respect and appeals to both law and mutuality. As a paralegal from Yambio commented: '[I tell the security personnel] What I only need from you is to make sure if they are arrested that they are taken to court. At some points he could agree and at other times disagree ... [it requires] building trust.' This was far from the standard human rights advocacy approach of publicising and condemning violations; it was a gentler form of persuasion, an improvised sort of humanitarian negotiation. As one activist put it: 'I have to be a mediator, I have to know the rights of the person and respect also.'[34]

Conclusion

The conditions of social and political fragmentation in South Sudan are extremely disabling for civic and legal activists. Beyond the risks of violence and arrest discussed in this chapter, there are also inevitable personal and emotional costs, and economic hardships. In this hostile environment, activists have developed networks, knowledge and adaptive capacities as strategies of self-protection and tools with which to assist people experiencing injustices at the hands of the law, in courts and prisons.

While they generally lack economic resources, the people who take up this challenging work are invariably urban social elites who have accumulated heterogeneous forms of cultural and social capital. They have become adept in the arts of negotiation and networking and have cultivated plural connections with people in various political spheres, drawing on both international human rights organisations and customary authorities alike, despite the normative distance between them. Perhaps most strikingly, they foster and rely upon allies within the government, including within security institutions that are otherwise notorious for intimidating or threatening citizens and civil society. All these activities required the subtle skills of intermediaries versed in multiple languages and cultures and distinct political registers, and able to shift and translate between them.

This chapter also highlights the extent to which, outside of the court settings, law was embodied in people in positions of power and authority, whether chiefs, government officials, security officers or representatives of international organisations. Leveraging law in favour of rights and justice meant persuading these authorities to act on particular cases of injustice. The activists did not dwell on the morality, ethnicity or the political allegiances of the individuals they dealt with, they simply tried to harness their support practically, hoping that: 'If you tell them the right things then maybe… At the end there may be a positive outcome.'[35]

In these practical and prosaic ways, activists tried to bridge the existing gulf between the law and the rights of ordinary citizens, making 'convivial' use of networks and negotiation. Such intricate social processes, and their seeming contradictions, help to explain why the 'rule of law' and human rights cannot simply be imposed or imported from above. They suggest that law, citizenship and contracts between people and authority are being repeatedly constituted through processes of interaction, even in the midst of political and legal turbulence. But they also reveal the acute challenges that citizen activists are exposed to in South Sudan as they try to counter injustices and broker survival, relying on little but their own inventive tactics.

CONCLUSION

'No condition is permanent'[1]

This book has explored the persistent power of law in a conflict arena, both as a political instrument for the ruling elite and as a tool for civilians struggling for justice and rights. It has documented the workings and contestations of the law in practice, focusing upon government-held towns over a period of five years from 2014 to 2019 – a time of intense conflict. By observing experiences and practices of the law 'from below', it has opened up a distinctive perspective on South Sudan's present conditions and future political possibilities as well as new insights and questions relevant to law and citizen activism in other conflict settings. It has also highlighted the extraordinary experiences and contributions of an energetic cohort of South Sudanese lawyers, paralegals and community activists who have monitored routine injustices and promoted social and legal changes during a civil war and amid pervasive violence. South Sudan's legal activists may be far from securing rights and justice, but they are engaged in principled attempts to counteract the proliferation of violence and to stabilise and constrain the excesses of the law.

There are several lessons we can draw from this about the relations between law, state and society. Firstly, although the book does not examine the dynamics of the war itself – and does not look into the conduct of South Sudan's opposition forces in the areas that were under their control during the same period – it does provide a window onto the relations between law and authority in South Sudan that are of more general relevance. In particular, it highlights the continuities between contemporary modalities of government and previous regimes including Sudanese and colonial governments. It suggests that while presiding political elites enter into transactional 'political marketplace' logics[2] in their competition to claim the state, once in government they are able to call upon law as a serviceable remnant of more institutionalised authoritarian systems. South Sudan's government has sustained itself in power against its competitors not only by means of violence, but also through 'legal politics'.[3] It has exploited the symbolic power of the law to construct a veneer of legality that enables it to transact with external powers, including international agencies and corporations; while it strives to dominate society by means of legal instruments and institutions.

Secondly, however, the law is never merely an instrument of power; it is also a field of political struggle – since law is routinely being made and contested within institutions and society. In addition, law is a resource, a form of 'symbolic capital' that can be harnessed in struggles in the wider political field.[4] It is central to the constitution and the legitimisation of political authority; to ordering relations between the state and society; and to shaping relations between people within society. The special characteristic of law is its duality: it consistently presents itself as sitting above political authority and in so doing serves both a hegemonic function and a political opening for people to try to place constraints upon power.[5] The book confirms these already well-established insights from socio-legal theorists, by revealing the prevalence of durable relations between law and the state, and legal imaginaries and contestations over law in society, even in this extreme case of a war-torn state.

In South Sudan, the struggles over law are far more multifaceted and vigorous than in other settings, and they are happening at speed. Law is plural and complex in every sense. This applies formally, in that there are plural sources of law, being administered by plural authorities, including customary authorities, statutory authorities and humanitarian agencies; and there are also various types of courts and they each draw upon various sources of law. But this plurality also applies within society even more radically. The state and many statutory laws are new, and people have often lived under various legal regimes, either in Sudan or in neighbouring countries. Moreover, customary law is not a singular phenomenon – it refers to multiple ethnicised and localised laws and authorities. The law is therefore fundamentally unsettled and being deployed and contested by different actors at various levels.

South Sudan's official institutions of justice, including the ministry, the judiciary and the bar association, are either weak or have been forced into subservience to the interests of a ruling clique. They were newly established in the run-up to independence and have been staffed by personnel who had either limited experience of the administration of justice; long experience of trying to administer the law under difficult and undemocratic conditions, under the previous Khartoum regime, with its expertise in authoritarian legal manoeuvres; or had worked under the military administration of the SPLM/A. Despite this, legal professionals have made important efforts to resist and constrain political efforts to harness law as an instrument. This includes the courageous public critiques of the government made by some judges and the less visible efforts of human rights lawyers to represent numerous people who have been arbitrarily detained for political reasons. There is no doubt that some legal professionals have maintained independence and acted with integrity, either by taking a stand directly in opposition to human rights violations or by simply trying to administer the law fairly; but in several important cases they have been dismissed or forced to resign.

Yet the bulk of the administration of justice is carried out by the chieftaincy and this institution provides a resilient and distinctive modality of government that has a history of evolving in interaction with, and 'contracting', predatory and violent regimes, as historian Cherry Leonardi has shown.[6] 'Customary' courts and chiefs have their origins in colonial native administration, but have generally operated at the fringes of power, and with roots firmly in society, and their legitimacy and authority depends not only on government but also upon serving the community, or at least a good number of its most powerful members. The chieftaincy varies from place to place in this fragmented and diverse country in terms of its characteristics and relations to power. But what defines and underpins its legitimacy are the customary courts, with their accessible, public and deliberative processes, which have proven extraordinarily resilient in the administration of justice and have continued to function, certainly in towns, for almost the entirety of the conflict.

Local courts have served as the mainstay of the justice system and the primary source of law and social regulation during the conflict. Based on an extensive archive of court reports gathered by South Sudanese researchers, the book has revealed the everyday workings of both statutory and customary courts in towns. The findings suggest that the courts act as forms of civil authority, social regulation, and a dispute settlement and conflict prevention mechanism within society. They juggle the consequences of political violence, instability, and social and economic deprivation on a shoestring, and try to devise makeshift temporary solutions. The cases people take to the courts are distressing, highlighting social disturbance and the proliferation of everyday forms of violence. But they also indicate the enduring social value attached to legality and persistent efforts by ordinary people to solve matters peacefully.

While legal complexity and uncertainty have created opportunities for military authorities, the courts are playing a role in ordering society and promote some forms of civil order and stability. Importantly, my findings also suggest that despite legal pluralism there were many commonalities in the administration of the law in practice. Different local courts draw upon heterogeneous sources of law in similar ways. They tend to apply the law intuitively, making its plurality into a more consistent form of hybridity, and administer similar settlements, in a mix of punishments and compensation payments to the victim or complainant, including cattle or money in cases such as adultery or murder ('blood compensation').

This ongoing hybridisation or 'harmonisation' of the law in courts seems promising in its potential to counteract political turbulence, but it is undermined by a political order which extends beyond the elite 'kleptocracy' and is dominated by 'hegemonic militarised masculinity'. This is evident in three ways. Firstly, the town courts prove to be generally unable to bring military and political elites to account on political or conflict-related issues. They can rarely rule against military figures even on more quotidian matters of property and, when they do, these decisions are difficult to implement given the shortcomings of security agencies, including the police. Secondly, customary courts can extend their power over elites when it comes to social matters, especially those relating to relationships between men and women, so we did record some prosecutions of politicians or soldiers involved in rape, domestic abuse and divorce cases. But the settlements in such cases are not necessarily in favour of the women concerned; rather they tend to privilege the concerns of the family. This relates to the third issue, that in this highly unstable context, families and kinship networks are the most reliable sources of trust, reciprocity and mutual support, and are also readily mobilised in disputes, sometimes violently. Like the political and security authorities of the state, they can also threaten the authority of courts or provide them with social support, guaranteeing decisions. Local courts and customary laws are therefore predisposed to defer to male elders, as local forms of patriarchal power that underpin their authority. We can see this in their consistently harsh treatment of women seeking divorces or accused of adultery, and young people involved in extra-marital relationships.

However, social changes are underway even during this time of war, and the courts and laws are already pivotal in resistance to the dominant politics of extraction, violence and patriarchy. The book has shown how lawyers and citizen activists have been striving to resist injustices, at great personal risk, on specific issues and cases, including land rights, women's rights, arbitrary detention and the use of the death penalty. Their capacity to act and effect change in this complex and unstable political environment depends on access to an eclectic mix of cultural and social resources and a 'convivial' approach defined by pragmatism and negotiation. It is the work of urbanised and educated people, who are mobile but have preserved strong ties into their 'home' communities. In their work, they draw upon and confront plural sources of law, and foster connections with a diverse array of authorities, including humanitarian actors, chiefs, police and government security agents.

The everyday legal activism described here complements justice projects and networks emerging at national and transnational levels, including broad agendas to establish transitional justice mechanisms and processes, and specific, concrete initiatives, such as the prosecution of the soldiers responsible for murder, rape and theft at the Terrain hotel[7] or the efforts by 'victims of the oil war' to bring Swedish oil company Lundin Petroleum to account.[8] In a similar fashion to these other struggles, local legal activism faces constant setbacks and will take time to yield any measurable gains. Yet it matters politically in a constructivist sense, because it promotes the spread of human rights norms.[9] South Sudanese approaches to legal activism described in the book present their own vernacular imaginings of rights, law and citizenship that derive from, and are attuned to, their political and cultural context. They engage productively with locally tenacious and valued customary systems, working to encourage 'a self-propelled process of improvement from within' as Francis Deng envisaged.[10] They also rely upon and cultivate a set of practices which are 'convivial' in their approach, defined by a compassionate and flexible sociability, involving networking and negotiation.

The book cannot speak to the salience of legal activism in South Sudan beyond the urban settings under government authority which were the focus of the research. The possibilities for political agency and citizen activism are surely more constrained in rural peripheries. Basic life-chances are tied to rural economies and people turn to a wider array of customary and spiritual authorities. To understand this wider picture we must look to accounts from the rural hinterlands and the experiences of people for whom interaction with the state is an assault upon their 'moral universe', as Jok Madut Jok observes.[11] Inequalities and differences between urban areas and rural communities, including in terms of access to education, are also fuelling the current war, and some young men at the margins have learnt to 'live by the gun';[12] they cling to its temporary power, and believe that it 'pays to rebel'.[13]

Nevertheless, the repeated wars experienced by South Sudanese people demonstrate that military might can yield only temporary and unstable domination, and can never 'substitute for power'.[14] They undermine arguments for the liberating potential of anti-colonial violence, for which Franz Fanon is best known, and instead confirm his clinical insights into the psychological torment violence inflicts upon both its victims and its perpetrators, as well as his warning that it is impossible to win a liberation from the 'colonialist war machine with the bare minimum of arms'.[15] In this context, history and reason dictate that fundamental change must come 'from below', through the productive power of persuasion and collaborative action.[16] Legal activism is one of the potential means towards this end.

African citizens have long been reckoning with the challenge of how to dislodge undemocratic, violent or arbitrary governments. As Mark Massoud has argued, 'the only effective catalyst for democracy' has been the people power of nonviolent revolutions.[17] Sadly, time and again these transformations prove difficult to sustain; even if the ruler is defeated, the system seems to survive, relying in no small part on the colonial state's legacy of law. Political transformation also requires more routine forms of practical and normative struggle within society, including to counteract the practices of authoritarian rule by law and to adapt valued 'informal' customary or religious laws and courts so that they might respond to the demands of the present and the equal rights of all citizens. It is significant that ordinary people have often been able to imagine law as a means to 'constrain the power of state officials' even in colonial times. As Zimbabwean historian George Hamandishe Karekwaivanane argues, they 'alert us to the possibilities for the struggle for rights ... to be defined from below'.[18]

This book has provided an account of contemporary injustices, rooted in historically violent and predatory practices of law and government. It has also traced the repertoires of legal activists working to challenge basic human rights violations under the extraordinarily harsh conditions of a civil war. Such efforts to transform the everyday life of the law deserve attention and support. They help some people to survive in the present, and they edge the system incrementally towards justice in the future.

APPENDIX

A note on methods

This book is mainly based on field research gathered in South Sudan between April 2014 and August 2017, including ethnographic and collaborative action research with South Sudanese lawyers, paralegals and activists. I made eight short field research trips to South Sudan. I also met with South Sudanese refugees in the region, twice in Cairo and three times in Uganda. In addition, a team of South Sudanese lawyers, paralegals and civic activists helped shape the research design, as well as contributing directly to producing substantial original research data. We organised and participated in a series of action research workshops, held in partnership with staff from Justice Africa, South Sudan Law Society (SSLS), Community Empowerment for Progress Organisation (CEPO), or South Sudan Women Lawyer's Association (SSWLA). The overarching aims of the research design were to capture 'situated processes of knowing and making legality'.[1]

Collaborative action

The collaborative action strand of the research, including the court observations, drew on ideas from feminist praxis and emancipatory research methodologies that build in concerns about justice and social change at all stages of the research process, striving to work in solidarity with activist struggles and to share power and resources with participants.[2] More generally, the research was informed by scholars who have sought to pursue what Didier Fassin terms an 'engaged practice open to the world and its problems'[3] in conflict settings, including the civil society approach adopted by Mary Kaldor of the Justice and Security Research Programme (JSRP) and Conflict Research Programme (CRP).[4] As Eghosa Osaghae and Gillian Robinson argue, there is an extra imperative to develop methodological forums 'in which outsiders and insiders can learn from each other' in conflict settings.[5] There is also an additional challenge in managing risks in these settings, and the collaborative action approach was compatible with the short immersions in the research environment, known as 'rapid' or 'focused ethnography' and used by other research teams in difficult and insecure research contexts.[6]

The main collaborative research activity was the court observation project in which South Sudanese researchers observed and recorded cases in their local town courts. The project emerged from discussions with a human rights lawyer, who was concerned about limited documentation of court proceedings and the need for lawyers to keep track of proceedings in both statutory and customary courts, which are not always recorded and are rarely easily accessible. It benefited from insights from Tiernan Mennen and his team of researchers, based on their previous work observing courts on South Sudan.[7] It also mirrored and reinforced aspects of the ongoing work of the SSLS, CEPO and Pact, which had each trained cohorts of paralegals and activists, and sought to monitor court proceedings as part of programmes aimed at promoting legal empowerment and access to justice. The court observer team was recruited through their networks, with the particular help of SSLS and Justice Africa.

The project encompassed a year of court observations of statutory and customary courts in Juba, Nimule, Torit, Yambio, Yei, Rumbek and Wau, and in displacement camps in Juba and Melijo by 19 court observers beginning in July 2015 and ending in July 2016; it also drew on the work of two court observers in Bentiu. Most of the observations were recorded by local researchers who were already working as volunteer paralegals. The court observers were given guidance on documentation, as well as ethics and risks. The court observations reports were all anonymised to exclude names of researchers and participants in court cases, in order to minimise risk of potential harm. The reports are identified by initials and dates in citations. The processes observed were all public processes which the observers were able to attend freely, but they consulted and informed relevant authorities, obtaining consent where appropriate. The majority of the reports gathered have been digitised and will be shared as a resource for other South Sudanese researchers, lawyers and analysts. The team gathered close to 700 reports in total. I surveyed 513 digitised reports and 83 paper copies out of this wider pool. These reports are the main source for Chapter 3.

The second element of collaboration was a series of action research workshops aimed at gathering research insights but also promoting critical reflection and mutual learning and exchanges. These involved between 12 and 65 participants on each occasion. The first workshop was in Juba in April 2014, in partnership with Justice Africa, CEPO and SSWLA, which brought together 65 civil society activists for the South Sudan Civil Forum II: Reflections on Justice and Reconciliation. In April 2015, Justice Africa, SSLS and JSRP convened a paralegal workshop in Nimule with more than 20 participants. In Juba in July 2015, we held a workshop with a group of 19 paralegals, together with six other participants, including a women's rights activist, three lawyers and a high court judge, to train paralegals as researchers in court observation, establishing the 'court observation research project' in partnership with CEPO and SSLS. We also convened a wider group of legal and civil society activists, bringing together over 50 participants to reflect critically on approaches and priorities for 'researching justice in South Sudan'. In January 2016, the same court observer project team met again to reflect on their experiences in Juba. In August 2017, we convened a further meeting of 12 court observers in Juba. Additionally, together with two of the court observers, we organised a second workshop, bringing together some 20 paralegals and chiefs from Nimule. In between these forums and workshops, I communicated with some of the research participants and court observers by means of messages or phone calls via email, Facebook or WhatsApp.

As well as the workshops, a number of informal meetings and discussions were held either to inform the research questions and design, or to clarify and supplement existing findings with either paralegals or community activists. In Nimule, in four *bomas* in April 2014, we organised focus groups with the support of chiefs, community activists and a lawyer from SSWLA, bringing together over 80 participants. In August 2014, Justice Africa, SSWLA and community leaders organised workshops on access to justice in five *bomas*, bringing together over 100 participants. I met with five paralegals and eight members of the community watch group in PoC3 Juba in July 2015. In May 2017, I met with some of the court observation team individually and others in a small group in Juba. In August 2017, I met a group of ten community activists and chiefs in Adjumani, Uganda; I also met with eight community activists from Wau in Cairo. I interviewed eight people and held two focus group discussions in Hai Game, Juba in April 2014 and July 2015. All of these research visits were accomplished within short periods, lasting from one week to a maximum of three weeks.

Interviews and life histories

I interviewed 80 individuals, with a mix of life history and semi-structured interviews. Most of these interviews were with men; they included only seven women. This reflects the realities of gender inequalities in South Sudan, including relating to education, and women's participation in the particular forms of activism that were the focus here, although women are active in many other roles in civil society. It also reflects the fact that the interviews were obtained by means of snowball sampling and are not intended to provide a representative sample, being further shaped by the constraints of the conflict setting. Most of the interviewees were young men; the youngest was 21. The life history interviews asked people to trace the experiences that led them to their current roles and situations in order to reveal the meanings they drew from past events and to situate their possibilities for action within social and political relations.[8] Especially in conflict settings, we need to be attentive to the ways in which memory is socially constructed and participant responses are shaped partly by the interests and presence of the researcher.[9] Where possible I cross-checked interviews with relevant documentation, including letters. The life history approach was also central to uncovering a 'view from below'.[10]

The interviews were conducted in conformity with the established principles for ethical social science research, including confidentiality and informed consent. In consequence, the material is anonymised, with first names or pseudonyms used as attributions, respecting the wishes of the research participant and the agreement made in each case. In addition, I deliberately left out details of names, ethnic identities, and events, localities and interviews where they are unnecessary to explaining the issues, especially where I judge the material to be most sensitive.

Funding and support

The field research was supported by the JSRP, a UK Department for International Development (DFID)-supported international research consortium, under a grant held by the LSE. In 2017–19, the research benefited from support and interactions with researchers in the CRP, another DFID-supported international research consortium, including Naomi Pendle, Hannah Logan and Alex de Waal. It includes two interviews carried out with CRP researchers and has benefited from insights from the CRP South Sudan research team, and an interview gathered by one of their members in Malakal, as well as from the rich insights of members of the South Sudan

Research Panel and the various contributors to the CRP 'Law from Below' panel discussion held in Arusha, Tanzania in July 2018. In addition to the field research, I consulted an array of documentary sources, including primary sources such as letters and meeting records, which were essential to verifying some of the events and which were obtained through the connections established by the collaborative action research or by existing links within NGOs. I also use published sources, including news reports judiciously, cross-checking various news sources on the same event, although I only select and reference those needed to support the point made in the book.

This book is in many ways the product of a collective effort, but it is inevitably shaped by my own perspectives and analysis as a UK-based researcher positioned at a great distance from the events and issues. Any analytical flaws, errors or omissions are my own. Like other 'activist scholars', I find there are irreconcilable tensions between efforts to act in solidarity with struggles for justice and the demands, approaches and timelines of academia.[11] My South Sudanese colleagues and research participants very generously shared and discussed their ideas and experiences with me throughout this project. I only hope the book might be of some use in their ongoing and future conversations, writings and endeavours.

NOTES

Preface

1   Republic of South Sudan 2012.
2   E.g. Collier et al. 2018.
3   Gilroy 1993; Mbembe 2017.
4   Donham 2007, p.34.
5   Donham 2007, p.27.
6   Ibid.
7   De Waal 2016a.
8   North et al. 2009; World Bank 2011.
9   Faundez 2016, p.408.
10 Agamben 1998, p.5.
11 Odinkalu 2006; Maru 2006.
12 ICAI 2015.
13 Abdelsalam 2000, 2004; Ibrahim 2008; Massoud 2014.
14 Abdelsalam 2000.
15 Mamdani 1996.
16 Ibrahim 2008.
17 El-Affendi 1991; Abdelsalam 2004; Berridge 2017.
18 Ibrahim 2008; Fluehr-Lobban 2009.
19 El-Affendi 1990.
20 African Rights 1997, p.10.
21 Deng 1987.
22 Benjamin 1968, p.255.

Introduction

1   YA, interviewed in Juba, August 2017.
2   Lawlessness is a trope in commentary on South Sudan, e.g. https://www. theguardian.com/global-development/poverty-matters/2014/aug/15/south-sudan-famine-lawlessness
3   See Massoud 2014, pp.19–24. South Sudan was formerly part of Sudan and both countries continue to share a similar predicament in differing ways,

encapsulated in the saying that the effect of independence was to make: 'one system two countries [into] two countries one system'.

4   Checchi et al. 2018 find that there were 382,900 excess deaths in this period and 190,000 deaths from violent injuries.

5   See United Nations High Commissioner for Refugees (UNHCR) data on South Sudanese refugees which records 2,281,588 in April 2019: https://data2.unhcr.org/en/situations/southsudan#_ga=2.28412408.530561710.1554290673-1865632357.1554290673; Internal Displacement Monitoring Centre (IDMC) data records 1,899,000 internally displaced people up to December 2017: http://www.internal-displacement.org/countries/south-sudan

6   Nordstrom 1997.

7   This conception of the duality of law may well be socially understood, but is also explored in Comaroff 1994.

8   Dwyer and Zeilig 2012, p.4.

9   Branch and Mampilly 2015, p.176. Also see de Waal and Ibreck 2013.

10   See Karekwaivanane 2017; Grewal 2016; Madhok 2017.

11   It is notable the Sudans have frequently served scholars as a 'case' that illuminates human societies and establishes new methods of understanding them. This includes work on the Nuer by the anthropologists Evans Pritchard (1940) and Sharon Hutchinson (1996) which is foundational to anthropology. They have also been a testing ground for aid responses and for scholarship that is seminal in critiquing these, including famine studies by de Waal (2005) and Keen (1994). And Sudanese scholars have been especially important in furthering cross-cultural perspectives on law and human rights, including Deng (2009) and An-Na'im (1992).

12   See MacGinty and Richmond 2013.

13   De Herdt and Olivier de Sardan 2015.

14   http://www.thenewhumanitarian.org/news-feature/2019/03/12/south-sudan-war-civilians-despite-six-months-supposed-peace; https://unmiss.unmissions.org/human-rights-investigators-rush-south-sudan%E2%80%99s-bentiu-following-spate-rapes

15   See de Waal et al. 2017.

16   See Massoud 2014.

17   This concept draws on work elaborating on Bourdieu's theory of structure and agency; Behague et al. 2008, p.492; Crossley 2003.

18   Bourgeois 2001, p.20.

19   By which I mean addressing structural violence defined by hunger, discrimination and social injustices as well as direct violence, see Galtung 1969.

20   Nagy 2008, p.287.

21   Theros and Kaldor 2018.

22   Lund 2006, p.689.

23   Ginsberg and Moustafa 2008; Mampilly 2011.

24   Bell 2015, p.2.
25   Bell 2015, p.1.
26   Pring 2017, p.225.
27   Kasfir 1998.
28   Ferguson cited in Lewis 2001, p.7.
29   See de Waal and Ibreck 2013.
30   Kasfir 1998, p.7.
31   This concept is a central strand of work on the CRP programme. Also see Theros and Kaldor 2018, pp.14–16.
32   Green 2012, pp.181–2.
33   Nordstrom 1997, pp.xviii–6.
34   Massoud 2014, p.228.
35   Massoud 2014.
36   See Leonardi 2015a.
37   Seidel and Sureau 2015, p.614.
38   See GoSS 2011, and for some criticisms Seidel and Sureau 2015; http://www.sudantribune.com/South-Sudan-constitution-under,38845; http://www.sudantribune.com/spip.php?article58216
39   See Deng 2013.
40   Mennen 2010; Ibreck et al. 2017.
41   Southern Sudan Civil Society Initiative 2005.
42   See Justice Africa 2015, p.1. Also see the account of the post-independence civil society dialogues from Flora McCrone: https://www.peaceinsight.org/blog/2013/12/constitutional-dialogue-south-sudan/
43   See de Waal 2014.
44   See Boege et al. 2009; Luckham and Kirk 2013.
45   Leonardi 2015a, p. 6; p.3.
46   Leonardi 2015a; Kindersley 2016.
47   Leonardi 2007, p.392.
48   Sureau 2013, p.258. Sureau finds that in Torit the spatial area of the town expanded by 745% from 2005 to 2012. Note that statistics are limited, but many sources agree that levels of urbanisation increased dramatically after 2005, especially in Juba, see Martin and Mosel 2011, p.3.
49   Thomas 2015, p.143.
50   Sureau 2013.
51   https://www.crisis.acleddata.com/south-sudan-june-2016-update/
52   AUCISS 2014, p.138-140. <with unspaced en between page range numbers
53   See UN Commission for Human Rights in South Sudan, 6 March 2017, https://www.amnesty.org/en/latest/news/2017/07/south-sudan-ongoing-atrocities-turn-countrys-breadbasket-into-a-killing-field/
54   https://www.ohchr.org/Documents/Countries/SS/UNMISSReportJuly 2016_January2017.pdf

55 See Turse 2016.

56 A famine declaration in parts of Unity state in February 2017 identified the worst affected areas, but the lethal combination of warfare and economic crisis dismantled coping strategies right across the country.

57 See Desai 2015, pp.8–11.

58 Thomas 2015, p.17.

59 Massoud 2014.

60 Guyer 2004, p.8.

61 Raeymaekers 2014.

62 Guyer 2004, p.8.

63 The concept of conviviality draws from Nyamnjoh 2017.

64 Scott 1990.

65 Raemaekers 2014, p.67.

66 See the note on methods in the Appendix for further details.

67 The approach was also informed by Tiernan Mennen, Edmund Yakani and their colleagues' ground-breaking research. See for instance Mennen 2010; Haki 2011.

68 Inter alia Merry 1990; Ewick and Sibley 1998; de Herdt and Olivier de Sardan 2015; Raeymaekers 2014.

69 Massoud 2014, Leonardi 2015a, Hutchinson 1998.

70 De Waal 2014, 2015; Thomas 2015.

71 This phrase was on a recent Facebook post of an activist group in South Sudan; it is often attributed to Wole Soyinka but also used in Nigerian and other African protests.

72 https://reliefweb.int/report/south-sudan/troika-statement-conflict-south-sudan-12-january-2018

73 The term was coined by Majak D'Agoot: https://www.youtube.com/watch?v=-IDZ2m63xIg

74 http://www.smallarmssurveysudan.org/fileadmin/docs/issue-briefs/HSBA-IB28-Spreading-Fallout.pdf

75 See ARCISS and R-ARCHISS.

76 My account of these events is based on discussions with a local lawyer and friend of the daughter of one of the accused, as well as the following media sources: https://radiotamazuj.org/en/news/article/spla-operations-commander-dies-of-food-poisoning-in-wau; https://radiotamazuj.org/en/news/article/diocesan-official-released-on-bail-after-being-arrested-on-suspicion-food-poisoning-in-wau; https://radiotamazuj.org/en/news/article/doctor-arrested-in-wau-after-ruling-out-food-poisoning-in-army-officer-s-death; http://www.gurtong.net/ECM/Editorial/tabid/124/ctl/ArticleView/mid/519/articleId/21163/Doctors-In-Wau-Lay-Down-Tools-Following-Arrest-Of-Their-Colleague.aspx; https://radiotamazuj.org/en/news/article/court-fines-doctor-31-cows-for-army-general-s-death-in-wau

77 United Nations Commission on Human Rights in South Sudan 2018, pp.74–86.

78 During 'protest actions and reprisal attacks' 24 people were killed and 60 injured, 11 of them at the hands of state security and the rest in 'inter-ethnic clashes' according to Amnesty International 2013.

79 The SPLM MP John Richard was accused of organising the protest, imprisoned without charges for four months and then convicted, despite a lack of evidence, to two years in prison. Following his release, he spent over a year in Juba, but eventually went into exile. I interviewed him in Cairo, February 2019.

80 Anonymous, 'Sudan's Secret Slaughter', cited in Africa Watch 1990, pp.68–70.

81 See Chapter 5 for a discussion of compensation rates.

82 Almquist Knopf (2016) among others has called for South Sudan to be administered as an international trusteeship.

83 Facebook, https://www.facebook.com/tamazuj/posts/1572129016157776

84 Facebook chat, 2 February 2018.

Chapter 1

1 https://www.nytimes.com/2016/06/08/opinion/south-sudan-needs-truth-not-trials.html

2 ARCISS 2015.

3 Human Rights Watch 2017.

4 https://www.theguardian.com/global-development/2016/jun/10/south-sudan-leaders-controversial-new-york-times-article-aides-say-riek-machar

5 http://www.theeastafrican.co.ke/news/South-Sudan-wants-paul-malong-out-of-peace-talks/2558-4381092-yyvmau/index.html

6 https://www.un.org/sc/suborg/en/sanctions/2206/materials/summaries/individual/paul-malong-awan

7 http://www.sudantribune.com/spip.php?article64718;https://uk.reuters.com/article/uk-southsudan-unrest/south-sudan-frees-rebel-chiefs-associates-to-back-peace-deal-idUKKCN1N713F

8 https://www.ohchr.org/en/NewsEvents/Pages/DisplayNews.aspx?NewsID=24268&LangID=E

9 As did local commanders, for instance Young (2016, p.33) describes the efforts of an SPLA-IO leader who sought to 'educate the fighters on the need to respect community values and the law'. See also Chapter 2.

10 http://africanarguments.org/2016/07/11/whos-behind-south-sudans-return-to-fighting/

11 See Jackson and Rosberg 1982.

12 For an explanation of the political marketplace logic and of 'turbulence' see de Waal 2015.

13 Bourdieu 1990, p.64. Note that Bourdieu first theorised the logic of practice based on his ethnography of Kabyle law and society in Algeria. See Bourdieu 1990, 1986a and 1986b.

14 Tamanaha 2004, p.2.

15 Comaroff and Comaroff 2016, p.32.

16 Weber 1919.

17 Keene 2002.

18 Lund 2006, p.689.

19 Hoffmann and Duschinski 2014; Ginsberg and Moustafa 2008.

20 Merry 1990, p.8.

21 Tamanaha 2004, p.14.

22 Keene 2002.

23 Mamdani 1996, p.298.

24 Ekeh 1975.

25 Comaroff, 1994, p.xiii.

26 Law and Society 1988 cited in Engel 1998, p.129.

27 Merry 1990, p.4; Ewick and Silbey 1998, p.17.

28 Pirie and Scheele 2014, p.2; Merry 1990, p.10.

29 Merry 1990, p.10.

30 Ewick and Sibley 1998, p.18.

31 Ewick and Silbey 1998, p.20.

32 See Bourdieu 1986a, 1986b.

33 Luckham and Kirk 2013, p.1.

34 Macdonald and Allen 2015, p.283.

35 Lund 2006.

36 Macdonald and Allen 2015, p.301.

37 Mayntz 2010.

38 Von Benda-Beckmann and von Benda-Beckmann 2016, pp.6–7.

39 Macdonald and Allen 2015, p.302.

40 Comaroff and Comaroff 2016, p.36.

41 Rajagopal 2008, pp.1348–49.

42 Isser 2011, p.3.

43 https://www.iied.org/legal-tools-sharing-lessons-innovation; Maru 2006.

44 Desai 2015, pp.8–11.

45 Comaroff and Comaroff cited in Hoffman and Duschinski 2014, p.506.

46 De Souza Santos and Rodriguez-Garavito 2005, p.2.

47 De Souza Santos and Rodriguez-Garavito 2005.

48 Grewal 2016, p.180.

49 Houtzager 2005, p.218.

50 Racialised divisions were forged within the north and between peoples of northern and southern Sudan producing 'Arab' and 'African' identities: Thomas 2015, p.59.

51 Ibrahim 2008, p.7.
52 Massoud 2014, p.53.
53 Massoud 2014, pp.54–58.
54 Rolandsen and Leonardi 2014, p.612.
55 Cited in Poggo 2009, p.93.
56 Cited in Collins and Herzog 1961, p.130.
57 Cited in Biong Deng 1999, p.60.
58 Leonardi 2015a, pp.87–92.
59 Leonardi 2015a, pp.101–102.
60 Deng cited in Leonardi 2015a, p.102.
61 Rolandsen and Daly 2016, p.72.
62 Rolandsen and Daly 2016.
63 Cited in Rolandsen and Leonardi 2014, p.616.
64 Thomas 2015, p.100.
65 Rolandsen and Daly 2016, pp.101–105.
66 De Waal 2004.
67 Cited in de Waal 1997, p.84.
68 Hutchinson 1996, p.338; 2000.
69 Rolandsen and Daly 2016, p.106.
70 Ibrahim 2008, p.43.
71 Magistrate or judge in a Sharia court.
72 Poggo 2009, p.93.
73 Leonardi 2015a, p.167.
74 Addis Ababa 1972, Ch. IV, Art.11.
75 See Kindersley 2016.
76 Rolandsen 2005, p.155.
77 African Rights 1997.
78 Kuol 1997, p.54.
79 Leonardi 2015a, pp.174–175.
80 Rolandsen 2005, p.117.
81 Leonardi 2015a, p.656.
82 Leonardi 2015a, p.657.
83 Leonardi 2015a, pp.158–159.
84 Leonardi 2015a, p.173.
85 Kindersley 2016, p.123.
86 Kindersley 2016, p.228.
87 De Waal 2013, pp.216–217.
88 De Waal 2013, pp.216–217.
89 Massoud 2014, p.124.
90 Massoud 2014.
91 Massoud 2014, p.129.
92 Mamdani 2016.

93 Jok 2012.
94 ICJ 2013.
95 DPKO 2014, p.39.
96 Massoud 2014, p.226.
97 United Nations Commission on Human Rights in South Sudan 2017.
98 Johnson 2016.
99 I am grateful to David Deng for this observation on the constitution.
100 This demand resonated with the views of ordinary people as an SSLS survey showed: see Deng et al. 2015.
101 https://www.reuters.com/article/us-southsudan-un/justice-for-atrocities-in-south-sudan-just-a-signature-away-u-n-investigator-idUSKCN1GP2J6?feedType=RSS&feedName=worldNews
102 https://www.nytimes.com/2016/06/08/opinion/south-sudan-needs-truth-not-trials.html
103 Lobel 2007, p.88.

Chapter 2

1   UNDP 2013b.
2   I borrow this concept from Zoe Cormack's work on borders, 2016, p.517.
3   I heard this claim repeatedly from people between 2014 and 2017. Also see Justice Africa: http://justiceafrica.org/voices-on-issues-related-to-divorce-security-the-justice-system/
4   http://www.idlo.int/news/highlights/south-sudan-coming-grips-new-legal-system; Mennen 2016; Deng et al. 2015.
5   This resembled the 'anti-politics machine', a term Ferguson (1990) used to describe how technical international development programmes that may fail to address poverty and powerlessness but serve to expand the power of the state and the possibility of further development interventions.
6   Massoud 2014, p.221.
7   http://www.joshuacraze.com/blog/2016/4/13/the-mission-of-forgetting
8   UN Panel of Experts 2017, p.21.
9   See de Waal 2014.
10 AUCISS 2014, p.90.
11 Inter alia UN Commission on Human Rights in South Sudan 2018; Amnesty International 2017.
12 http://www.sudantribune.com/spip.php?article58216
13 ICJ 2013, pp.27–38.
14 https://sudantribune.com/spip.php?article39854
15 Notably Justice Ambrose Riny Thiik of the Jieng Council of Elders.
16 https://www.irinnews.org/opinion/2016/11/25/genocidal-logic-south-sudan's-"gun-class"

17 See Kuyok 2015, pp.612–613.

18 Abdelsalam and de Waal 1999.

19 http://www.sudantribune.com/INTERVIEW-Avoid-taking-law-in-own,33722

20 http://www.sudantribune.com/spip.php?article45537

21 https://www.pulse.ng/news/world/in-south-sudan-rebel-chief-issues-war-call-from-exile-id5529854.html

22 https://www.facebook.com/thenationalcourier/posts/juba:-parliament-approves-new-appointees/799076026924101/

23 http://www.sudantribune.com/Unveil-list-of-75-corrupt,42907

24 http://www.sudantribune.com/spip.php?article57062. Note that the Rule of Law sector, encompassing the ministry, ostensibly received a substantial share of the budget allocation, generally second only to spending on security and defence. But the internal distribution of the funds within this sector was weighted towards security actors. An estimate of spending in 2014–15 suggested that 1.573 billion SSP were being spent on police, prison and fire service, Attipoe et al. 2014, p.5.

25 Johnson 2016, pp.83–86.

26 YA, interviewed in Juba, August 2017. Note that another independent lawyer (interviewed in May 2017) also raised concerns about the fire.

27 https://www.transparency.org/gcb2013/country?country=south_sudan

28 Johnson 2016, location 2161.

29 Ibid. Another example was the Terrain case, discussed in Chapter 3.

30 http://www.sudantribune.com/spip.php?article58216

31 https://radiotamazuj.org/en/news/article/national-alliance-lawyers-say-chief-justice-too-biased-to-rule-in-28-states-case

32 It was repeatedly adjourned. Also note that a few months later Dr Lam Akol resigned from the transitional government and formed a new rebel movement.

33 https://uk.reuters.com/article/uk-southsudan-security-idUKKBN15X0B3?il=0

34 http://www.thecitizen.co.tz/News/Third-S-Sudan-official-resigns/1840360-3820274-format-xhtml-50wrr6z/index.html

35 http://www.sudantribune.com/spip.php?article62351

36 Other reports suggested their pay was equivalent to US$50. Interviewed in Juba, August 2017.

37 http://www.eyeradio.org/justices-judges-strike-seeking-removal-chief-justice/

38 Interview with spokesperson of the strike committee in Juba, August 2017.

39 YA, interviewed in Juba, August 2017.

40 It was thought that some 30 out of 171 judges continued to work, mainly in Juba. Interview with spokesperson of the strike committee in Juba, August 2017.

41 South Sudan Human Rights Commission 2017, p.28.

42 Focus group discussion with legal activists in Juba, August 2017.

43 https://africasustainableconservation.com/2017/04/25/south-sudan-security-chief-wants-chief-justice-sacked/

44 Interview with the spokesperson of the strike committee in Juba, August 2017.

45 Republican Decree no 100/2017.

46 https://radiotamazuj.org/en/news/article/south-sudan-judges-call-off-strike-unconditionally

47 https://www.reuters.com/article/us-southsudan-strike/south-sudan-judges-end-strike-to-return-to-huge-legal-backlog-idUSKCN1BI2KZ

48 Interviewed in Juba, May 2017.

49 http://www.southsudannation.com/justice-under-fire-the-dismissal-of-13-justices-judges-from-the-judiciary-of-south-sudan/

50 http://www.monitor.co.ug/blob/view/-/4186638/data/1809407/-/112durnz/-/Sudan.pdf

51 https://radiotamazuj.org/en/news/article/supreme-court-judge-resigns-citing-interference

52 The Sentry 2016, p.7.

53 The FHRI listed some 20 participants in its meetings in October to December 2015 (FHRI reports to Justice Africa, October, November and December 2015). JAHRO listed 11 founder members at its registration (JAHRO, certificate of registration, 2 October 2015). Some of the lawyers participated in both organisations. For insights into the work of the South Sudan Law Society see: https://www.facebook.com/South-Sudan-Law-Society-SSLS-129189833927950/

54 Some lawyers were determined to stay on in Juba despite threats, in the belief that their presence could help ordinary people and each other, as I learned in separate conversations with two lawyers in Juba, in May and August 2017.

55 FHRI internal report to Justice Africa, 18 December 2015.

56 http://www.eyeradio.org/security-suspends-elections-lawyers-leadership/

57 Interviewed in Juba, May 2017.

58 http://www.eyeradio.org/lawyers-strike-suspension-bars-election/

59 Supreme Court, SC/Adm.Review No. 03/2015.

60 Interviewed in Juba, May 2017.

61 http://www.gurtong.net/ECM/Editorial/tabid/124/ctl/ArticleView/mid/519/articleId/9678/Bar-Association-Complain-Of-Right-To-Commission-Oath.aspx

62 http://www.eyeradio.org/bar-association/

63 Madut 2016.

64 YA, interviewed in Juba, August 2017.

65 See Legal Watch Associates for one analysis of this case: http://sudantribune.com/spip.php?article61020

66 http://www.sudantribune.com/spip.php?article62307

67 https://www.hrw.org/sites/default/files/related_material/Commentary%20 on%20the%20NSS%20Bill%20-%20October%2014%2C%202014.pdf

68 http://docs.southsudanngoforum.org/sites/default/files/2016-07/ natsecbill2014_0.pdf

69 The NSS was not bound by the ARCISS peace deal and this may have been another reason why it proved a strategic instrument for government in this period.

70 https://reliefweb.int/sites/reliefweb.int/files/resources/AFR6546322016 ENGLISH.pdf

71 Several of my interlocutors were convinced that their phones and emails were monitored. The fact that phone wiretapping was prevalent was established in a case in the Court of Appeal: http://www.sudantribune.com/spip.php? article62576

72 United Nations Commission on Human Rights in South Sudan 2018, p.11.

73 https://odihpn.org/magazine/a-thousand-papercuts-the-impact-of-ngo-regulation-in-south-sudan/

74 https://www.kenyatalk.com/index.php?threads/south-sudan-national-security-service-most-feared-prison.37357/

75 https://foreignpolicy.com/2015/08/26/radio-silenced-in-the-worlds-newest-country-press-freedom-south-sudan/

76 http://www.gurtong.net/ECM/Editorial/tabid/124/ctl/ArticleView/mid/519/ articleId/16039/Civil-Society-Demands-Legal-Aid-Access-To-UNMISS-Detained-Journalist.aspx; http://africanarguments.org/2016/08/01/south-sudan-the-uns-deafening-silence-over-its-jailed-journalist/

77 https://www.news24.com/Africa/News/ai-wants-35-men-held-by-south-sudan-released-20160416

78 https://www.ecoi.net/en/file/local/1039019/1226_1459329400_ afr6536752016english.pdf

79 A dean at the University of Juba who was in custody for five months without charges and released in April 2016, wrote a public appeal to the president for the release of the remaining detainees: http://www.sudantribune.com/spip. php?article61894

80 https://uk.reuters.com/article/uk-southsudan-trial/south-sudan-sentences-rebel-leaders-spokesman-to-death-idUKKBN1FW1M6

81 https://www.amnesty.org/en/latest/news/2018/02/south-sudan-quash-death-sentence-for-former-opposition-spokesman/

82 https://www.voanews.com/a/south-african-death-penalty-south-sudan/4268204.html

83 https://www.amnesty.org/en/documents/afr65/9369/2018/en/

84 Human Rights Watch 2015.

85 Deng and Willems 2015, p.14.

86 https://radiotamazuj.org/en/news/article/tambura-detainees-demand-legal-adjudication

87 https://www.hrw.org/news/2019/01/23/disappearances-south-sudanese-critics-demand-response

88 UNSC 2019, p.15.

89 https://www.ohchr.org/en/NewsEvents/Pages/DisplayNews.aspx?NewsID=24268&LangID=E

90 http://www.sudantribune.com/spip.php?article67256

91 https://uk.reuters.com/article/uk-southsudan-prisoners/prisoners-seize-control-of-part-of-south-sudan-detention-centre-idUKKCN1MH087

92 https://www.change.org/p/freedom-for-peter-biar-ajak

93 Commission on Human Rights in South Sudan 2019, p.4.

94 We can only approximate the number of chiefs given that there were no records before the war; there were changes and disputes on administrative boundaries, with the creation of 32 states; new chiefs were appointed in sites of displacement; and there is a blurred line between chiefs and elders (who sit on court panels). Given that the Republic of South Sudan Bureau of Statistics lists 516 *payams* and the Republic of South Sudan Ministry of Health lists 2,500 *bomas*, we could estimate a number in excess of 3,000 chiefs.

95 Baker and Scheye 2009, p.173.

96 Leonardi 2015a.

97 The value of the SSP was depreciating rapidly during this period. Some estimates indicate the salary was worth little more than the equivalent of US $10. See https://tradingeconomics.com/south-sudan/currency

98 Interview with chief JE, northern Uganda, August 2017.

99 Kindersley 2018, p.12. This was also confirmed in my interviews with chiefs.

100 See Christian Aid (2018) for an example of chiefs who refused to respond to SPLA demands to assist recruitment; also Nuer chiefs from Unity criticised the 28 states policy and accused the president of trying to install a 'Dinka tribal empire': https://reliefweb.int/report/south-sudan/unity-state-traditional-chiefs-warn-massive-conflicts-over-imposed-28-tribal

101 See inter alia RVI 2018; and Kindersley 2018.

102 For instance, this appeared to be the case in mid-2016 in Ganyiel, Southern Unity State, Justice Africa (2017) where young people were rejecting the authority of chiefs in favour of spiritual leaders such as prophets ('magicians').

103 In a speech given in 2009, cited in Leonardi 2015a, p.1.

104 https://www.reuters.com/article/us-southsudan-war-casualties/volunteers-gather-names-of-south-sudans-uncounted-war-dead-idUSKBN1EE1CS Surveys by the Office of Deputy Coordinator of Humanitarian Affairs 2016 and Deng et al. 2015 provide some of the best insights into crisis impacts.

105 Small Arms Survey 2016.

106 Amnesty International 2016, https://www.amnesty.org.uk/files/fi08716_4.pdf

107 http://sudantribune.com/spip.php?article61163; https://radiotamazuj.org/en/
news/article/joseph-bakosoro-freed-from-prison
108 https://www.ssnationaldialogue.org/bio/wilson-peni-rikito-gbudue-azande-king/
109 Interviewed in northern Uganda, August 2017.
110 http://www.sudantribune.com/spip.php?article57540
111 Mamdani 1996, 2016.
112 Leonardi 2015a.
113 http://jmecsouthsudan.org/index.php/press-release/item/113-traditional-elders-are-agents-of-peace-and-reconciliation
114 https://www.nation.co.ke/news/africa/Igad-to-involve-traditional-leaders-in-ending-South-Sudan-war/1066-3470282-s2in01z/index.html
115 See RVI 2018.
116 Search for Common Ground 2017, p.8.
117 See Christian Aid 2018.
118 See UNDP 2010.
119 Interviews in Nimule 2014; northern Uganda 2017; see also http://riftvalley.net/event/south-sudan-chiefs-speak#.W2ROfdhKhp8
120 Interviewed in northern Uganda, August 2017.
121 Justice Africa 2016, p.49.
122 Two journalists were injured in the protest, said to have been organised by the South Sudan Council of Chiefs: https://www.voanews.com/a/two-journalists-beaten-in-south-sudan-protest/4241835.html
123 Dinka-Nuer West Bank Peace and Reconciliation Conference 1999.
124 https://www.un.org/sc/suborg/en/sanctions/2206/materials/summaries/individual/paul-malong-awan
125 http://www.sudantribune.com/spip.php?article63958; he subsequently became the most high-profile opponent of peace talks.
126 Massoud 2014, p.212.
127 Massoud 2014, pp.128–129.
128 See 'the power of law' in Chapter 1.

Chapter 3

1 Like the working-class Americans in Sally Merry's (1990) study, ordinary citizens in South Sudan displayed their legal consciousness by going to the court.
2 The towns were Juba, Nimule, Torit, Yambio, Yei, Rumbek and Wau, and in displacement camps in Juba, Bentiu, and Melijo during 2015 and 2016. See Appendix for further details.
3 Kindersley 2019.
4 See Chapter 2.

5   A summary of some of the issues is available here: https://reliefweb.int/sites/
    reliefweb.int/files/resources/South_Sudan_2018_Humanitarian_Needs_
    Overview.pdf
6   South Sudan is divided into the following administrative divisions with the
    largest being the state, then in descending order of size, the county, *payam* and
    boma.
7   See the Laws of Southern Sudan: Judiciary Act (2008) and the Laws of
    Southern Sudan: Local Government Act (2009).
8   Leonardi et al. 2010; Deng 2013 outline the structures and provide rich
    insights into the courts in the period immediately prior to the war. They have
    informed much of the rest of this discussion alongside ethnographic research.
9   See Chapter 2 and Mamdani 2016.
10 Customary judgments were supposed to be subject to the Transitional
    Constitution and the law. Also note that adultery was listed as a crime in the
    Penal Code (2008) yet customary *payam* courts (ordinarily supposed to try
    only civil cases) were empowered to try such cases, see Braak 2016, p.33.
11 Deng 2010, p.286.
12 http://www.sudantribune.com/INTERVIEW-Avoid-taking-law-in-
    own,33722
13 Leonardi et al. 2010, p.17.
14 Leonardi et al. 2010, p.18.
15 They had proliferated under SPLM/A administration in the 1990s to the
    extent that the chief justice and local authorities worried about their impacts
    and sought to rein them in. See Leonardi et al. 2010, pp.19–20.
16 Residents of Nimule, for instance were resisting the reclassification of their
    payam as a town council at the beginning of the war.
17 Up to 90% according to the best estimate, Deng 2013, p.18.
18 Customary court fees varied and rose over time as the value of the SSP
    plummeted; in September 2015 Kator B was charging 25 SSP for a summons,
    15 SSP to each of the parties for a court fee. In the Juba PoC in November
    2015, the Nuer court charged 100 SSP for court fees and 50 SSP for a referral.
19 These were Bari, Mundari, Madi, Acholi, Latuko, Kakwa, Balanda, Lango,
    Muru, Pojulu, Baka, Dinka, Shilluk and a Nuba (a group originally from the
    border areas associated with Sudan).
20 See Ibreck and Pendle 2016, 2017.
21 See Turse 2016, pp.44–47 for details of this massacre.
22 Kindersley 2019, pp.18–20.
23 See Leonardi 2015a, p.656.
24 See Fadlalla 2009; this UNDP-sponsored ascertainment and harmonisation
    project is discussed by Mennen 2016.
25 UNDP 2013a.
26 See Bourdieu 1990.

27 Deng 2010, pp.303–304.

28 This was also the orientation of other customary institutions see Deng 2010, p.296.

29 Based on a review of all court reports. A sample batch of 30 criminal cases in statutory courts from four different towns in 2015 indicated that both sides were represented by a lawyer in only one case and one side (a church diocese) was represented by a lawyer in one case.

30 https://www.idlo.int/news/highlights/south-sudan-coming-grips-new-legal-system

31 Laws of Southern Sudan: Code of Civil Procedure Act 2007.

32 Note that brother could also be used to refer to more distant relative.

33 See the Southern Sudan Penal Code 2008, 206.

34 Court report: EJJ16/04/2015.

35 Court report: EJJ06/10/2015.

36 This argument is made by Wilson 2014. See also Pendle 2018.

37 Deng 2013, p.27.

38 See Chapter 2.

39 Interviewed recorded by local CRP researcher in Malakal, July 2018; Edna is a pseudonym.

40 For instance, Human Rights Watch https://reliefweb.int/report/south-sudan/war-crimes-both-sides

41 See https://www.un.org/sg/en/content/sg/note-correspondents/2016-08-05/note-correspondents-board-inquiry-report-malakal

42 Interviewed recorded by CRP researcher in Malakal, July 2018.

43 https://reliefweb.int/report/south-sudan/rule-law-restored-malakal

44 The PoC update from March 2018 lists 24,417 civilians in the site: https://reliefweb.int/report/south-sudan/unmiss-poc-update-19-march-2018 Overall there were close to 200,000 people in PoC sites around this period. See Ibreck and Pendle (2017) for a discussion of customary courts within UN PoCS.

45 The purpose of the 'wildlife' was conservation and wildlife management but the service was armed, operated in urban areas and was militarised in that it had absorbed some former rebel fighters after the CPA.

46 https://radiotamazuj.org/en/news/article/trial-of-spla-soldiers-accused-of-rape-receives-mixed-reaction

47 http://www.sudantribune.com/spip.php?article55760

48 https://radiotamazuj.org/en/news/article/south-sudan-govt-human-rights-investigation-ended-report-filed-with-president

49 Interviewed in Juba, August 2017.

50 https://www.hrw.org/report/2014/12/10/ending-era-injustice/advancing-prosecutions-serious-crimes-committed-south-sudans

51 https://www.hrw.org/news/2013/05/24/south-sudan-no-justice-protester-killings. Other opponents of the relocation were tried for murder in a special

court, and 11 of them were convicted and sentenced to death. Human rights lawyers and community leaders had mobilised to defend those arrested. But based on interviews in Juba in July 2015 and August 2017, they faced intimidation and surveillance. Also see End Impunity Organization 2013.

52 Turse 2016, p.67.

53 Turse 2016, pp.78, 21. A lawyer involved in the investigation felt there was collusion as a result of their ethnicity and suspected that the soldiers had simply returned to 'Dinkalands'.

54 https://radiotamazuj.org/en/news/article/president-kiir-reverses-orders-to-shoot-rapist-soldiers

55 https://www.news24.com/Africa/News/delayed-verdict-in-south-sudans-deadly-hotel-rampage-20180504

56 http://new.radiotamazuj.org/en/news/article/terrain-case-verdict-adjourned-until-further-notice

57 Commission on Human Rights in South Sudan 2019, p.202.

58 https://www.reuters.com/article/us-southsudan-security/military-investigates-after-south-sudan-villagers-claim-gang-rape-by-soldiers-bishop-idUSKBN15Y0TO

59 Observed by a local researcher in Juba, January 2015. Notes on file with the author.

60 According to the SPLA Act (2009) section 37 (4): 'Whenever a military personnel commits an offence against a civilian or civilian property, the civil court shall assume jurisdiction over such an offence.'

61 Pendle 2018.

62 Such regulation was originally wielded by spiritual authorities including prophets. But chiefs' courts had also increasingly played a role. See Hutchinson (2000, p.10) on the impact of the spread of the gun.

63 Hutchinson 2000.

64 See Hutchinson and Pendle 2015; Pendle 2015.

65 Wild et al. 2018. The most disastrous case was the *Mathiang Anyoor*, see Pendle 2015. These poorly trained young fighters wreaked havoc killing and abusing civilians, and many later perished in the service of Dinka elites in government.

66 Court report: JTA24/11/2015.

67 Police were generally involved in the prosecutions that took place in statutory courts, but not necessarily those in customary forums.

68 https://www.cmi.no/file/3253-Justice-and-Conflict-in-South-Sudan---Pilot-Survey---Briefing-Paper.pdf; see Leonardi et al. (2010, p.47) for previous complaints about police corruption.

69 Based on interviews and a review of the court report data. Also for instance see Justice Africa 2015, pp.5, 11.

70 Court report: LBN7/10/2015.

71 Court report: JTA06/01/2016.

72 Recounted at a court observers' forum, July 2015.

73 Badiey 2014, pp.135, 169, 171.

74 Customary regimes are generally characterised by flexible and overlapping rights in land, and treat land as heritage and the basis of community and spiritual relations, as well as a source of livelihoods.

75 Deng 2016, p.5.

76 Deng 2011.

77 Leonardi and Santschi 2016, p.141.

78 De Waal et al. 2017.

79 Interview recorded by Justice Africa in Juba, 2015. Peter is a pseudonym.

80 Ibreck et al. 2017, pp.16–17.

81 Deng 2016, p.16.

82 Court report: OGL25/11/2015.

83 Court report: OGL17/11/2015

84 Court report: NG25/03/2016.

85 Court report: AMA17/06/2016.

86 Court report: AMA13/06/2017.

87 Court report: NG24/03/2016.

88 Court reports: AMA09/05/2016; NG25/03/2016; NG29/02/2016.

89 Court report: AW26/10/2015; JTA12/01/2016.

90 Court report: AW18/11/2015.

91 Court report: OGL31/08/2015.

92 Beswick 2001, p. 37.

93 Court report: BAMB15/06/2016; Court report: AW13/01/2015.

94 See survey by Scott et al. 2013 taken in 2009–11; Care 2014.

95 Mennen 2010; UNDP 2008.

96 UNDP 2013a, pp.64, 102–104.

97 See Kane et al. 2016; Grabska 2014.

98 Court report: AMA26/01/2016.

99 See Porter 2016.

100 Ogbu 1978.

101 Leonardi 2007, p.402.

102 Matfess 2017, p.47.

103 See Ibreck and Pendle 2016; Case of fight in Dinka court.

104 AD interview with chief, Shirikat, August 2018. See also Luedke and Logan 2018.

105 The imprisonment was often paid in monetary equivalent or sometimes house arrest under customary authority as the chiefs could not imprison people within the PoC. Court report: GP24/02/2016.

106 Deng 2010, p.286.

107 GP29/02/2016.

108 AMA29/03/2016.

109 Court report: AJS7/2015.

110 Court report: AW10/03/2016.

111 Pendle 2018, p.111. Across a range of cases, adultery payments were fairly consistent around 6,000–7,000 SSP. The cost for a young man to compensate a women for a child (and to thereby have custody and 'ownership' of them) was around 5 cows or 5000 SSP. See Court report:GP02/05/2016. Compensation varies but 31 cows is a good average.

112 Pendle 2018.

113 See Chapter 5.

114 Jok 1999, p.432.

115 Beswick 2001, p.50.

116 Pinaud 2014.

117 Pendle 2018, p.111; https://paanluelwel.com/2018/06/19/high-bride-price-is-the-main-driver-of-rampant-conflicts-in-south-sudan/

118 Sommers and Schwartz 2011.

119 South Sudan Household Survey 2006, cited in Scott et al. 2013.

120 Luedke and Logan 2018.

121 https://eyeradio.org/traditional-leaders-in-south-sudan-to-review-high-bride-price/

122 Court report: BKY3/08/15.

123 Court reports: EJJ07/06/2015; EJJ04/12/2015.

124 Court report: WNR10/05/2016.

125 Court report: SRM09/10/2016; SRM7/2016.

126 Court report: AJS04/08/2015.

127 Court report: LBN17/05/2016.

128 See Deng 2013.

129 Focus group in Nimule town, April 2014.

130 See Chapter 5.

Chapter 4

1 Discussion on 'law from below' at the Conflict Research Programme, South Sudan Research Panel, Tanzania, July 2018.

2 https://www.suddinstitute.org/our-research-2/our-research/; see also Stringham and Forney 2017.

3 For example SSLS, CEPO, End Impunity.

4 See Chapter 3.

5 See Chapter 2.

6 See Abdelsalam and de Waal (1999) for an insight into the 'civil project' for a new Sudan. This brought together civil society groups and SPLM elites and produced a draft constitution that informed the CPA version.

7 See Chapter 2 on Bourdieu.

8 GoSS 2011, articles 11, 12, 15, 18, 21, 28, 171.

9   See Keck and Sikkink (1998) on 'political opportunity' structures.

10 I provide some insights into this in later chapters, based on interactions with paralegals in other towns, and longer-term research in Nimule.

11 See Appendix.

12 See Bourdieu 1986a, 1986b.

13 Sunstein 1996, p.9.

14 Cited in Dwyer and Zeilig 2012.

15 Egidio Osvaldo letter to Executive Director, Juba Payam, 5 January 2010.

16 Focus group discussions, Hai Game, July 2015.

17 See Badiey 2014; Mennen 2012.

18 Letter from director general of the directorate of survey to legal advisor, Ministry of Physical Infrastructure, 30 March 2010.

19 Letter from Hon. Speaker Juba city legislative council to mayor, Juba city council, 10 October 2011.

20 Letter from chief executive officer Juba city council to minister of physical infrastructure, December 2011.

21 Resolution of the State Council of Ministers No. 204 for the year 2012, 16 July 2012.

22 Committee report on land dispute of Hai game between the citizens and the Central Equatoria Wild Life, 8 October 2012.

23 Minister letter to commissioner of wildlife, CES, 16, July 2012.

24 Director of directorate of survey, CES, 31 July 2013.

25 Field report on plot no 50 at Hai Gam [sic] area, 23 January 2014.

26 Memo, March 2014.

27 Godfrey field notes 'visit of the state minister of finance', 10 July 2014.

28 Interviews in Juba, January 2016.

29 Interview with chief P. Juba, July 2015; GB, facebook message, 16 July 2018; comment from elderly resident in Hai game, July 2015.

30 Boone 2014, p.115.

31 Note that my research indicates that the Madi community resisted the demarcation of customary land in the town of Nimule, at least until 2016. Other urban land contests include Wau and Malakal, both have ethnic dimensions and have erupted in violence.

32 See Deng 2011.

33 See Ibreck and Pendle 2017 on the regimes of 'customary protection' that emerged under 'UN governance'.

34 I visited the site in July 2015, and interviewed, met and discussed the situation repeatedly with members of this group in the years that followed, including in workshops by email and social media. I have also been sent photographs, videos, reports and testimonies. See Appendix on methods.

35 Inter alia see Arenson 2016; Civic 2015; Justice Africa 2016.

36 See Ibreck and Pendle 2016, 2017.

37 Jansen 2016.

38 Malkki 1995.

39 Lecadet 2016, p.18.

40 Cormack forthcoming; https://www.thebritishacademy.ac.uk/blog/arts-vital-social-projects-self-care-south-sudan; see also CRP 2019.

41 This refers to the four Nuer 'sections' from different localities of South Sudan.

42 See Ibreck and Pendle 2016, p.17; CIVIC 2016; United Nations Independent Special Investigation 2016.

43 http://www.sudantribune.com/spip.php?article55604

44 Report on security updates at POC3 2016–17.

45 Ibreck and Pendle 2016, 2017. See also Chapter 3.

46 Pact had worked in partnership with South Sudan Law Society on access to justice programmes producing groundbreaking research and activities, see Deng 2013.

47 They had many other roles and commitments, for instance two were teachers, two law students, one an employee of a humanitarian organisation, one was the founder of a drama group and another was a member of the N4 security team.

48 Interview with Chotlith, May 2017.

49 PoC group discussion August 2017; Interviews with Chotlith and Bangoang, May 2017.

50 See for instance Levitt and Merry 2016.

51 See Chapter 3.

52 Grabska 2013; Hutchinson and Pendle 2015.

53 https://www.independent.co.uk/news/world/politics/south-sudan-sexual-violence-new-female-chief-rebecca-nyandier-chatim-womens-rights-a8383861.html

54 We provided $200 under the Conflict Research Programme for coordination, note-taking and refreshments.

55 Narrative Report on Two Days Chief and community leadership Forum, 2 July 2018.

56 Emily Wax, 'In Sudan, sitting in one prison to escape another', Washington Post Foreign Service, Wednesday, 10 August 2005.

57 See Leonardi 2015b.

58 See Justice Africa 2016; Luedke and Logan 2018.

59 See Chapter 1.

60 See Jok and Hutchinson 1999.

61 Human Rights Watch 2012.

62 https://unmiss.unmissions.org/transforming-south-sudan%E2%80%99s-prisons

63 http://www.ss.undp.org/content/south_sudan/en/home/projects/access-to-justice-and-rule-of-law.html

64 A lawyer estimated 117, meeting in Juba, August 2018. HRW estimates a total of 200 death row prisoners in South Sudan in 2012.

65 Amnesty International 2018.

66 Letter from father and the relatives of the late and father and the relatives of the murderer [names withheld], 'Request for dismissal of death sentence', 21 March 2017.

67 Southern Sudan Penal Code 2008, 9b.

68 Amnesty International 2017.

69 http://www.southsudannation.com/national-dialogue-of-the-deaf-and-blind-is-a-waste-of-time/

70 https://www.reuters.com/article/us-southsudan-unrest-uganda/south-sudanese-troops-butchered-civilians-shot-children-refugees-idUSKBN1771Y0

71 Interview with JR, Juba, May 2017.

72 The names and case records were provided to the author and are on file.

73 See Deng 2013, p.8.

74 Forum in Juba August 2017; meeting in Gulu August 2017.

75 https://www.rememberingoneswelost.com/

76 Butler 2006.

77 De Waal 2016b.

78 I heard this term used by several activists to describe the arbitrary character of the regime. See also http://www.southsudannation.com/rule-of-law-has-died-in-south-sudan-as-rule-of-man-now-rules/

79 Madhok 2017.

Chapter 5

1   De Souza Santos and Rodriguez-Garavito 2005, p.6.

2   Sen 2009, p.vii. I am grateful to Henry Radice for the reminder of Sen's relevance.

3   Madhok 2017, p.502.

4   Ewick and Sibley 1998, pp.231, 230, 239, 244.

5   Krause 2017, p.281; Baines and Paddon 2012, p.242.

6   See Appendix.

7   http://apanews.net/index.php/en/news/south-sudan-has-one-of-worlds-highest-illiteracy-rate-unesco

8   See Debos 2011, p.411.

9   Chotlith and Awech were interviewed in Juba, May 2017 and Thon in Nimule, August 2017.

10 Sections are a sub-division of clans.

11 https://www.theguardian.com/global-development/2017/jun/08/south-sudan-battle-for-cattle-is-forcing-schoolgirls-to-become-teenage-brides

12 http://www.undp.org/content/dam/southsudan/library/Documents/CSAC%20Reports/UNDP-SS-Lakes-State-Summary-Report.pdf

13 http://nyamile.com/2018/01/10/open-letter-from-rumbek-community-in-diaspora-to-president-of-republic-of-south-sudan-mr-salva-kiir-mayardit-and-the-international-community/

14 https://www.oxfam.org/en/south-sudan/pushing-peace-south-sudan

15 This area suffered the split within southern opposition movements and fighting between Nuer groups as well as Anyanya II and SPLA, as well as targeting by the Sudan government as it attempted to suppress rebellion in the Nilotic areas. See Johnson 1994, pp.127–128.

16 See HRW 1994.

17 Deng et al. 2015, p.24.

18 Hammond and James cited in Kindersley 2015, p.228.

19 International Legal Assistance Consortium 2011, p.14.

20 Interview with high court judge, May 2017.

21 See Anyang and Sworo 2016 for an overview of the development of paralegalism in South Sudan.

22 Interview with Edmund Yakani, August 2017.

23 UNDP for instance trained 40 paralegals, including nine women: http://www.undp.org/content/undp/en/home/ourwork/ourstories/paralegals-bring-justice-to-women-in-south-sudan.html CEPO also began its work with a focus on legal aid through 'justice and confidence centres', and continued to promote legal aid services and to develop programmes for paralegal training, including training 19 paralegals in Wau before the war broke out.

24 Interview with SSLS staff member, August 2017.

25 In part this was because after December 2013 donor priorities shifted to humanitarian response rather than access to justice (which was not defined as a humanitarian issue, interview with SSLS staff member August 2017). See Kitson 2016, p.81.

26 Also see Anyang and Sworo 2016; and http://catholicradionetwork.org/?q=node/26377

27 See appendix for details of the forums and the court observation project.

28 This definition of a network is adapted from Keck and Sikkink 1998.

29 I am grateful to the Bridge research team at the Conflict Research Programme, LSE for explaining 'tagging'.

30 One of the Nimule paralegals ran for election as a chief in 2018 (and gained support although he did not win) and one of the lawyers was approached to stand for election as a chief, although he declined as it would prevent him from carrying out some of his legal work.

31 Based on visits to Nimule, Juba PoC, Hai game in Juba and Adjumani.

32 See Ewick and Sibley 1998, p.132.

33 See RVI 2018, p.23.

34 In contrast to some of those discussed by Madhok 2017 and de Souza Santos and Rodriguez-Garavito 2005.

35   Nyamnjoh 2017, pp.265–266.

Chapter 6

1   Interviewed in May 2017.
2   Boege et al. 2009.
3   Simone 2001, p.104.
4   See Ibreck and de Waal 2013; Verweijen 2017.
5   Mbembe 1992, p.5.
6   Lund 2006, p.700.
7   Note that negative stereotypes and hate speech were common https://medium. com/@donnasojok/south-sudans-unholy-trinity-ethnicity-hate-speech-and-social-media-c5073eb30d7c
8   Yakani cited in Turse 2016, pp.107, 111.
9   Court observers' forum, Juba, July 2015.
10   Interviewed in May 2017.
11   See Nyamnjoh 2017.
12   http://www.sudantribune.com/spip.php?article62576
13   My research focused on government areas but there is evidence that citizen activists were targeted in opposition-held areas also https://radiotamazuj.org/ en/news/article/south-sudan-rebels-release-activists-detained-in-wau
14   Interview in Juba, August 2017.
15   Interview with TR, May 2017.
16   https://cpj.org/data/people/isaiah-diing-abraham-chan-awuol/
17   https://www.aa.com.tr/en/africa/human-rights-activist-killed-in-south-sudan-/643683
18   Deputy chairman of the Ma'di community.
19   Interview with JIL in Uganda, August 2017.
20   Facebook phone call and messages, February 2017.
21   Focus group discussion in Kampala, August 2017.
22   Turse 2016, pp.108–109.
23   Paralegal forum in Nimule, April 2015.
24   Interviewed in Kampala, August 2017.
25   Interviewed in Juba, May 2017.
26   Interviewed in Nimule, August 2017.
27   Interviews with BT, Juba May 2017 and BMB and C, Uganda August 2017.
28   Interviewed in Uganda, August 2017.
29   See Roth 2004.
30   Massoud 2014, pp.194–95.
31   See de Waal 2015.
32   See Schomerus and Allen 2010, p.23.
33   Paralegal forum in Nimule, April 2015.

34 Interview in Kampala, August 2017.
35 Interviewed in May 2017.

Conclusion

1 This phrase was on a recent Facebook post of an activist group in South Sudan; it is often attributed to Wole Soyinka but also used in Nigerian and other African protests.
2 De Waal 2015.
3 Massoud 2014.
4 Bourdieu 1986a, 1986b. See Chapter 1.
5 Merry 1990, p.8.
6 Leonardi 2015a.
7 https://www.theguardian.com/world/2018/sep/06/south-sudan-soldiers-jailed-for-and-in-hotel-attack
8 https://www.paxforpeace.nl/stay-informed/in-depth/unpaid-debt/voices-of-the-victims/we-as-a-community-are-crying-and-nobody-is-hearing-us; https://www.business-humanrights.org/en/swedish-prosecutors-to-question-lundin-petroleums-ceo-for-companys-possible-complicity-in-south-sudan-war-crimes-company-comments
9 Keck and Sikkink 1998.
10 Deng 2010, p.312.
11 Jok 2017; and see Thomas 2015; Hutchinson and Pendle 2015.
12 Debos 2011, p.7.
13 Stringham and Forney 2017, p.197.
14 Arendt 1958.
15 Fanon 1963, p.145.
16 Arendt 1970.
17 Massoud 2014, p.229.
18 Karekwaivanane 2017, p.247.

Appendix

1 Fletcher 2016.
2 See Gergen 2015; Centre for Social Justice and Community Action 2012; Adshead and Dubula 2016; Fletcher 2016; Coleman 2015.
3 Fassin 2017, p.9
4 See for instance Theros and Kaldor 2018.
5 Osaghae and Robinson 2005, p.21.
6 See Skårås and Breidlid 2016.
7 Mennen 2010.
8 Dhunpath 2000, pp.543–544; Mills cited in Plummer 2001, pp.6–7.

9   Kindersley (2015) finds that life stories of Sudanese refugees gathered since the 1960s tended towards generic simplified accounts, shaped by mutual expectations of the narrator and the editor of a concept of refugee victimhood.

10 Plummer 2001; Ssali and Theobald 2016; Hatch and Wisniewski 1995, p.117.

11 See Coleman 2015.

REFERENCES

Abdelsalam, A.H. (2000) 'Constitutional Challenges of the Transition', in A.H. Abdelsalam and de Waal, A. (eds) *The Phoenix State: Civil Society and the Future of Sudan*, Trenton, NJ: Red Sea Press.

Abdelsalam, A.H. (2004) 'Islamism, State Power and Jihadism in Sudan', in de Waal, A. (ed.) *Islamism and its Enemies in the Horn of Africa*, London: Hurst.

Abdelsalam, A.H. and de Waal, A. (eds) (1999) *The Phoenix State: Civil Society and the Future of Sudan*, Trenton, NJ: Red Sea Press.

Addis Ababa Agreement (1972) The Addis Ababa Agreement on the Problem of South Sudan, https://peacemaker.un.org/sites/peacemaker.un.org/files/SD_720312_Addis%20Ababa%20Agreement%20on%20the%20Problem%20of%20South%20Sudan.pdf

Agreement on the Resolution of the Conflict in the Republic of South Sudan (2015) Addis Ababa, Ethiopia, 17 August, https://unmiss.unmissions.org/sites/default/files/final_proposed_compromise_agreement_for_south_sudan_conflict.pdf

Adshead, M. and Dubula, V. (2016) 'Walking the Walk? Critical Reflections from an Afro-Irish Emancipatory Research Network', *Educational Action Research*, 24(1): 115–133.

African Rights (1997) *Justice in the Nuba Mountains of Sudan: Challenges and Prospects*, August, London: African Rights.

Africa Watch (1990) Denying 'the Honor of Living', Sudan: A Human Rights Disaster, London: Africa Watch.

African Union Commission of Inquiry on South Sudan (AUCISS) (2014) *Final Report of the African Union Commission of Inquiry on South Sudan*, Addis Ababa, 15 October, http://www.peaceau.org/uploads/auciss.final.report.pdf

Agamben, G. (1998) *Homo Sacer: Sovereign Power and Bare Life*, transl. Heller-Roazen, D., Stanford, CA: Stanford University Press.

Almquist-Knopf, K. (2016) 'Salvaging South Sudan's Sovereignty (and Ending its Civil War)', *Council on Foreign Relations Blog*, https://www.cfr.org/blog/salvaging-south-sudans-sovereignty-and-ending-its-civil-war

Amnesty International (2013) *South Sudan: Civil Unrest and State Repression Human Rights Violations in Wau, Western Bahr El Ghazal State*, https://www.amnesty. org/download/Documents/16000/afr650012013en.pdf

Amnesty International (2016) *Urgent Action: Three Freed, Four More Arbitrarily Detained*, 4th update on UA: 87/16 Index: AFR 65/5293/2016 South Sudan, https://www.amnesty.org.uk/files/fio8716_4.pdf

Amnesty International (2017) *South Sudan: Ongoing Atrocities Turn Country's Breadbasket into a Killing Field*, https://www.amnesty.org/en/latest/news/2017/07/south-sudan-ongoing-atrocities-turn-countrys-breadbasket-into-a-killing-field/

Amnesty International (2018) *South Sudan: One of Just Two Executing States in Sub-Saharan Africa in 2017*, https://www.amnesty.org/en/latest/news/2018/04/south-sudan-one-of-just-two-executing-states-in-sub-saharan-africa-in-2017/

An-Na'im, A.A. (ed.) (1992) *Human Rights in Cross-Cultural Perspectives: A Quest for Consensus*, Philadelphia: University of Pennsylvania Press.

Arendt, H. (1958) *The Human Condition*, Chicago, IL: Chicago University Press.

Arenson, M. (2016) *If We Leave We Are Killed: Lessons Learned from South Sudan Protection of Civilian Sites 2013–2016*, International Organization for Migration, https://publications.iom.int/system/files/pdf/if_we_leave_o.pdf

Attipoe, O., Choudhary, B. and Jonga, N. (2014) An Analysis of Government Budgets in South Sudan from a human development perspective Discussion Paper, August, https://www.undp.org/content/dam/southsudan/library/Discussion%20Papers/SS-Discussion%20paper%20final.pdf

Badiey, N. (2014) *The State of Post-Conflict Reconstruction: Land, Urban Development and State-building in Juba, Southern Sudan*, Rochester, NY: Boydell and Brewer Ltd.

Baines, E. and Paddon, E. (2012) '"This Is How We Survived": Civilian Agency and Humanitarian Protection', *Security Dialogue*, 43(3): 231–247.

Baker, B., and Scheye, E. (2009) 'Access to Justice in a Post-Conflict State: Donor-supported Multidimensional Peacekeeping in Southern Sudan', *International Peacekeeping*, 16(2): 171–185.

Behague, D.P., Kanhonou, L.G., Filippi, V., Legonou, S. and Ronsmans, C. (2008) 'Pierre Bourdieu and Transformative Agency: A Study of how Patients in Benin Negotiate Blame and Accountability in the Context of Severe Obstetric Events', *Sociology of Health and Illness*, 30(4): 489–510.

Bell, C. (2015). *Governance and Law: The Distinctive Context of Transitions from Conflict and its Consequences for Development Interventions* (PSRP Briefing Paper No. 4), Edinburgh: Global Justice Academy, University of Edinburgh.

Benjamin, W. (1968) 'Theses on the Philosophy of History', in *Illuminations: Essays and Reflections*, trans. Zohn, H., New York: Schocken.

Berridge, W.J. (2017) *Hasan Al-Turabi: Islamist Politics and Democracy in Sudan*, Cambridge: Cambridge University Press.

Beswick, S. (2001) '"We Are Bought Like Clothes": The War over Polygyny and Levirate Marriage in South Sudan', *Northeast African Studies*, 8(2): 35–61.

Biong Deng, L. (1999) *Famine in the Sudan: Causes, Preparedness, and Response: A Political, Social and Economic Analysis of the 1998 Bahr el Ghazal Famine*, Brighton: University of Sussex, Institute of Development Studies.

Boege, V., Brown, A. and Clements, K.P. (2009) 'Hybrid Political Orders, Not Fragile States', *Peace Review*, 21(1): 13–21.

Boone, C. (2014) *Property and Political Order in Africa: Land Rights and the Structure of Politics*, Cambridge: Cambridge University Press.

Bourdieu, P. (1986a) 'The Forms of Capital', in Richardson, J. (ed.) *Handbook of Theory and Research for the Sociology of Education*, Westport, CT: Greenwood.

Bourdieu, P. (1986b) 'The Force of Law: Toward a Sociology of the Juridical Field', *Hastings Law Journal*, 38: 805–853.

Bourdieu, P. (1990) *The Logic of Practice*, trans. Nice, R., Cambridge: Polity Press.

Bourgois, P. (2001) 'The Power of Violence in War and Peace: Post-Cold War Lessons from El Salvador', *Ethnography*, 2(1): 5–34.

Braak, B (2016) *Exploring Primary Justice in South Sudan: Challenges, Concerns, and Elements that Work*, https://www.universiteitleiden.nl/binaries/content/assets/rechtsgeleerdheid/instituut-voor-metajuridica/south-sudan-report-vs-2016.10.27.pdf

Branch, A. and Mampilly, Z. (2015) *Africa Uprising: Popular Protest and Political Change*, London: Zed Books.

Butler, J. (2006) *Precarious Life: The Powers of Mourning and Violence*, London: Verso.

Checchi, F., Testa, A., Warsame, A., Quach, L. and Burns, R. (2018) *Estimates of Crisis-Attributable Mortality in South Sudan*, December 2013–April 2014, A Statistical Analysis, September, London School of Hygiene and Tropical Medicine, https://crises.lshtm.ac.uk/wp-content/uploads/sites/10/2018/09/LSHTM_mortality_South_Sudan_report.pdf

Christian Aid (2018) *In It for the Long Haul: Lessons on Peacebuilding in South Sudan*, https://www.christianaid.org.uk/sites/default/files/2018-07/In-it-for-the-long-haul-lessons-peacebuilding-south-sudan-jul2018.pdf

Centre for Civilians in Conflict (CIVIC) (2015) *Within and Beyond the Gates: The Protection of Civilians by the UN Mission in South Sudan*, https://civiliansinconflict.org/wp-content/uploads/2017/09/SouthSudanReport_Web.pdf

Centre for Civilians in Conflict (CIVIC) (2016) *Under Fire: The July 2016 Violence in Juba and UN Response*, https://civiliansinconflict.org/wp-content/uploads/2017/09/civic-juba-violence-report-october-2016.pdf

Centre for Social Justice and Community Action (2012) *Community-based Participatory Research: A Guide to Ethical Principles and Practice*, Durham University National Co-ordinating Centre for Public Engagement,

November, https://www.dur.ac.uk/resources/beacon/CBPREthicsGuideweb November2012.pdf

Coleman, L.M. (2015) 'Ethnography, Commitment, and Critique: Departing from Activist Scholarship', *International Political Sociology*, 9(3): 263–280.

Collier, P., Besley, T. and Khan, A. (2018) Escaping the Fragility Trap. Report of the Commission on State Fragility, Growth and Development, chaired by David Cameron, Donald Kaberuka and Adnan Khan, London School of Economics, International Growth Centre and University of Oxford, Blavatnik School of Government.

Collins, R. and Herzog, R. (1961) 'Early British Administration in the Southern Sudan', *The Journal of African History*, 2(1): 119–135.

Comaroff, J. (1994) 'Foreword', in Lazarus-Black, M. and Hirsch, S.F. (eds) *Contested States, Law, Hegemony and Resistance,* New York and London: Routledge.

Comaroff, J., and Comaroff, J.L. (2016) Reflections on the Anthropology of Law, Governance and Sovereignty in von Benda-Beckmann, F. and von Benda-Beckmann, K. (eds) *Rules of Law and Laws of Ruling*, London: Routledge.

Conflict Research Programme (2019) The Future of Protection of Civilians Sites: Protecting displaced people after South Sudan's Peace Deal, Memo, February.

Cormack, Z. (2016) 'Borders Are Galaxies: Interpreting Contestations over Local Administrative Boundaries in South Sudan', *Africa*, 86(3): 504–527.

Crossley, N. (2003) 'From Reproduction to Transformation: Social Movement Fields and the Radical Habitus', *Theory, Culture and Society*, 20(6): 43–68.

Debos, M. (2011) 'Living by the Gun in Chad: Armed Violence as a Practical Occupation', *The Journal of Modern African Studies*, 49(3): 409–428.

De Herdt, T. and Olivier de Sardan J.P. (eds) (2015) *Real Governance and Practical Norms in Sub-Saharan Africa: The Game of the Rules*, London: Routledge.

De Waal (1997) *Famine Crimes: Politics and the Disaster Relief Industry in Africa*, London: James Currey, African Rights and the International African Institute.

De Waal, A. (2004) 'Counter-Insurgency on the Cheap', *London Review of Books*, 26(15), 5 August.

De Waal, A. (2005) *Famine that Kills: Darfur, Sudan*. Revised edition, Oxford: Oxford University Press.

De Waal, A. (2013) 'Sudan's Elusive Democratisation: Civic Mobilisation, Provincial Rebellion and Chameleon Dictatorships', *Journal of Contemporary African Studies*, 31(2): 213–234.

De Waal, A. (2014) 'When Kleptocracy Becomes Insolvent: Brute Causes of the Civil War in South Sudan', *African Affairs*, 113(452): 347–369.

De Waal, A. (2015) *The Real Politics of the Horn of Africa: Money, War and the Business of Power*, Cambridge and Malden: Polity Press.

De Waal, A. (2016a) 'Writing Human Rights and Getting it Wrong', *Boston Review*, 6 June, http://bostonreview.net/world/alex-de-waal-writing-human-rights

De Waal, A. (2016b) Introduction to the Political Marketplace for Policymakers JSRP Policy Brief 1, March, http://www.lse.ac.uk/internationalDevelopment/research/JSRP/downloads/JSRP-Brief-1.pdf

De Waal, A. and Ibreck, R. (2013) 'Hybrid Social Movements in Africa', *Journal of Contemporary African Studies*, 31(2): 303–324.

De Waal, A., Ibreck, R., Pendle, N., Logan, H. and Robinson, A. (2017) *Conflict Research Programme: South Sudan Synthesis Paper*, October, London School of Economics and Political Science, http://eprints.lse.ac.uk/100159/1/De_Waal_South_Sudan_Published.pdf

De Sousa Santos, B. and Rodríguez-Garavito, C.A. (2005) 'Law, Politics and the Subaltern in Counter-Hegemonic Globalisation', in De Sousa Santos, B. and Rodríguez-Garavito, C.A. (eds) *Law and Globalization from Below: Towards a Cosmopolitan Legality*, Cambridge Studies in Law and Society, Cambridge: Cambridge University Press.

Deng, D.K. (2011) '"Land Belongs to the Community": Demystifying the "Global Land Grab in Southern Sudan"', The Land Deal Politics Initiative Working Paper, Sussex: IDS.

Deng, D.K. (2012) South Sudan Country Report Findings of the Land Governance Assessment Framework (LGAF), November, Juba: South Sudan Law Society.

Deng, D.K. (2016) '"Between a Rock and a Hard Place": Land Rights and Displacement in Juba, South Sudan', South Sudan Law Society, http://land.igad.int/index.php/documents-1/countries/south-sudan/gender-5/979-between-a-rock-and-a-hard-place-land-rights-and-displacement-in-juba-south-sudan-2016/file

Deng, D. and Willems, R. (2015) *Legacies of Enforced Disappearances in South Sudan, Briefing Paper*, Intersections of Truth, Justice and Reconciliation in South Sudan, November, http://upeace.nl/cp/uploads/downloadsprojecten/The%20Legacy%20of%20Enforced%20Disappearances%20in%20South%20Sudan%20-%20Briefing%20Paper.pdf

Deng, D.K, Lopez, B., Pritchard, M. and Ng, L.C (2015) *Search for a New Beginning: Perceptions of Truth, Justice, Reconciliation and Healing in South Sudan*, June, South Sudan Law Society https://www.undp.org/content/dam/southsudan/library/Rule%20of%20Law/Perception%20Survey%20Report%20Transitional%20Justice%20Reconciliation%20and%20Healing%20-.pdf

Deng, F. (1987) *Tradition and Modernization: A Challenge for Law among the Dinka of Sudan*, New Haven: Yale University Press.

Deng, F. (2010) *Customary Law in the Modern World: The Crossfire of Sudan's War of Identities*, London: Routledge.

Deng, M.A.W. (2016) The Importance of Judicial Independence to the Administration of Justice: The Case of South Sudan, Policy Brief, 5 July, https://www.suddinstitute.org/publications/show/577cab35eff46

Department of Peacekeeping Operations (DPKO) (2014) *Justice and Corrections Update*, Office of Rule of Law and Security Institutions (OROLSI) and Criminal Law and Judicial Advisory Service (CLJAS).

Desai, M. (2015) *Subaltern Movements in India: Gendered Geographies of Struggle Against Neoliberal Development*, London: Routledge.

Dhunpath, R. (2000) 'Life History Methodology: "Narradigm" Regained', *International Journal of Qualitative Studies in Education*, 13(5): 543–551.

Donham, D. (2007) 'Staring at Suffering: Violence as a subject', in Bay, E.G. and Donham, D.L. (eds) *States of Violence: Politics, Youth, and Memory in Contemporary Africa*, Charlottesville: University of Virginia Press.

Dwyer, P. and Zeilig, L. (2012) *African Struggles Today: Social Movements Since Independence*, Chicago, IL: Haymarket Books.

Ekeh, P.P. (1975) 'Colonialism and the Two Publics in Africa: A Theoretical Statement', *Comparative Studies in Society and History*, 17(1): 91–112.

El-Affendi, A. (1990) 'Discovering the South: Sudanese Dilemmas for Islam in Africa', *African Affairs*, 89: 371–389.

El-Affendi, A. (1991) *Turabi's Revolution: Islam and Power in Sudan*, Leicester: Grey Seal.

End Impunity Organization (2013) Press Statement, 4 April, Juba.

Engel, D.M. (1998) 'How Does Law Matter in the Constitution of Legal Consciousness?', in Garth, G.B. and Sarat, A. (eds) *How Does Law Matter?*, Evanston, IL: Northwestern University Press.

Evans-Pritchard, E.E. (1940) *The Nuer: A Description of the Modes of Livelihood and Political Institutions of a Nilotic People*, London: Oxford University Press.

Ewick, P. and Sibley, S. (1998) *The Common Place of Law: Stories from Everyday Life*, Chicago: Chicago University Press

Fadlalla, M. (2009) *Customary Laws in Southern Sudan: Customary Laws of Dinka and Nuer*, New York and Bloomington: iUniverse.

Faundez, J. (2016) 'Douglass North's Theory of Institutions: Lessons for Law and Development', *Hague Journal of the Rule of Law*, 8: 373–419.

Fanon, F. (1963) *The Wretched of the Earth*, trans. Farringdon, C., London: Penguin Books.

Fassin, D. (2017) 'Introduction: When Ethnography Goes Public', in Fassin, D. (ed.) *If Truth Be Told: The Politics of Public Ethnography*, Durham, NC and London: Duke University Press.

Ferguson, J. (1990) *The Anti-Politics Machine: 'Development', Depoliticization and Bureaucratic Power in Lesotho*, Cambridge: Cambridge University Press.

Fletcher, R. (2016) 'FLaK: Mixing Feminism, Legality and Knowledge', *Feminist Legal Studies*, 23(3): 241–252.

Fluehr-Lobban, C. (2009) 'Rectifying the Neglect of Sudan's Judiciary', *Making Sense of Sudan*, 18 March, http://africanarguments.org/2009/03/18/rectifying-the-neglect-of-sudans-judiciary/

Galtung, J. (1969) 'Violence, Peace, and Peace Research', *Journal of Peace Research*, 6(3): 167–191.

Gergen, K.J. (2015) 'From Mirroring to World-Making: Research as Future Forming', *Journal for the Theory of Social Behaviour*, 45(3): 287–310.

Gilroy, P. (1993) *The Black Atlantic: Modernity and Double Consciousness*, London: Verso.

Ginsburg, T. and Moustafa, T. (eds) (2008) *Rule by Law: The Politics of Courts in Authoritarian Regimes*, Cambridge: Cambridge University Press.

Government of South Sudan (GoSS) (2011) The Transitional Constitution of the Republic of South Sudan, https://www.wipo.int/edocs/lexdocs/laws/en/ss/ss013en.pdf

Grabska, K. (2013) 'The Return of Displaced Nuer in Southern Sudan: Women Becoming Men?', *Development and Change*, 44(5): 1135–1157.

Grabska, K. (2014) *Gender, Home and Identity: Nuer Repatriation to Southern Sudan*, Martlesham, Suffolk: Boydell & Brewer.

Green, D. (2012) *From Poverty to Power: How Active Citizens and Effective States Can Change the World*. 2nd edition, Rugby: Practical Action Publishing and Oxfam, UK.

Grewal, K.K. (2016) *The Socio-Political Practice of Human Rights: Between the Universal and the Particular*, London: Routledge.

Guyer, J.I. (2004) *Marginal Gains: Monetary Transactions in Atlantic Africa*, Chicago: University of Chicago Press.

Haki (2011) *Combatting Gender-Based Violence in the Customary Courts of South Sudan*, https://static1.squarespace.com/static/53f7ba98e4b01f78d142c414/t/53ffdb13e4b0bf4098a1194d/1409276691505/Combatting+GBV+in+South+Sudan_Haki.pdf

Hatch, J.A. and Wisniewski, R. (1995) 'Life History and Narrative', *International Journal of Qualitative Studies in Education*, 8(1): 3–4.

Hoffman, B. and Duschinski, H. (2014) 'Contestations Over Law, Power and Representation in Kashmir Valley', *Interventions*, 16(4): 501–530.

Houtzager, P.P. (2005) 'The Movement of the Landless (MST), Juridical Field, and Legal Change in Brazil', in de Sousa Santos, B. and Rodríguez-Garavito, C.A. (eds) *Law and Globalization from Below: Towards a Cosmopolitan Legality*, Cambridge: Cambridge University Press.

Human Rights Watch (2012) *'Prison Is Not For Me': Arbitrary Detention in South Sudan*, 21 June, https://www.hrw.org/report/2012/06/21/prison-not-me/arbitrary-detention-south-sudan

Human Rights Watch (2015) *South Sudan: Arbitrary Detention, Torture; Military, National Security Service Routinely Beat Detainees*, 18 May, https://www.hrw.org/news/2015/05/18/south-sudan-arbitrary-detention-torture

Hutchinson, S.E. (1996) *Nuer Dilemmas: Coping with Money, War, and the State*, Berkeley: University of California Press.

Hutchinson, S.E. (1998) 'Death, Memory and the Politics of Legitimation: Nuer Experiences of the Continuing Second Sudanese Civil War', in Werbner, R. (ed.) *Memory and the Postcolony: African Anthropology and the Critique of Power,* London: Zed Books.

Hutchinson, S.E. (2000). 'Nuer Ethnicity Militarized', *Anthropology Today,* 16(3): 6–13.

Hutchinson, S.E. and Pendle, N.R. (2015) 'Violence, Legitimacy, and Prophecy: Nuer Struggles with Uncertainty in South Sudan', *American Ethnologist,* 42(3): 415–430.

Ibrahim, A. (2008) *Manichaean Delirium: Decolonizing the Judiciary and Islamic Renewal in Sudan, 1898–1985,* Leiden: Brill.

Ibreck, R. and Pendle, N. (2016) *Customary Protection? Chiefs' Courts as Public Authority in United Nations Protection of Civilian Sites, South Sudan* (October), Working Paper, Justice and Security Research Programme, LSE.

Ibreck, R. and Pendle, N. (2017) 'Community Security and Justice under United Nations Governance: Lessons from Chiefs' Courts in South Sudan's Protection of Civilians Sites', *Stability: International Journal of Security and Development,* 6(1): 1–17.

Ibreck, R., Logan, H. and Pendle, N. (2017) *Negotiating Justice: Courts as Local Civil Authority during the Conflict in South Sudan,* Working paper, Justice and Security Research Programme, LSE.

Independent Commission for Aid Impact (ICAI) (2015) 'Review of UK Development Assistance for Security and Justice', London, ICAI, Report 42, March, https://icai.independent.gov.uk/wp-content/uploads/ICAI-Report-UK-Development-Assistance-for-Security-and-Justice..pdf

International Commission of Jurists (ICJ) (2013) *South Sudan: An Independent Judiciary in an Independent State?,* https://www.refworld.org/pdfid/530cb3604.pdf

International Legal Assistance Consortium (2011) Pre-Assessment Mission, South Sudan Report, 6–13 December.

Isser, D.H. (2011) 'Introduction: Shifting Assumptions from Abstract Ideals to Messy Realities', in Isser, D.H. (ed.) *Customary Justice and the Rule of Law in War-Torn Societies.* Washington, DC: US Institute of Peace Press.

Jackson, R.H. and Rosberg, C.G. (1982) 'Why Africa's Weak States Persist: The Empirical and the Juridical in Statehood', *World Politics,* 35(1): 1–24.

Jansen, B.J. (2016) 'The Refugee Camp as Warscape: Violent Cosmologies, "Rebelization", and Humanitarian Governance in Kakuma, Kenya', *Humanity: An International Journal of Human Rights, Humanitarianism, and Development,* 7(3): 429–441.

Johnson, D.H. (1994) 'Destruction and Reconstruction in the Economy of the Southern Sudan', in Harir, S. and Tvedt, T. (eds) *Short-cut to Decay: The Case of the Sudan,* Uppsala: Nordiska Africainstitutet.

Johnson, H.F. (2016) *South Sudan: The Untold Story from Independence to the Civil War*, London: I.B. Tauris.

Jok, J.M. (1999) 'Militarization and Gender Violence in South Sudan', *Journal of Asian and African Studies*, 34(4): 427–442.

Jok, J.M. (2012) 'Negotiating Security: Gender, Violence and the Rule of Law in Post-War South Sudan', in Stein, H. and Fadlalla, A.H. (eds) *Gendered Insecurities, Health and Development in Africa*, London: Routledge.

Jok, J.M. (2017) *Breaking Sudan: The Search for Peace*, London: OneWorld.

Jok, J.M. and Hutchinson, S.E. (1999) 'Sudan's Prolonged Second Civil War and the Militarization of Nuer and Dinka Ethnic Identities', *African Studies Review*, 42(2): 125–145.

Justice Africa (2015) *Justice in Practice*, https://blogs.lse.ac.uk/jsrp/files/2015/05/FINAL_JA-SouthSudanSpring2015.pdf

Justice Africa (2016) *Violence Begets Violence: Justice and Accountability for Sexual and Gender-Based Offences in South Sudan*, http://justiceafrica.org/wp-content/uploads/2016/08/Violence-Begets-Violence-SGBV-South-Sudan-Draft1.pdf

Justice Africa (2017) *They Left Us with Spears and Came Back with Guns: Armed Youth, Cattle Raiding and Community (In)security in Southern Unity State, South Sudan*, http://justiceafrica.org/wp-content/uploads/2016/06/Armed-Youth-Cattle-Raiding-and-Community-Insecurity-in-Southern-Unity-FINAL.pdf

Kane, S., Kok, M., Rial, M., Matere, A., Dieleman, M. and Broerse, J.E. (2016) 'Social Norms and Family Planning Decisions in South Sudan', *BMC Public Health*, 16(1): 1183.

Karekwaivanane, G.H. (2017) *The Struggle over State Power in Zimbabwe: Law and Politics since 1950*, Cambridge: Cambridge University Press.

Kasfir, N. (1998) 'Civil Society, the State and Democracy in Africa', *Commonwealth and Comparative Politics*, 36(2): 123–149.

Keck, M. and Sikkink, K. (1998) *Activists Beyond Borders: Advocacy Networks in International Politics*, Ithaca, NY: Cornell University Press.

Keen, D. (1994) *The Benefits of Famine: A Political Economy of Famine and Relief in Southwestern Sudan 1983–89*, Princeton: Princeton University Press.

Keene, E. (2002) *Beyond the Anarchical Society: Grotius, Colonialism and Order in World Politics*, Cambridge: Cambridge University Press.

Kindersley, N. (2015) 'Southern Sudanese Narratives of Displacement, and the Ambiguity of "Voice"', *History in Africa*, 42: 203–237.

Kindersley, N. (2016) *The Fifth Column? An Intellectual History of South Sudanese Communities in Khartoum, 1969–2005*, PhD thesis, Durham University.

Kindersley, N. (2018) *Politics, Power and Chiefship in Famine and War: A Study of the Former Northern Bahr el-Ghazal State, South Sudan*, Nairobi: Rift Valley Institute.

Kindersley, N. (2019) 'Rule of Whose Law? The Geography of Authority in Juba, South Sudan', *The Journal of Modern African Studies*, 57(1): 61–83.

Krause, J. (2017) 'Non-Violence and Civilian Agency in Communal War: Evidence from Jos, Nigeria', *African Affairs*, 116(463): 261–283.

Kuol, M.A. (1997) *Administration of Justice in the SPLA/M Liberated Areas: Court Cases in War-torn Southern Sudan*, Buxton Trust Fellow, Refugee Studies Programme, University of Oxford, February.

Kuyok, K.A. (2015) *South Sudan: The Notable Firsts*, Bloomington: AuthorHouse.

Lecadet, C. (2016) 'Refugee Politics: Self-Organized "Government" and Protests in the Agamé Refugee Camp (2005–13)', *Journal of Refugee Studies*, 29(2): 187–207.

Leonardi, C. (2007) '"Liberation" or Capture: Youth in between "Hakuma", and "Home" during Civil War and Its Aftermath in Southern Sudan', *African Affairs*, 106(424): 391–412.

Leonardi, C. (2015a) *Dealing with Government in South Sudan, Histories of Chiefship, Community and State*, Woodbridge, Suffolk: James Currey, Boydell and Brewer Ltd.

Leonardi, C. (2015b) 'Points of Order? Local Government Meetings as Negotiation Tables in South Sudanese History', *Journal of Eastern African Studies*, 9(4): 650–668.

Leonardi, C. and Santschi, M. (2016) *Dividing Communities in South Sudan and Northern Uganda Boundary Disputes and Land Governance*, Nairobi: Rift Valley Institute.

Leonardi, C., Isser, D., Moro, L. and Santschi, M. (2010) *Local Justice in Southern Sudan*, Nairobi: Rift Valley Institute and Washington, DC: United States Institute for Peace.

Levitt, P. and Engle Merry, S. (2016) 'The Vernacularization of Women's Human Rights', in Vinjamuri, L., Snyder, J. and Hopgood, S. (eds) *Human Rights Futures*, Cambridge: Cambridge University Press.

Lewis, D. (2001) 'Civil Society in Non-Western Contexts: Reflections on the "Usefulness" of a Concept', *Civil Society Working Paper 13*, October, London School of Economics and Political Science.

Lobel, O. (2007) 'The Paradox of Extralegal Activism: Critical Legal Consciousness and Transformative Politics', *Harvard Law Review*, 120: 937–958.

Luckham, R. and Kirk, T. (2013) 'The Two Faces of Security in Hybrid Political Orders: A Framework for Analysis and Research', *Stability: International Journal of Security and Development*, 2(2): 1–30.

Luedke, A.E. and Logan, H.F. (2018) '"That Thing of Human Rights": Discourse, Emergency Assistance, and Sexual Violence in South Sudan's Current Civil War', *Disasters*, 42: S99–S118.

Lund, C. (2006) 'Twilight Institutions: Public Authority and Local Politics in Africa', *Development and Change*, 37(4): 685–705.

Macdonald, A. and Allen, T. (2015) 'Social Accountability in War Zones – Confronting Local Realities of Law and Justice', *International Journal on Minority and Group Rights*, 22(3): 279–308.

MacGinty, R. and Richmond, O.P. (2013) 'The Local Turn in Peacebuilding: A Critical Agenda for Peace', *Third World Quarterly*, 34(5): 763–783.

Madhok, S. (2017) 'On Vernacular Rights Cultures and the Political Imaginaries of Haq', *Humanity: An International Journal of Human Rights, Humanitarianism, and Development*, 8(3): 485–509.

Madut, C.R. (2016) Judicial Circular No. 1 On the Appearance of Advocates Before the Courts, 2 November, Office of the Chief Justice, https://www. facebook.com/SSBALAW/photos/pcb.364782887205042/364782563871741/ ?type=3&theater

Malkki, L.H. (1995) *Purity and Exile: Violence, Memory, and National Cosmology among Hutu Refugees in Tanzania*, Chicago: University of Chicago Press.

Mamdani, M. (1996) *Citizen and Subject: Contemporary Africa and the Legacy of Late Colonialism*, Princeton: Princeton University Press.

Mamdani, M. (2016) 'Who's to Blame in South Sudan?', *Boston Review*, 28 June, http:// bostonreview.net/world/mahmood-mamdani-south-sudan-failed-transition

Mampilly, Z.C. (2012) *Rebel Rulers: Insurgent Governance and Civilian Life during War*, New York: Cornell University Press.

Martin, E. and Mosel, I. (2011) City Limits: Urbanisation and Vulnerability in Sudan Juba case study January, Humanitarian Policy Group (HPG), London: Overseas Development Institute (ODI).

Maru, V. (2006) 'Between Law and Society: Paralegals and the Provision of Primary Justice Services in Sierra Leone', New York, Open Society Justice Initiative.

Massoud, M. (2014) *Law's Fragile State: Colonial, Authoritarian and Humanitarian Legacies in Sudan*, Cambridge: Cambridge University Press.

Matfess, H. (2017) *Women and the War on Boko Haram: Wives, Weapons, Witnesses*, London: Zed Books.

Mayntz, R. (2010) 'Legitimacy and Compliance in Transnational Governance', *MPifG Working Paper 10/5* Max-Planck-Institut für Gesellschaftsforschung.

Mbembe, A. (1992) 'Provisional Notes on the Postcolony', *Africa*, 62(1): 3–37.

Mbembe, A. (2017) *Critique of Black Reason*, trans. Dubois, L., Durham, NC: Duke University Press.

Mennen, T. (2010) 'Lessons from Yambio: Legal Pluralism and Customary Justice Reform in Southern Sudan', *Hague Journal on the Rule of Law*, 2(2): 218–252.

Mennen, T. (2012) Customary Land Rights in South Sudan Information, Counselling and Legal Assistance (ICLA) Project South Sudan, March, http:// docs.southsudanngoforum.org/sites/default/files/2016-10/9195246_0.pdf

Mennen, T (2016) Study on the Harmonisation of Custormary Laws and the National Legal System in South Sudan, 13 March, South Sudan: UNDP.

Merry, S.E. (1990) *Getting Justice and Getting Even: Legal Consciousness among Working-Class Americans*, Chicago: University of Chicago Press.

Nagy, R. (2008) 'Transitional Justice as Global Project: Critical Reflections', *Third World Quarterly*, 29(2): 275–289.

Nordstrom, C. (1997) *A Different Kind of War Story*, Philadelphia: University of Pennsylvania Press.

North, D., Wallis, J.J. and Weingast, B.R. (2009) *Violence and Social Orders: A Conceptual Framework for Interpreting Recorded Human History*, Cambridge: Cambridge University Press.

Nyamnjoh, F.B. (2017) 'Incompleteness: Frontier Africa and the Currency of Conviviality', *Journal of Asian and African Studies*, 52(3): 253–270.

Odinkalu, C.A. (2006) 'Poor Justice or Justice for the Poor? A Policy Framework for Reform of Customary and Informal Justice Systems in Africa', in Sage, C. and Woolcock, M. (eds) *The World Bank Legal Review: Law, Equity, and Development*, Washington, DC: Martinus Nijhof.

Ogbu, J.U. (1978) 'African Bridewealth and Women's Status', *American Ethnologist*, 5(2): 241–262.

Osaghae, E. and Robinson, G. (2005) 'Introduction', in Porter, E.J., Robinson, G., Smyth, M., Osaghae, E. and Schnabel, A. (eds) *Researching Conflict in Africa: Insights and Experiences*, Tokyo: United Nations University Press.

Pendle, N. (2015) 'They are Now Community Police: Negotiating the Boundaries and Nature of the Government in South Sudan through the Identity of Militarised Cattle-keepers', *International Journal on Minority and Group Rights*, 22(3): 410–434.

Pendle, N. (2018) 'The Dead Are just to Drink From': Recycling Ideas of Revenge among the Western Dinka, South Sudan', *Africa*, 88(1): 99–121.

Pirie, F. and Scheele, J. (eds) (2014) 'Justice, Community, and Law', *Legalism: Community and Justice*. Oxford: Oxford University Press.

Pinaud, C. (2014) 'South Sudan: Civil War, Predation and the Making of a Military Aristocracy', *African Affairs*, 113(451): 192–211.

Plummer, K. (2001) 'The Call of Life Stories in Ethnographic Research', in Atkinson, P., Coffey, A., Delamont, S., Lofland, J. and Lofland, L. (eds) *Handbook of Ethnography*, London: Sage.

Poggo, S.S. (2009) *The First Sudanese Civil War: Africans, Arabs and Israelis in the Southern Sudan, 1955–73*, New York: Palgrave Macmillan.

Porter, H. (2016) *After Rape: Violence, Justice, and Social Harmony in Uganda*, Cambridge: Cambridge University Press.

Pring, J. (2017) 'Including or Excluding Civil Society? The Role of the Mediation Mandate for South Sudan (2013–2015) and Zimbabwe (2008–2009)', *African Security*, 10(3–4): 223–238.

Raeymaekers, T. (2014) *Violent Capitalism and Hybrid Identity in the Eastern Congo*, Cambridge: Cambridge University Press.

Republic of South Sudan (2012) *Fragility Assessment: Summary Results*, Juba.

Rajagopal, B. (2008) 'Invoking the Rule of Law in Post-conflict Rebuilding: A Critical Examination', *William & Mary Law Review*, 49: 1347–1376.

Rift Valley Institute (RVI) (2018) *Now We Are Zero: South Sudanese Chiefs and Elders*

Discuss their Roles in Peace and Conflict, South Sudan Customary Authorities Project, Nairobi: RVI.

Rolandsen, Ø. (2005) *Guerrilla Government: Political Changes in the Southern Sudan during the 1990s*, Uppsala: Nordiska Afrikainstitutet

Rolandsen, Ø.H. and Daly, M.W. (2016) *A History of South Sudan: From Slavery to Independence*, Cambridge: Cambridge University Press.

Rolandsen, Ø.H. and Leonardi, C. (2014) 'Discourses of Violence in the Transition from Colonialism to Independence in Southern Sudan, 1955–1960', *Journal of Eastern African Studies*, 8(4): 609–625.

Roth, K. (2004) 'Defending Economic Social and Cultural Rights: Practical Issues Faced by an International Human Rights Organization', *Human Rights Quarterly*, 26: 63–73.

Schomerus, M. and Allen, T. (2010) *Southern Sudan at Odds with Itself: Dynamics of Conflict and Predicaments of Peace*, London: Development Studies Institute, London School of Economics and Political Science.

Scott, J. (1990) *Domination and the Arts of Resistance: Hidden Transcripts*, New Haven and London: Yale University Press.

Scott, J., Averbach, S., Modest, A., Hacker, M., Cornish, S., Spencer, D. and Parmar, P. (2013) 'An Assessment of Gender Inequitable Norms and Gender-based Violence in South Sudan: A Community-based Participatory Research Approach', *Conflict and Health*, 7(1): 4.

Search for Common Ground (2017) 'Baseline Evaluation of the "Facilitating Access to Justice in South Sudan"', Prepared for Search for Common Ground, Smart Edge Research and Consulting, 4 August, https://www.sfcg.org/wp-content/uploads/2017/09/INL-Baseline-Report-7-Sept-2017.pdf

Seidel, K. and Sureau, T. (2015) 'Introduction: Peace and Constitution Making in Emerging South Sudan on and Beyond the Negotiation Tables', *Journal of Eastern African Studies*, 9(4): 612–633.

Sen, A.K. (2009) *The Idea of Justice*, Cambridge, MA The Belknap Press of Harvard University Press.

Skårås, M. and Breidlid, A. (2016) 'Teaching the Violent Past in Secondary Schools in Newly Independent South Sudan', *Education as Change*, 20(3): 98–118.

Small Arms Survey (2016) *Conflict in Western Equatoria*, Human Security Baseline Assessment (HSBA) for Sudan and South Sudan, https://reliefweb.int/sites/reliefweb.int/files/resources/HSBA%20F%26F%20Western%20Equatoria%20final%20check.pdf

Sommers, M. and Schwartz, S. (2011) *Dowry and Division Youth and State Building in South Sudan,* Special Report, United States Institute of Peace.

South Sudan Human Rights Commission (2017) *Annual Report,* Juba: South Sudan.

Southern Sudan Civil Society Initiative (2005) The Constitution of Southern Sudan, Draft Constitution, http://www.gurtong.net/LinkClick.aspx?fileticket=lOqRv9hqgv8%3D&

Southern Sudan Penal Code (2008) *Act 9 The Penal Code Act,* Ministry of Legal Affairs and Constitutional Development, Acts Supplement to *The Southern Sudan Gazette* No. 1 Volume I, 10 February 2009, https://www.wipo.int/edocs/lexdocs/laws/en/ss/ss014en.pdf

Ssali, S.N. and Theobald, S. (2016) 'Using Life Histories to Explore Gendered Experiences of Conflict in Gulu District, Northern Uganda: Implications for Post-Conflict Health Reconstruction', *South African Review of Sociology,* 47(1): 81–98.

Stringham, N. and Forney, J. (2017) 'It Takes a Village to Raise a Militia: Local Politics, the Nuer White Army, and South Sudan's Civil Wars', *The Journal of Modern African Studies,* 55(2): 177–199.

Sunstein, R.C. (1996) 'Social Norms and Social Roles', *Columbia Law Review* 96(903): 904–967.

Sureau, T. (2013) 'New Forms of Exclusion in Torit: Contestation over Urban Land', in Grawert, E. *Forging Two Nations Insights on Sudan and South Sudan,* Ethiopia: OSSREA and BICC.

The Sentry (2016) 'War Crimes Shouldn't Pay: Stopping the Looting and Destruction in South Sudan', https://thesentry.org/reports/warcrimesshouldntpay/

Tamanaha, B.Z. (2004) *On the Rule of Law: History, Politics, Theory,* Cambridge: Cambridge University Press.

Theros, M. and Kaldor, M. (2018) 'The Logics of Public Authority: Understanding Power, Politics and Security in Afghanistan, 2002–2014', *Stability: International Journal of Security and Development,* 7(1): 1–22.

Thomas, E. (2015) *South Sudan: A Slow Liberation,* London: Zed Books.

Turse, N. (2016) *Next Time They'll Come to Count the Dead: War and Survival in South Sudan,* Chicago: Haymarket Books.

United Nations (2017) Panel of Experts on South Sudan, Final Report Panel of Experts on South Sudan, 13 April, United Nations Security Council S/2017/326.

United Nations Commission on Human Rights in South Sudan (2017) *Report of the Commission on Human Rights in South Sudan* 6 March, A/HRC/34/63 Human Rights Council, Thirty-fourth session.

United Nations Commission on Human Rights in South Sudan (2018) *Report of the Commission on Human Rights in South Sudan,* 23 February, A/HRC/37/CRP.2 Human Rights Council, Thirty-seventh session.

United Nations Commission on Human Rights in South Sudan (2019) *Report of the Commission on Human Rights in South Sudan* 25 February–22 March, A/HRC/40/69, Human Rights Council, Fortieth session.

United Nations Development Programme (UNDP) (2010) Leadership, trust and legitimacy in Southern Sudan's Transition after 2005, *Global Event Working Paper,* New York: UNDP.

United Nations Development Programme (UNDP) (2013a) Training Manual for Traditional Authorities on Customary Law in South Sudan (2010 version

revised), http://www.undp.org/content/dam/southsudan/library/Reports/
Manual%20for%20Traditional%20Authorities%20on%20Customary%20
Law%20in%20South%20Sudan%20(1).pdf

United Nations Development Programme (UNDP) (2013b) *Access to Justice
Perception Survey*, Executive Summary, August, http://www.undp.org/content/
dam/southsudan/library/Reports/southsudanotherdocuments/Executive%20
Summary%20of%20perception%20survey.pdf

United Nations Independent Special Investigation (2016) *Executive Summary of the
Independent Special Investigation into the Violence which Occurred in Juba in 2016
and UNMISS Response.*

UN Security Council (UNSC) (2019) *Final Report of the Panel of Experts on South
Sudan* Submitted Pursuant to Resolution 2428 (2018), 9 April.

Von Benda-Beckmann, F. and von Benda-Beckmann, K. (eds) (2016) *Rules of Law
and Laws of Ruling*, London: Routledge.

Warburg, G.R. (1990) 'The "Sharia" in Sudan: Implementation and Repercussions,
1983–1989', *The Middle East Journal,* 44(4): 624–637.

Wild, H., Jok, J.M. and Patel, R. (2018) 'The Militarization of Cattle Raiding in
South Sudan: How a Traditional Practice became a Tool for Political Violence',
Journal of International Humanitarian Action, 3(1): 2–11.

Wilson, J.H. (2014) *Blood Money in Sudan and Beyond: Restorative Justice or Face-
Saving Measure?*, PhD thesis, Faculty of the School of Continuing Studies
and of the Graduate School of Arts and Sciences, Georgetown University
Washington, DC.

World Bank (2011) *World Development Report 2011: Conflict Security and
Development*, Washington DC: World Bank.

Young, J. (2016) 'Popular Struggles and Elite Co-optation: The Nuer White
Army in South Sudan's Civil War', *Small Arms Survey*, Graduate Institute of
International and Development Studies, Geneva.

INDEX

www.ingramcontent.com/pod-product-compliance
Ingram Content Group UK Ltd.
Pitfield, Milton Keynes, MK11 3LW, UK
UKHW020732280225
455688UK00012B/611